Celestial Bodies in Orbit

Memoirs of
The Unknown Stripper

By Eve Littlepage

Dedicated, with love, to

The One

CONTENTS

ACKNOWLEDGEMENTS

My sincere thanks to all who take the time to read my story. I hope you enjoy reading it as much as I enjoyed sharing it!

Life is like a labyrinth we journey through on the way to finding ourselves. The people we meet along the way are the stones that form the labyrinth walls. Unlike stones, they are not inanimate objects. They come to life and form sparks with our own energies. Sometimes the sparks are quite beautiful, like fireflies or fireworks. Other times, they cause frightful explosions. These sparks and explosions prompt us to make unexpected twists and turns, guiding us through our maze, changing us along the way.

I dearly thank all of the characters I have written about in this memoir. Many others have been omitted from the story, but not from my gratitude. They all have played a part in my journey, as I have in theirs.

There are people I wish to specifically thank, without whose support I never would have completed this work: My husband Arturo, who has been there for me in more ways than there are stars in the cosmos; The many friends who patiently listened when the book was just a formless thought; My manuscript readers, whose perceptive comments helped me immensely: Alan B., Bob B., Dean L., Fern T., Jill Solomon, Karen Johnson, Lindsey Boss, Morwen T.F., SherryAnne, and Wren W.; Members of various writing groups who offered feedback on excerpts, including: Boots Baumbaugh, Gordon Kuhn, Julieanna B., and Mary Wanser; and also Ginny East, who facilitated one of these groups, for her encouragement and for sharing her expertise on creative writing.

An exuberant thanks to my editor, Linda Maree, and to the Goddess for making sure our paths crossed. Linda's positive and enthusiastic feedback has been a blessing as she shared her intelligence, insight, and grammatical skills with me. I only wish I had another book ready to edit so I could continue working with her!

My deepest gratitude to Kickstarter and all of the kind, generous people who Backed my Kickstarter Campaign and helped to spread the word about it. You are all amazing!

For many years I worked as an event coordinator. I had to rely on a huge network of people to create an event. I thought, Instead of working on an event that I need to count on so many others to complete, I will write a book. Then I will be counting on no one but myself to get it done.

Cocooning myself in my writing den for hours, days, weeks, I typed my heart out, alone. Yet in the end, this lone-wolf endeavor took the efforts and support of a team of wonderful people to bring it to fruition.

I am humbled when I contemplate the inter-connectedness and inter-dependence of us all. I am honored and grateful to be part of the vibrant web of beautiful spirits who have shared my journey through the labyrinth.

- Eve Littlepage

AUTHOR'S NOTES

This is the true story of my ten-year career as a striptease dancer. It is told interview-style, using my nom-de-plume Eve Littlepage, to a fictional author named Stella Mars. Stella, her house, parlor, and tape recorder are fictive elements. However, the story 'Eve' tells to Stella is a real account of what happened to me. About two-thirds of the names of the characters have been changed to protect the innocent, the guilty, and the in-betweens.

I have opted to capitalize the words Witchcraft and Pagan, as I feel they have been in lower case for far too long.

Time and again when I was a striptease dancer I heard other dancers lament, "Why is a painting of a naked woman deemed 'Art,' but a live naked woman considered obscene?" I have no answer, but I like how my favorite poet, e.e. cummings, summed it up for himself: "… a pretty girl who naked is, is worth a million statues."

- Eve Littlepage

1. ROAD TO STUPIDVILLE

I remember my first time. Though decades have passed, it's still as clear as a full moon on a winter night. You'd think I was facing a firing squad. I stood behind the velvet curtain, frozen in a time warp that made each second seem like an hour. Every hair on my body was buzzing. I thought I would pass out.

I jumped a mile when someone barely touched my shoulder. It was Tina, a young woman with cinnamon-colored skin and exotic green eyes. From her accent, I guessed she was from the Caribbean. Tina had been around the scene a while, and was playing stage mother, patting me gently on the back, saying, "Don't worry 'bout a thing, Honey. You go on out there, just look over their heads—they'll think you're looking at them—and smile, smile, SMILE! You'll do just fine."

I strained to take a breath, but my lungs were locked. No matter how much I tugged at the black velvet camisole, I couldn't make it cover more than the trunk of my body. The core of my female shape was hidden by the skimpy costume, and I was still backstage. But I already felt exposed, as if a roomful of men's eyes were reaching through the curtain like greedy fingers, grabbing at my body and groping my breasts. I was going to lose my lunch any second now. I looked around for a bucket or a trash can. *Why don't they give out barf bags to first-timers?*

Tina, bless her kind heart, had tried her best to calm me down, but it was useless. My heart was thumping as loud as thunder. Then the music was on and it was time to *do something.* I glanced toward the stairs. There was still time to change my mind, leap down those three little steps and run. Yes, I could run, back to the life I was desperate to change. It was hell, but it was a hell I knew.

Suddenly a switch flipped in my head and I was super-cool, weighing the situation as calmly as choosing what to eat for breakfast. Logic had swept my fear aside, as I realized I was terrified of the UNKNOWN: *How would I feel dancing naked in front of a room full of strangers? How would the audience react? How will my life change if I go through with it? What if I trip and go hurtling off the stage?* These were all unknowns to me.

I *did know* that if I split then, I'd be back on the treadmill looking for another waitress job. And I'd be back on the terror-mill living with Eddie. That was all it took.

I flung the curtain wide and strutted out.

Smiling, looking over their heads, I sashayed around to the jukebox song I had selected for my debut. The music carried me from that point on '... *doo doo dooo doo do do ... I've got to ruuun to keep from hiiiding ...* ' The words of the Allman Brothers' tune seemed to fit my running and hiding mood, '*... and I'm not gonna let 'em catch me no, not gonna let 'em catch the Midnight Riiider..* '

I thought I'd just do it for a little while: a few weeks, maybe a couple of months. I had no idea a *little while* would be *ten years* of my life. I was such a naive little twit.

* * * * *

Thus it was that Eve Littlepage began to tell me her story.

My name is Stella Mars. Eve had initially contacted me to co-author her memoir. However, my role evolved more into a transcriber than writer. As my typing skills were superior, we decided I should be the one to type Eve's words as they were captured onto my tape recorder. In March of 2010 I sat down with Eve to hear her account of her days as a striptease dancer. That was how Eve had supported herself when we first met, in the early 1980s.

I had been living in Boston with a man named Max at the time. Max's son Doug had brought Eve over for dinner to introduce her to Max and I. We had several other guests that night. Eve was quiet and shy, but her smile lit up the room. She looked like she was in her late teens, medium height and slim. With her sparkly blue eyes and cascade of blonde curls, it wasn't hard to see why Doug was smitten with her. I found out later she was actually in her early thirties. I had wondered how she managed to look so sweet and innocent, especially after I found out about her 'profession.'

I remember how animated Eve had become that night in '82 when our dinner conversation turned to a new book our friend had written, about the I Ching. "This is unbelievable!" she had said. "I've been reading the I Ching for over ten years, but hadn't met any other people who even heard of it until I met you folks!" Eve told us she had wondered if the book had fallen out of the sky and she was the only one on the planet who knew about it. She said that people would look at her like she was batty when she explained that it was a book based on ancient Oriental wisdom and that you asked a question and threw coins to find out what part to read for your answer. "I was starting to think I was crazy too," Eve had exclaimed, "and now you tell me you not only know about it, but your friend wrote a book about it. This is so exciting!" Eve's shyness evaporated as she told us about how she had discovered the I Ching and about the wild year she had had in 1972, ten years before that first time we met.

I had thoroughly enjoyed Eve's company back then, and now welcomed the opportunity to become reacquainted with her.

"What I remember most about my first encounter with you, Eve," I said, as we settled into the comfy sofa in my parlor, "is that you had been more interested in discussing metaphysics than in talking about stripping. You told us that you had been living with a mind control and meditation teacher in Manhattan a couple of years before you became a stripper. As I recall, it was an intriguing tale, though the details are a little hazy. Could you refresh my memory?"

"Sure, I'd be glad to Stella," Eve replied. "When I lived in New York City in '72 I met people from all walks of life who were interested in every facet of psychic phenomenon imaginable. It was like studying for a master's degree in the occult.

"A different group came every weekend for the three-day mind control intensive. I helped the teacher by acting as a hostess: making sure everyone was comfortable, getting food and beverages ready, that kind of thing. In exchange, I got free room and board in a cool loft space, and got to take the mind control class over and over again. There was plenty of time in between the sessions to talk to people, and they were eager to talk about all the weird stuff they were into.

"There was a cab driver who was interested in clairvoyance. A woman who called herself Lady Zaria read Tarot cards. Sharon, who worked with Stanley Krippner at the Maimonides Dream Lab, filled me in on the experiments they were doing to test people with psychic abilities.

"One of my favorite characters was Bryce Bond. His day job was radio host on a classical station, but his passion was chasing UFOs. Some psychic would predict that extraterrestrials were going to land in a remote place in England, so Bryce would assemble a film crew and fly the whole bunch over to the UK and sit and wait in a cornfield for the spacemen to land.

"Psychokinesis, levitation, pyramid power, divination, Witchcraft and shamanism—you name it—they were into it. Some of the people seemed like they were just released from Bellevue, but many were very intelligent, well educated, and appeared to be fairly normal. It was a fascinating year, and a different educational experience than any college I could have attended.

"But all of my explorations into the paranormal didn't help me to predict the twisted path my life would take after that," Eve said with a wry grin. "Maybe I should have polished my crystal ball a little better."

As Eve paused to drink some water, I thought back to her brief relationship with Doug. He had brought her to our apartment several times, but their affair had ended after a few months. Doug wouldn't volunteer much about why they stopped seeing each other. He was so sullen when I asked him about Eve I decided not to pursue it any further. Doug was sullen much of the time anyway. I didn't have to stretch my imagination to understand why such a beautiful, bubbly young lady wouldn't want to hang around him for too long.

Poor Doug. He had hoped Eve would be the one to turn his life around. I had tried to help him understand that no person outside of yourself can make you happy; that you need to find your own happiness from within, and once you do, you may be lucky enough to find someone to share that happiness with. It had been futile to share my insight with him. It's hard to hear gems of vibrant truth when you're mired in the swampland of unrequited love.

I'd sometimes wondered what happened to Eve after that, but assumed she hadn't given me much thought over the years. Why would she? So, I was impressed that she managed to find me, as I had relocated from Boston to Savannah.

Now here she was, back in my life thirty years later. No longer the ingénue, Eve's long golden locks had dulled to a light brown and were clipped to chin-length. Her face and figure were fuller, but not overly-so for a woman in her late fifties. The wide-eyed look in her blue eyes had been replaced with something hard to define, perhaps a serenity born of experience — not jaded, but lit with a deep knowing.

Her smile was the most unchanged thing about her. I should say smiles, as they varied from a slight upward curve of the lips to an open ear-to-ear grin, enhanced by a slight creasing on either side of the mouth. We call them 'laugh lines' but they are etched from years of reacting to a spectrum of emotions: shock, pain, and horror, as well as joy and rolling-on-the-floor laughter. Whatever Eve had gone through since our first meeting, time had not diminished her cheerful demeanor.

Eve had contacted me just a few months prior. I was pleasantly surprised to get her email:

> Dear Stella,
> You probably don't remember me. It's been many years since we met. I used to date Max's son Doug. I have a project I'm working on and wondering if you might be willing to help me? I thought of you because even though we only knew each other briefly, I felt we had a strong connection. Perhaps I should have dated you instead of Doug (lol). But seriously, I always liked your energy, and you're the only published author I know. I want to write about my days as an ecdysiast (a.k.a. striptease dancer). I am turning to you because I don't have much experience as a writer and I want to keep my identity secret. I am looking for someone to co-author my story. If you are open to it, please give me a call so we can explore the idea further.
> Kind regards,
> Eve Littlepage

Eve's email couldn't have come at a better time. It seemed an eternity since anything I'd worked on had truly sparked my interest. Writing travel guides and co-authoring cookbooks were helping to supplement my pension, but it had been a decade since I'd written my last romance novel. Since then, my inner muse had been doing a great imitation of Sleeping Beauty. Now, because of Eve's note, my slumbering muse had sprung back to life. I was exhilarated by the prospect of learning about the 'Adventures of Eve' and helping her to document them. There were questions I had yearned to ask when we had first met, all those years ago, but it hadn't seemed polite to pry too much at the time. Now here she was, thirty years later, welcoming me to explore a chapter in her life she had hidden from most people.

Eve had included her contact info and without thinking twice, I invited her to stay with me for a month to get the work started. I had plenty of room and welcomed the company in the spacious old Victorian I had inherited from my aunt. Besides, we both agreed it would be more pleasant to be in Savannah than Boston in late March. After taking a day for Eve to settle in, we were finally ready to start working together on her memoir. We set ourselves up in my parlor, using my trusty old tape recorder and an interview-style process to help spark her memory.

"It's funny about those early days," Eve told me. "Some things, like that first time on stage, I remember like it was yesterday. Much of it after that is a big blur, like fragments of a foggy dream. Well, of course I was in a fog. I hated what I had become, so I did a lot of drinking and getting stoned on whatever was in front of me to deal with it. I remember sitting at the bar at the Surf Club, the first place I danced in. I was thinking about my life: how I had been into yoga, health food, cosmic consciousness and whatnot, just a year or so before this. I'm sitting in this dark bar, no windows to let in the beautiful sunshine, noticing the sickening stench of the place: alcohol-stained carpets, cigarette smoke, and stale perfume—and thinking to myself: *How did a wholesome country girl like me end up in a depressing place like this?* Then I heard a voice, in my head, but it seemed like it came from outside of me. It said: *IF YOU HELP AT LEAST ONE PERSON, THEN THAT IS WHY YOU ARE HERE.*

"It yanked me out of despair and gave me a flash of hope, and a feeling I was being guided. Things didn't exactly get rosy after that. They got much worse before they got better. Yet that voice and that strange moment gave me strength to keep on going through some difficult times. It wasn't until years later I understood more about it. I was having a spiritual awakening, though I was still in too much of a fog to see it at the time."

It was inspiring to listen to Eve recount such a pivotal moment. It made me realize how often adverse circumstances ended up helping me, or someone around me, after all. I never heard any 'voices' that told me my suffering was for a reason. I wasn't sure I envied her experience. Hearing voices would probably unnerve me and make me question my sanity, more than offer me solace.

"What happened next?" I asked. "How did things

get worse before they got better?"

"I'll get to that soon enough, Stella," said Eve, "but I'd like to give you more background first, if that's okay?"

"Yes, of course," I replied. "I want you to tell your story in your own words. I may ask questions for clarification, or to help you if you seem stuck. But I want you to feel in control of this process. Please continue as you wish."

"Thank you Stella, that's helpful. I wasn't sure how this would work, having someone co-author. So, the voice told me I was there for a reason, but I want to share with you the other factors which led me to that first day, and subsequent ten-year stint as a striptease artist."

Eve kicked off her shoes and shifted around on the sofa, tucking her legs under her in a lotus position. Drawing a deep breath, she eyed the tape recorder on the coffee table. Still gazing at the little black box, she continued, shaking her head slowly. "It's amazing how far I strayed from my childhood ambitions. You see, by the time I was ten years old, I was convinced I wanted to become a nun. Hard to believe, I know!" she laughed. Looking up from the table, Eve continued with a bemused expression on her face. "The truth is, after five years in Catholic school, I really wanted to be a saint, like St. Francis or St. Theresa. Of course, I knew I could never be good enough, or holy enough, so I would settle for being a nun. Then I transferred to public school in sixth grade and everything changed. I discovered boys and

decided being a nun might not be so much fun after
all." Eve grinned, then took a sip of water before she
went on. "I'm not into describing my whole
childhood here, just a little history to help you
understand how I got from being that shy, devout
little Catholic girl, to ten years later making a living in
a smoky barroom, dancing naked in front of
strangers."

The bemused expression faded. Eve was a bit
subdued as she went on. "Don't get me wrong, I have
a lot of happy memories of my childhood. I grew up
in a big family; eight kids, nice suburban
neighborhood, two generally good parents who did
the best they could. They were so young when they
started a family, on some level we were all growing
up together.

Where it went bad, was that my mother was an
alcoholic, hitting bottom on booze at the same time I
was hitting puberty. Mom took a lot of the frustration
over her problems out on me. I thought she hated me,
not realizing until years later it was herself, her own
behavior, she hated."

Eve paused, taking a long peering look out the
window. My instincts told me there was something
significant she was leaving out. From the look on her
face I knew she wasn't ready to share whatever secret
had her fighting back tears. She swallowed hard and
shook off the mood.

"Added to the mix, the chaotic era it was: the height
of the Vietnam War and the Peace Movement, and it
was a perfect set-up for my tumble into rebellion. I

started drinking and partying at the age of fourteen, hanging around with townies, hippies, and any social misfits I could find. Sometimes I stayed out all night because I was afraid of what my parents would do if they caught me drinking. It would have been better for all of us if I had showed up at bedtime, drunk, instead of sneaking in at dawn, hung over. Booze may help you escape momentarily, but it's also the quickest road to 'Stupidville.'

"I had been a straight-A student in junior high. By high school I was more interested in drinking, dating, and rock 'n roll than reading, writing, and arithmetic. I managed to graduate, in spite of my mother kicking me out of the house in my senior year. She had freaked out one night when I came home late and screamed at me to get out. Mom was fed up with my partying, but I knew she had a good buzz going herself that night. It was tough. I lived with friends, went to school in the morning and worked six days a week in a department store for minimum wage. Didn't have a car. I walked, bummed rides, or hitchhiked to get around.

"I moved back home briefly, but by the time I was eighteen I was pretty much out on my own. I didn't know how damaged I was until years later. I had very low self-esteem, but nobody was talking about that back in those days. I fancied myself an adventurer, a rebellious explorer. I was going to find some other way to live. I didn't know what I *wanted*, but I knew what I *didn't want*. I didn't want the house in the suburbs, the yard full of kids, the white picket fence.

"Well, that's not exactly true. I *did know* what I wanted, I just didn't think it was possible, so I put it out of my head. Then, one time when I was living home again temporarily, Dad asked me what I wanted to do with my life. I had a momentary surge of courage. I looked him square in the eye and said, 'I WANT TO BE AN ACTRESS!'

"I had finally blurted out my biggest secret. Throughout my childhood I had longed to be a movie star. Every time I was alone in the house, I'd play albums of musicals and sing and dance around the living room, fantasizing that I was Eliza Doolittle, or Maria from the Sound of Music.

"I hid my dream from family and friends, afraid of being laughed at, or accused of the sin of vanity. Of course, there was nothing for me to be vain about. I couldn't sing, except comedy, and my dancing was as graceful as a rodeo clown. My lack of talent hadn't stopped me from hoping I would be discovered someday, but my lack of confidence had kept me from admitting it to anyone, until that moment.

"I had hoped my father would take me seriously, maybe even offer to help me go to school for theater arts. Instead, he shook his head from side to side, waving his arms the way a football ref signals a missed field goal. 'No, no, NO, Eve-Marie, we're talking about EATING here,' he said, giving me a look that meant 'end of conversation.' My heart fell to my feet. All my insecurities came flooding back. I thought, *He's right. I'm not pretty or talented enough. I'd probably starve. Just forget about it.*

"It stung like the lash of a whip, to finally blurt out my secret dream only to be shot down. It would be a long time till I would again dare to admit I had *any* dreams, even to myself.

"The next couple of years I moved around a bit, tried different jobs: office work, waiting tables, exercise instructor in a health club. I had that wild year I told you about in the city, with the mind control teacher. I barely managed to keep a roof over my head and feed myself, but got by somehow. Then I hit a rough patch. I went from barely getting by to falling flat on my face. Jobless and broke, I moved home again. I was glad to be home, and wanted to make a change from my vagabond gypsy lifestyle. I had missed being around my siblings, and especially wanted to get closer to my younger sisters. I hoped I could pass along some of the hard lessons I'd learned to them, keep them from getting hurt, and hurting themselves, like I had.

"It was not to be. Before I could talk to Mom about the reformation that was happening inside me, she threw me out of the house again—for the last time. It was after I had been out until about 3:00 a.m.. I didn't think it was such a big deal. I was twenty-one and had been on my own doing whatever I wanted to for a few years. My mother hadn't told me she expected me to come home 'at a decent hour,' so I was shocked when she flew into a rage, screaming that I was a bad influence on my younger sisters and I should *'get the hell out—out Out OUT!'* I couldn't plead with her. She wouldn't listen, just wanted me out ASAP. Her words burned me to the core, especially since I was ready to pull my life together and cool it on the partying.

"This time I didn't just move out of the house, I moved out of state. I'd been briefly dating a guy I liked okay, but wasn't in love with. Eddie wanted to move to Cape Cod. I didn't know what else to do, and wanted to put some miles between me and my pain, so I went with him. I was so crushed by my mother's last rejection of me, I wanted to run and not look back. I left with not much more than the clothes on my back and a couple of dollars in my pocket. I didn't care what would happen, or that the man I was leaving with was virtually a stranger to me. Even after I found out he was a convicted felon I still decided to leave with him. That's how desperate I was."

"He was a convicted felon?" I asked Eve. I concealed my surprise, trying to keep a detached demeanor. I wanted her to feel comfortable telling me anything, without fear that I would judge or condemn.

"Not only was he a criminal, Stella, but a stupid one. He got caught robbing a bank—no disguise, security cameras everywhere. But I was even more stupid, staying with him after I'd found out," Eve said, with a self-mocking smirk. "Oh yeah, I was on the highway to Stupidville for sure."

2. THE 'UN-REAL' WORLD

"Why did you stay with Eddie then?" I asked Eve.

"The way he explained it, the robbery was a one-time mistake he genuinely regretted," she replied. "He said he was completely reformed and would never do anything like that again. Because I was desperate, I chose to believe him. We both had reasons for wanting to move away, get a fresh start and forget the past. We admitted that we weren't in love. It was too soon to be sure about our feelings for each other for the long run. Neither one of us had much money. It would be easier to move if we had each other to depend on. We made a pact to stay together for at least six months, help each other make a new life on the Cape. At the end of six months, we would review our situation. If either of us wanted out, the other would let them go, without any struggle or blame, or making a scene.

"We moved to Hyannis and found jobs in the restaurant business. I waited tables, he cooked. We lived in the basement of a rooming house. Eddie jazzed up the dull room by shingling a wall with cedar and I hung tie-dyes and Indian-print bedspreads to make it homey. We were two blocks from the ferry to Nantucket and the Vineyard. When the breeze blew from the east, the salty sea air was refreshing. Other days the west wind brought a sweet mix of floral and spice from the candle factory up the street. No wonder they called it Pleasant Street.

"Things were pretty good for a while. We managed to pay rent, eat well, and always had plenty of weed — as there were a lot of partying people around. Eddie and I grew closer, or at least more comfortable with each other. He was on his best behavior — kind to me, helpful around the house, steadily employed. When the six-month review came up, we decided to stay together. We didn't make a long-term commitment, but saw no reason to part ways right then. It wasn't for another six months that I began to see signs of the disease that would take us spiraling downward.

"Everyone we hung out with was into partying so our daily drinking and pot smoking seemed fairly normal at the time. In the back of my mind, I knew I had to watch it — that I had what I called 'alcoholic tendencies' because of my family history. My mom and dad started going to Alcoholics Anonymous and got sober when I was about nineteen. I went to a few AA and Al-Anon meetings to make Mom happy, and because I was a little curious. The experience of going to those few meetings gave me some understanding of alcohol addiction, but I was totally ignorant about compulsive gambling and how destructive it could be.

"I don't know when Eddie's gambling got out of control. He was a good con man and was hiding a lot of things from me. For instance, there was a group of guys he played poker with once or twice a week. There wasn't much to do on the Cape in the winter, so I thought it was good for him to get out with his buddies. It wasn't until much later that I found out this 'great bunch of guys' he hung out with were burglarizing unoccupied vacation homes. God knows what else they were into; it was only by accident that I found out. I was horrified. I barely had two nickels to rub together, but I couldn't condone stealing.

"An opportunity came along for us to move near Boston. A young woman I met in Hyannis offered to put us up while we looked for jobs and a place of our own. It was hard to make a living year-round on Cape Cod in the early '70s, and I was eager to get away from this gang of hoodlums Eddie had taken up with. So we packed our few belongings and moved in with Goldie. It took about three months for us to save up enough to get our own place.

"Something happened between Goldie and Eddie; I never found out what. Things were going fine, then one day she seemed mighty pissed off and we were asked to leave immediately. Neither of them would tell me what was going on, but I have my suspicions."

Eve paused, her gaze fixed on the coffee table, her lips twisted into a half-smile. She seemed deep in thought, perhaps pondering an old mystery that she knew would never be solved.

"What suspicions, Eve?" I asked.

"I had suspected for a while that they were fooling

around. I had no real evidence, just something in the way they looked at each other, subtleties in body language, that sort of thing. I chose to ignore my instincts. What would it gain to confront them? Most likely I'd be the one out on the street if I brought it up. Besides, the only thing I was an expert in back then was avoiding confrontation. Most children of alcoholics learn how to do that before they hit kindergarten. But I had wondered why Goldie was so generous taking us in the way she had. Maybe she'd been screwing him all along.

"Whether they were into hanky-panky or not, I think Eddie conned her out of some cash. I had no idea at the time, but found out later that he had a habit of burning people all the time. He was dodging people he owed gambling debts to. He'd get someone to put up cash for a pot deal, then put them off saying he was waiting for the shipment to come in. He'd say he couldn't return their money, because he'd 'already given it to the dealer,' or some such bullshit. He was clever enough to hide his con games from me, and I was naive enough not to notice. It wasn't until we had been together for a year that my blindfold was removed.

"We got an apartment in Somerville after we left Goldie's. Eddie got a job as a cook in Harvard Square and I was waiting tables at a Middle Eastern restaurant—the Averof—in Porter Square. We were making just enough to keep a roof over our heads. One day the landlord calls and is wondering why we are two weeks late on the rent. I was stunned, because I had given Eddie the cash to pay it two weeks prior, and he swore he took care of it. When I confronted him about it, he told me it was tied up in a pot deal. He thought it would only take a couple of days, and he could turn the weed over for some extra cash, get our own stash, and still have the rent money when it was done. But the blah blah guy hadn't blah blah gotten back to him, and he was waiting for the shipment—you get the idea.

"It took a few more days before he finally admitted to me that he lost the money at the track. That was hard for me to swallow, to think he would take my hard-earned waitress tips and blow them on a damn horse race! On top of that, I was afraid we'd get evicted for not having rent. My stomach was churning enough acid to run a car battery.

"He must have sensed that I was thinking about leaving him. He became more possessive and controlling. It got to where I couldn't make a move without his consent. For example, I told him I was going to Boston to visit my friend Cookie and her boyfriend Tom. He asked me what time I'd be home. I told him I wasn't sure, but he badgered me to commit to a time. He said it was because he cared about me, and he only wanted a timeframe so he would know when he should start worrying, if I were late. That sounded reasonable enough, so I said I'd probably be home around 7:00 PM. Then he calls Cookie's house at 6:45, screaming at me because I hadn't left yet, and he says it takes forty-five minutes to take the T home and I'm going to be late.

"So this wasn't just someone caring about their mate, but trying to control them. I was such a wimp; I let him get away with this crap for a long time. I didn't see the signs, didn't know how abusive he would become. It happened so gradually that I just didn't notice how bad it was getting."

Eve took a moment to re-position herself on the sofa. Drawing her knees up close to her chest, she wrapped her arms around her legs, hugging them as if to shield herself from dark memories.

"You said he became abusive—do you mean physically?" I asked.

"Yes, I am getting to that, Stella. It's mentally—emotionally—hard for me to go back there, but the desperation I felt, being stuck in this relationship with him, has so much to do with why I became a dancer.

"I'd been with Eddie for about a year and a half, when I decided to take a trip home to visit my friends and family. Once I was away from him, I saw things more clearly, realized how unhappy I was with him. He had been on his best behavior the first year we were together, then the dark side of his nature began to emerge. My friend, Lydia, was worried about me. I didn't have to say much. She could see from the dark circles around my eyes and my bony body that I was a wreck. She didn't want me to feel stuck with this creep. Lydia offered to put me up for a while until I could get on my feet. So I made up my mind on that weekend trip that I was going to leave him. The only reason I was going back was to retrieve my clothes and what few belongings I had. Little did I know that going back was going to cost me much more than my few measly possessions were worth. How different my life might have turned out if I had not made that near-fatal decision.

"Up 'til then, I had been a wimp. The day I showed up to get my things, I was feeling very strong and resolute. I knew Eddie would be upset, but wasn't prepared for what happened next. He wasn't home when I first got there. I scurried around the apartment gathering what I could. I was heartsick about leaving Bunny behind — she was a stray cat we had taken in. It didn't fit into the plan to take her with me. I had to leave quickly, no time to make arrangements for custody of our pet. I wasn't afraid of Eddie, but hoped to get out before he got home to avoid a showdown. I planned to call him from a safe distance to say good-bye. It didn't work out that way. He came home before I finished packing.

"I don't remember what we said to each other, only what happened when he realized I was leaving. He had never laid a hand on me in anger, so I was shocked when he grabbed me by my upper arms and carried me through the front door out of the apartment. There was a long flight of stairs, then a landing, then another long flight of stairs that led to the main entrance of the building. Eddie had a death grip on my upper arms, so they were pinned down against both sides of me. He was about 6 feet, 180 pounds. He took my 5-and-a-half-foot, 120-pound frame and lifted me like I was a rag doll. He held me up in the air. I was certain he was going to toss me down the staircase. Then I felt a sharp whack across my lower back as he slammed my helpless body against the banister. With nauseating horror I realized I was suspended over the empty space between the stairwells and if he let go I would plummet headfirst straight down the twenty-foot drop. He had a crazed look in his eyes I had never seen before. He held me there, threatening to drop me unless I promised not to leave him. It was all I could do to squeak out, 'Okay, okay, I'll give you another chance. I promise I won't go. Just please stop hurting me.' It was so strange — the sudden puzzled look on his face, as if to say, *'Oh, was I hurting you? I hadn't realized ...'* as he set me down gently on my feet. The last thing I wanted to do was stay, but it would mean death if I didn't plan my exit carefully.

"So I stayed with him, for six hellish months more. Six months of waiting until I could find a way out of this freakish prison, wondering each day if I would have a chance to escape. Whatever charm he initially held for me, all I felt now was repulsion. I had to hide my true feelings and 'play along' until the right opportunity to run presented itself. It may be hard for you to imagine that I could not find a way to get out. But after that day, he kept a tighter rein on my every move and seldom left me alone for more than two minutes. He made sure I never had any cash on me. It's hard to get very far when you don't even have bus fare. The skeeviest thing was that I couldn't reject his sexual advances without arousing suspicion that I was planning to escape. So I went along with it, faking orgasms and dealing with my disgust by numbing myself with booze and weed.

"We were always broke, even though I was busting my ass waitressing. One day we had no food in the house. Eddie had no money, I had about four bucks. I sent him to the store to get a loaf of bread and tuna fish and he came back with nothing but beer and cigarettes. *I was fuming!* He didn't see any point in buying food if we couldn't eat anything better than tuna fish — said we might as well get a buzz and make sure we had smokes! I was so friggin' thin at the time my family and friends thought I was anorexic. I wasn't. An anorexic is underweight and still thinks they're fat. I knew I was too thin. I was such a nervous wreck living with this creep; I couldn't eat, half the time from nerves, the other half from being penniless.

"One day he came home all excited and said he had a great idea how we could make some easy money, but it would involve me and he wasn't sure how I'd feel about it. One of the other cooks he worked with was from Brazil, and was looking to get married to stay in the country. They thought it would be a great idea for me to marry him! Eddie said if I did it, it would only be on paper, and that the cook was willing to pay eight hundred dollars, which went a lot farther in 1973 than it does now.

"I was astounded by his 'proposal.' Up until then I thought Eddie cared about me, and that's why he wanted me to stay with him. I was finally getting a clue that it wasn't me he was afraid of losing. I was nothing more to him than a meal ticket and an easy piece of ass. I was crushed he would even suggest I marry this stranger for money, but I hid my feelings from him. I had absolutely no intention of going through with this harebrained scheme, but Eddie talked me into at least meeting the guy before I said 'no.'

"I had some picture in my mind that this Brazilian cook would be half my height, missing teeth, and speak broken English. I was thinking before I met him that even if I wanted to do it, no one would believe we could possibly be a couple, and I would probably end up in jail.

"When I met Luis, all my concerns melted away. His appearance was a pleasant surprise. He was slightly taller than me, with a slender build, dark handsome looks, and a knockout smile. I was charmed by his soft-spoken manner as he explained, in very articulate English, why he wanted to marry a U.S. citizen. He had a lovely American girlfriend. They were both students, and thought they might marry someday, but were not ready yet. His student visa was going to expire soon. He wanted to settle in the U.S. and, once he could afford it, bring his mother here from Brazil to give her a better life.

"*What a guy,* I thought. I could just tell from looking into those big brown eyes that he was truly a good soul. My instincts told me he was a good man: honorable, kind, generous, sincere, and many other qualities that Eddie lacked. I decided on the spot to go ahead with it. I genuinely wanted to help him out. That meant more to me than the money. I also knew we would be believable as a couple.

"The wedding was surreal. Eddie did not want to come. Luis and I went to a Justice of the Peace. It was a small dingy office in a huge downtown building. The walls were grayish green; not sure if it was paint or mold. Our witnesses were one of Luis' friends, Raphael, and Luis' American girlfriend Katie. We all politely ignored the pungent odor of stale urine and fresh whiskey surrounding the desk where the JP sat, or rather, swayed.

"I half-expected Eddie to show up and stop us before we went through with it. I couldn't fathom that anyone could arrange to have someone they loved married off to someone else. It confirmed that whatever he felt for me, it wasn't love.

"Luis and I said our 'I do's' after a mercifully short ceremony. We had a celebration dinner at an Italian restaurant with about ten of Luis and Katie's friends. You'd think Katie might have been uncomfortable with the situation, but she was grinning from ear to ear and thanking me profusely for helping them out. I smiled sweetly and thanked the wait staff for their endless congratulations, wondering who was writing this script.

"I wasn't sorry I did it. Luis was a good person and I sincerely wanted to help him. I never saw a dime of the money either. He gave the eight hundred dollars to Eddie. I was thinking we could at least get caught up on the rent and bills, but no. Without even mentioning it to me first, Eddie bought a stereo system with the money! To think he could 'sell me off' for the price of a stereo, that he presumed the money was all his to spend. I was sick with rage. It got me pissed off enough to stand up to him.

"It was then that I announced I was thinking of trying a new career. I told him I couldn't handle waitressing anymore, and if he wanted me to stay, he'd have to let me do something else. He asked me what I had in mind. I said I wanted to be a nightclub dancer. I looked at him defiantly, bracing myself, ready for his opposition. To my surprise, he thought it was a good idea. Of course he would think so — if his meal ticket could find a way to make more dough, why would he stand in her way?

"My disgust with him was complete by now. I was becoming stronger in my resolve to leave him, but knew I had to be careful how I did it. The memory of being dangled over the stairwell lingered, long after my bruises had faded. Whatever my plan, I needed to make more money in order to leave. I started making moves to find a job as a dancer. It was this whole combination of things — the desperate financial situation, feeling stuck in an abusive relationship, and still having a deep-down desire to be an actress — that led me to seek this new 'career path.'"

Eve paused her story to stretch and shift her position on the sofa. It gave me a moment to reflect on how a catalyst isn't always a singular event. Oftentimes there are several elements, like ingredients in recipe, that combine to create a turning point in our lives. I assumed from what Eve was saying that if poverty weren't an issue, or if she had been happy with her boyfriend, that her wish to be an actress wasn't enough in itself to catapult her into the striptease business.

"Didn't the idea of dancing in the nude bother you?' I asked Eve.

"Of course it did, Stella," she replied. "My mind was going in circles around the issue. I was influenced by the hippie movement to see the human body in its natural unclothed state as something beautiful, a divine creation that should be celebrated, not shamed. Yet, I hadn't eradicated my Catholic upbringing that told me nudity was a sin. Added to that, I was insecure about how my body looked, naked or clothed, but especially naked. Like millions of other young women, I had been brainwashed into worshipping an ideal of beauty that I would never achieve. I also struggled with Women's Lib, not wanting to betray my feminist ideals by buying into a system that treats women merely as sex objects. That may have bothered me most of all. But I put my internal arguments on that to rest with a shrug. What the hell, I told myself, men have been treating me as a sex object anyway, I might as well make some money at it.

"I answered an ad in the paper and ended up being sent by an agent named Roy Dee to the red-light district of Boston known as the Combat Zone. I can't remember the name of the club, because I didn't even make it as far as the audition. I was creeped-out the minute I walked in the place. I was expecting something more akin to the old Burlesque—Gypsy Rose Lee in a feather boa and sequins—flirty and sexy, but classy. The place Roy sent me to was more like a peep-show where the girls start out wearing next to nothing and a minute later they're showing the world parts of their anatomy that would make a gynecologist blush. There was a sickening stench in the place. Cigar smoke, sweat, and pussy, is the best way I can describe it. The guy who ran the place said it was my turn to audition. I took one look at 'the stage'—a long narrow runway with a row of guys swilling beers all around it—and thought I was gonna hurl any minute. I ran out of the place in tears, disgusted with myself and devastated that my life seemed to be going from bad to worse.

"I thought that was the end of my dancing career. I was wrong. Roy Dee called me and asked what happened, said the club manager told him I ran off without saying a word to anyone. I told him how I felt about the whole thing, and maybe it just wasn't for me. He said not to give up yet, that the Combat Zone was a tough scene, but there were other clubs in the suburbs that were more tame than the ones in Boston. He talked me into trying out a club on the North Shore. That's when I went to the Surf.

"It was different from the club in the 'Zone', still not a place I'd want Mother to see me in. It was dark and eerie, but I didn't have the sense of repulsion I had in the other place. It was a large room, and reminded me more of a restaurant the way it was set up, except for the stage at the far end. There was a bar with tall stools that ran along the left side of the room, and round tables with red cloths filled the lounge area in front of the stage.

"I was a skinny, wide-eyed twenty-two year old, terrified, but so desperate to change my life I was willing to give it a shot. The club manager, Peter, was a short, stocky, intimidating guy in his forties. I told him Roy sent me to audition. He took his cigar out of his mouth and asked me if I'd ever danced before. I said 'No, not like this,' glancing at the stage and the half-naked woman who was writhing around on it. He looked me up and down and said, 'A little scrawny, but you'll do all right. Where's your wardrobe?' 'What wardrobe?' I asked. He rolled his eyes around and shook his head. Pointing to a door in the corner, he told me to go into the dressing room and ask some of the girls back there to help me.

"That's when I met Kayleen. In a frantic flurry, she and Tina helped me get ready for my 'debut.' I would never have gotten on stage that first time if it wasn't for the two of them. Kayleen pulled a skimpy black velvet costume out of her suitcase and tossed it at me. 'Here put this on,' she commanded. 'What's your name?' 'Eve,' I replied. 'That your real name? Is that what you want to be announced as?' 'Oh God, NO!' I said. 'I hadn't thought about a stage name, definitely don't want to use my real name! God, let me think ...' 'There's no time,' she said. 'You gotta get out there. Peter will have a conniption! He hates an empty stage. How about Lisa? You kinda look like a Lisa.' 'Sure, great,' I said. 'You're shakin' like a leaf,' she said. 'Here, drink this.' Kayleen pushed a tall cold glass into my hand and without hesitation, I gulped down the vodka-and-something. The warmth of the liquor oozed through my body, but it barely took the edge off my panic. 'Good Luck!' I heard her call behind me as Tina led me out of the dressing room toward the stage. I glanced back at Kayleen to thank her and saw her rolling her eyes and shaking her head. By her gestures I could tell she didn't think this rookie would make it past the first inning.

"I probably wouldn't have been hired if they really gave a shit how good I was that first day. All that mattered to the bosses and to the customers was that it was my first time. It's not like anyone announced it. It was obvious, I'm sure. The word spread like lightning through the club that the 'new girl' was totally new to the business. It was a rare thrill for them to witness a 'virgin striptease.' I got through it, with Tina coaching me right up until I stepped out through the red velvet curtain. The customers hooted, hollered, and applauded as I shyly swayed around to the music, shedding a little more clothing with each song. I can clearly remember those few minutes behind stage and the first song I danced to — *Midnight Rider* — but the rest of it is vague — like a dream that evaporates as you awaken.

"Peter hired me, under the condition that I get a wardrobe and some proper shoes. I danced my first day barefoot. I was dismayed, as I was so broke I didn't know how I could afford a special wardrobe. Kayleen told me to ask Peter for an advance. I did and he paid me for my first day. As he handed me the cash he said, 'Remember honey, as long as you're a dancer, you'll always have money in your pocket.' These were magical words to me, after living on the edge for so long.

"Kayleen tipped me off on where to get a pair of dancer's spikes. They were specially-made high heels that would stand up to the abuse a dancer puts shoes through. They were stronger and safer than the dainty little heels you'd get at the neighborhood shoe store. They had a curved platform made of plywood — several layers of laminated wood — with a rubber sole. The leather uppers came in four colors: gold, silver, black, or red. I picked the silver ones, with ankle straps. 'Take a good look at your feet,' Kayleen said. 'What's wrong with them?' I replied, glancing downward. 'Nothing!' she laughed. 'It's just that they'll never look like that again, once you start dancin' in those shoes!' She was right. I wish I had 'before and after' pictures. Maybe some people think it's glamorous, getting up on stage in feathers and rhinestones. They'd think differently if they ever saw us backstage soaking our corns and blisters, not to mention how years of trotting around in spiked heels wreaks havoc on your knees and spine.

"I bought some underpieces—bra, jock, and g-string sets—from one of the other dancers. She made her own costumes, and some to sell for extra cash. I went to Filene's Basement and picked up a few odd outfits and lingerie that could be converted into an acceptable wardrobe. The first costume I got was a flashy red pantsuit. It was made of a stretchy knit and had a short bolero-type jacket. There was red fringe edging the whole jacket and more fringe on the hem of the pants. It was brighter and trashier than anything I'd ever worn before, but it would work for my new job. With the help of my co-workers, I added 'stripper zippers' to the sides of the pant legs and sparkled it all up with rhinestones. I loved the way the fringe swished around when I danced in it. It felt silky brushing against my arms and legs.

"The make-up and costumes helped me transform and adapt to my new role. The real me, little Eve-Marie Littlepage, was too meek and modest to be a stripper. I had to create a new character, like an actress does, to be able to get up there and bare it all. I put on the spikes, the sparkles, the phony grin, and this other personality came out to play—flirty, vampy, maybe a little naughty. The person on the stage was me, but not me. I was aware of this core being, the one inside me, who was watching this persona I created as if it was a cartoon character. I don't think I'm the only dancer who felt that way. We all would refer to jobs outside of the striptease business as the 'Real World'—as if it were universally accepted among us that the world we lived and worked in was somehow not valid, that is was the 'Un-Real World.'

"There was another crucial part of my 'costume,' my character-creating mask: drugs and booze. Nothing hard, but I had to have something to relax me before I could get on stage, something to give me courage. I got butterflies in my stomach every time. I had a drink, a hit off a joint, or both. I had to be careful not to get too wasted so I could keep my balance in those three-inch spikes! 'Come-Fuck-Me-Shoes' they used to call them. I never heard that expression before. There were a lot of expressions I heard in those bars that I never heard before."

Eve shook her head, amused by her last remark. "Sorry Stella, I hope my language doesn't offend you. I picked up a few swear words from my four brothers growing up, but working in strip clubs morphed my language to the point where every other word was the f-word. I can turn it off when I need to be more dignified, but if I'm relaxed and around friends I'm comfortable with, I still swear like a sailor."

"No offense taken," I replied, with a wink. "I've been known to use a colorful expletive myself, now and then. By the way, I'm in the mood for another cup of coffee. Can I get one for you too?" I asked.

"I'd fucking love one Stella!" Eve answered, and we both laughed as I headed off to the kitchen.

3. DEMON EYES

I was back in the parlor a few minutes later with hot coffee for both of us. As Eve continued to recount her early days as a striptease dancer, she was fidgeting and twisting a cotton handkerchief. There was a noticeable tightness around her lips and a furrow in her brow. Much as I wanted to hear more, I wondered if she was a bit fatigued. I asked if she needed to take a break.

"Bear with me Stella, I need to get through this next part. It's strange, I've talked about it before. I used to get weepy, but after awhile I could tell the story without much emotion at all, like it happened to someone else. Having it written down, where thousands of strangers might read it—it's just hard. Time may heal all wounds, but putting them in print can amplify them.

"I was working at the Surf about three weeks by then. Eddie liked that I was earning twice what I did waitressing. Things were getting more tense between us though. I was becoming stronger, more independent. There wasn't anything obvious I said or did, but he could sense it. He was more anxious if I was a little late coming home. He'd show up at the club unexpectedly, grill me about who I was sitting with, ask if they were hitting on me, stuff like that. I'd tell him we were just talking. He didn't believe me. He was probably worried that I was plotting to run away from him.

"I didn't have a plan yet, but I wasn't about to run off with some guy I met in the club. Don't get me wrong, some of the guys I met seemed nice enough. I just figured none of them would respect me, if they met me as a stripper. Besides, the last thing I wanted was to start another relationship once I got away from this one!

"The club atmosphere was gloomy, and I was uneasy in my new job, but it was heaven to me. That's how miserable I was — I couldn't wait to go to work in a sleazy strip joint every day just to get away from my 'charming' boyfriend.

"One day, two guys from Hyannis came to our apartment looking for Eddie. He had taken some money from them for a pot deal. He'd been putting them off for weeks, telling them the usual bullshit. Once again he had blown the money at the track, so he had no money or dope for them. When the bell rang he looked out the window and panicked when he saw them. They were tired of being put off and had driven three hours to track him down. It was the only time I saw Eddie afraid. He ducked into the hall closet, expecting me to tell them he wasn't home. I was thoroughly fed up with his BS by then. I let them in, then opened the closet door. 'Here he is,' I said, half-hoping they'd beat the crap out of him. You should've seen the look on his face—a comical combo of shock at my betrayal, and shame at his own cowardice.

"He made good on the 'deal' by giving them the stereo he'd bought with the money Luis had given us. First, he orchestrated selling me off in marriage to a foreigner, then gambled away the money we got for it! I was at my limit. I had to figure a way out of this relationship—some way that wouldn't get me killed.

"We lost that nice apartment too, because of the back rent we owed that he blew at the track. It was one of six units in a stucco building, built in the 1940s, with lots of character and warmth. It had five rooms, front and back porches, and a little yard in back. We moved into a bland two-room, semi-modern apartment in a drab area next to the highway. We left so fast we didn't take half our furniture with us. We only had a mattress on the floor in the bedroom, and a day bed and one chair in the other room—a combination living room and kitchen area.

"I was living in a depressing place, working in a degrading job, and stuck in an abusive relationship. It's no wonder I came down with some weird stomach flu that had me heaving for three days straight. My body was trying to purge the hell my life had become by vomiting endlessly. I couldn't keep anything down, not even water. I dropped to 110 pounds. As soon as I recovered enough to walk and keep some food down, I went back to work. I was quite weakened by the ordeal. I could have used a few more days to recuperate, but there are no paid sick days in that line of work.

"A week later I went out after work with a few of the other girls. Nothing too wild—Chinese food and a couple of drinks. I wasn't out very late, but Eddie gave me the third degree when I got home. He didn't believe I was out with my co-workers, but convinced himself there was another guy.

"I was so fed up I totally forgot about making a plan, or being careful. I glared back at him and yelled, *'I've had it! I cannot live with you anymore! I am getting out of here for good this time!'*

"My stomach knotted up like a clenched fist when I saw his face. He had that same maniacal look in his eyes the night he dangled me over the stairwell. I glanced toward the front door, only a few steps away. He rushed over to it and thrust the deadbolt into the lock.

"There would be no escape. I felt a thousand tiny needles pricking my body all over. My breath caught halfway between my heart and throat and stopped cold. I was certain he would murder me.

"He yanked me up in the air and hurled me against the wall. It knocked the wind out of me. I fell to the floor, gasping for air. He jerked me up and slammed me against the wall again. His arms were flailing around and I felt the sharp rap of fists pounding my arms and legs. He kept throwing me around and beating me for five or ten minutes that felt like eternity.

"He tossed me down on the floor and was coming at me again. I was on my back and recoiled into a fetal position. I thought he was going to pick me up and toss me again. Instead he kicked me square in my tailbone with steel-toed construction boots. My body shot back about ten feet across the floor from the searing pain—like a bolt of lightning had struck me. An electrical shock surged up my spine and shot out to every part of my body. He jumped down on top of me and grabbed my head with both hands. He twisted it sideways, nearly wrenching it off my shoulders. My neck was about to snap. I was sure I would be dead in a few seconds. *God, I didn't want to die, but I did want the torture to stop!*

"All of a sudden he stopped tearing at my neck and jumped to his feet. I thought he'd come to his senses—realized he'd almost killed me. I was astounded by what he did next.

"My poor little kitty, Bunny, had been cowering in the corner. He dashed across the room and grabbed her by the scruff of her neck. Then he suspended her from our third-floor apartment window, dangling her furry little body in the night air, glaring at me with a sinister smirk. He seemed to savor the look of horror and pleading, as my expression screamed a silent 'NO!'

"Then, he let go. He let her drop—thirty feet—into the parking lot below, and didn't take his eyes off me.

"I'll never forget his face—demon eyes staring at me—cold as death and burning with hellfire. I didn't know who it was behind those eyes. It couldn't have been the man I chose to live with, shared my bed with. I still can't believe it, but the incredible thing is, it saved my life."

"How so?" I asked. Eve had told me, when she was giving me an outline of her story, that she had been beaten. She hadn't told me until now that her cat had been brutalized too. I couldn't imagine how that saved her life.

"Well, Stella, up to this point he had been in control. He was the bully and I was his fearful, helpless victim. When he threw Bunny out the window, I felt this amazing shift within me. I had a surge of immense energy—the kind I'd heard stories about, like a mother who could lift a car off her trapped child. I knew those stories were true, because I was feeling super-human strength in me. I must have looked different too, because Eddie looked terrified of me. The tables were turned. I knew I had the power to tear his head off, but all I cared about was my cat. I ran to the door—I could have ripped it off the hinges—and unlocked it quickly. I was down three flights of stairs in two leaps, then outside into the parking lot.

"I expected to find my cat's lifeless body splayed out on the pavement. To my great relief, she was alive—trembling wildly in a juniper bush that had broken her fall a mere foot from the ground. I scooped the poor shaken thing up in my arms, and started sobbing. I was crying for joy that she was okay, at the same time crying at the horror of the whole episode.

"I snapped out of it as I realized I was OUT. He didn't seem to be running after me, and I wasn't going to wait around to see if he would. *But what to do?* I was traumatized, confused, yet all my senses were at a peak. I fished around the pocket of my jeans and found a dime. All I had was the clothes on my back, the cat in my arms, and ten cents in my pocket. I headed to the fast food place nearby to make a phone call—you could make a call for a dime back then." Eve chuckled at this last remark.

Her laughter did not camouflage the distress she felt while verbally reliving her nightmarish experience. I could see tears welling up, though she fought them back. One small tear escaped and trickled down her cheek. She wiped it quickly with the back of her hand. "I just need a moment, Stella, before I continue. Excuse me," she said. She grabbed a tissue from the box on the table and headed to the bathroom, sniffling a bit as she went.

I knew Eve was tired and probably ready to wrap things up for the day, especially after this heart-wrenching monologue. I didn't want to push her, but I was dying to know what she did end up doing next. *What would I have done — out on the street, beaten, shaken, with only my cat and a dime to my name?*

"Are you okay? We can stop for now if you'd like," I said, as she reentered the parlor. I was hoping otherwise, but it seemed the right thing to say.

Eve shook her head in reply as she got resettled. Stretching her legs out across the length of the sofa, she leaned back on cushions she had propped up against the arm of it. "Thank you Stella, I'm fine. I am sort of ragged out, but I can go on a bit longer. Aren't you curious about what happened next?" She raised one eyebrow and grinned slightly as she said this. I could see the impish sparkle returning to her eyes, and was relieved to see her relaxing again.

"Yes, indeed, I am most curious. If you have the energy to talk, I have the energy to listen." I mirrored her levity. The exchange of our smiles lightened the atmosphere. There was a refreshing crispness in the room, the way the air feels after a spring rain. "So there you were, in the fast food place. Who did you call?" I asked.

"Actually, I wasn't in the restaurant," Eve replied. "They wouldn't let me in because I had my cat with me. I was trying to avoid being murdered, and they're worried about someone getting a cat hair in their chintzy burger. The only help they offered was to point to the phone booth outside. I could barely dial the phone—between holding the cat, trembling like an earthquake, and keeping a lookout for Eddie.

"I called the Surf and asked for JD. He was Peter's brother, and the manager of the club. I knew he had a thing for me. I was attracted to him too, but had been careful not to let the flirtation go too far, afraid of what would happen if Eddie found out. I didn't know who else to turn to. Eddie had done a good job of alienating all my old friends, so I didn't even try to make new ones.

"JD met me in the parking lot of the shopping center across the street. I cried on his shoulder and told him what had happened, how dreadful it was to be with this guy, that I was desperate to leave but had nowhere to go. After I calmed down, he took me to a late-night breakfast place. I told him I didn't feel hungry, but he insisted. He seemed genuinely concerned about me. After what I'd been through—not just getting beat up, but Eddie's complete disregard for my well-being—it felt good having someone care. The fact that he was a member of a well-known Mafia family should probably have scared me. Quite the opposite though—I felt safe, protected.

"He said he could help me, but insisted I go back home that night. He would come to get me the next day. I was to pack some clothes but leave the cat—sorry, but he didn't like cats. *I was terrified! I begged him not to make me go back.* He said he was sure I'd be okay, that Eddie most likely had calmed down by then and was sorry for what he'd done. He gave me some money and his home phone number, and said to get the hell out and call him if it looked like I was going to get hurt again.

"I couldn't believe I was walking back into that apartment. I wished I hadn't eaten—my stomach was doing backflips. I was beyond grateful to find Eddie passed out in the living room on the daybed. He was snoring blissfully, in a deep drunken sleep. I tiptoed into the bedroom and collapsed on the mattress.

"The next morning it took a few seconds, as I was coming out of dreamland, to recall the horror of the night before. When I came into full consciousness, terror gripped me again, as I wondered if Eddie was still in the other room. I tried to get up. My fear level went off the charts when my body didn't respond to my mental wish to move. I concentrated on pressing my forefingers to my thumbs, but couldn't feel a thing. I tried to wiggle my toes. My body just didn't seem to be there. I couldn't lift my head up to see if it was, either.

"*I was paralyzed!* I had the sensation of being a disembodied head. I could hear, see, think, blink, but could not feel any part of my body below my neck! *How could this be? He'd hurt me badly, but I was able to walk last night. Maybe I'd been in shock and didn't feel the full effects right away.* My panic surged beyond what I thought possible. I was sure he was going to find me incapacitated and finish me off—crush my skull or choke me, as I lay there, defenseless.

"I summoned every bit of willpower imaginable, and prayed to God to help me get up and get out of this place—*to let me live.* Somehow I was able to roll over on my side, ease off the mattress and onto the floor. I was on my hands and knees, fierce pain screaming through my body. I managed to get on my feet, but couldn't straighten up. So I hobbled around, my body bent at a right angle, and looked into the other room. Eddie was gone. He left me a brief note, saying he was sorry, that he went to work but would be home at lunchtime. I looked at the clock. I had about an hour to get out. I needed every minute of it too. I was in agonizing pain and could barely walk. It took me forty-five minutes to pack a small suitcase that would have taken five minutes to fill if I wasn't hurt.

"JD told me to take a cab to his place—he would pay the fare. He grilled me a bit when I got there. He wanted reassurance that I had no intention of going back to the asshole. He'd seen girls before who got beat up and went running back to the jerk, and it would really piss him off if I did that. He said he was glad to help me out, but he was putting his neck on the line, and mine too. His brother Peter didn't like him getting involved with any of the staff—waitresses or strippers—and might fire us both if he found out I was staying with him.

"He left me alone in his apartment to rest while he went to work. He came back later with Chinese food. After we ate, he turned on soft jazz and put his arm around me as we stretched out on his bed. He said, 'We don't have to fool around, if you don't want to.' I said it was okay, and didn't let him know how much pain I was in. I don't know why I went through with it. I did want to sleep with him, but would've preferred waiting until my injuries were healed. I guess I wanted to give him something back for helping me. There's also something about taking a

new   lover   when   you've   ended   an   abusive
relationship—as if I could erase the aura of Eddie's
dark energy by sharing my body with another man. It
was my final declaration of independence."

4. LET THE BAGGAGE GO

"I should have gone to a hospital," continued Eve. "Instead, I spent three days after the trauma cloistering myself in JD's apartment. He had to work, so I was mostly alone, with a radio and TV for company. I spent most of the time sleeping, and reflecting on what had happened. I now understood why women who have been beat up or raped become man-haters. I did not want to do that. It didn't seem right to condemn an entire gender for the misdeeds of one man. That kind of bitterness can get into your blood until you wear it on your face like an ugly mask.

"I remember giving myself this 'pep-talk,' telling myself that ALL men did not do this to me, that I shouldn't let this incident affect my attitude toward other guys. I reinforced the idea by reminding myself of all of the good men in my life—like my four brothers, and my hometown buddies—who would never do such a cruel thing. I had to work at this though, because I was in such pain, both physically and mentally.

"I did some yoga and gentle stretching, hoping it would realign my spine as it healed. I had no health insurance. I was trying to be my own crisis counselor and physical therapist. Nowadays there are many shelters and organizations to help battered women, but it wasn't so back then.

"I didn't know what else to do. I couldn't bring myself to call my parents. I was feeling a lot of shame—embarrassed that I could have been so naïve, so stupid—to be with anyone who would brutalize me. I didn't want my Mom to be upset and blame herself for driving me out of the house and into the arms of a bully. I'm not sure I didn't blame her myself.

"I just wanted to hide. So I did, until JD told me, as kindly as he could, that I had to find another place to stay.

"Peter was not happy about JD keeping me at his apartment. Peter also told JD that if I took any more time off he couldn't guarantee I'd have a job. I needed the money, as I was now homeless and practically alone. It was clear to me that JD liked me but wasn't interested in anything long-term. That was fine with me. Much as I was drawn to him, I wasn't ready for another relationship.

"Somehow I managed to hobble back to work. I was having trouble walking, but I had to put on the spikes, fake the smile, and dance around naked. I tried to cover the bruises, but it was useless. Make-up couldn't hide the dark blue patches on my arms and legs. I could see the shock on the customers' faces when they saw that I was hurt. Their looks of pity did not comfort me, only intensified my humiliation.

"Peter, who rarely spoke to me, came over to me right after my show. He took his cigar out of his mouth and said, 'Holy shit, he really beat the crap outta you. Ya know, when JD told me, I didn't believe you was hurt that bad. A lot of chicks say their boyfriend beat 'em up, but they only got slapped around a little, but you got some nasty bruises on you. We don't like that shit around here—guys beatin' up on broads. Tell you what I'll do, you just say the word, and we'll break his kneecaps. Usually we charge for this kinda thing, but for you, we'll do it for nothing; you won't owe us a thing. Just let me know. I won't do it unless you want.'

"He was dead serious. In his tough-guy Mafioso way, he was being chivalrous. I was deeply moved by his offer. For a brief moment I toyed with the idea of saying the words that would cripple Eddie—permanently. I pictured it in my mind. In a dark alley, one guy would restrain him while the other clobbered his knees with a steel pipe. I saw the agony on his face as he crumbled to the ground, the sudden jerk as one of the goons gave him one last swift kick in the ribs.

"'Thank you Peter, that's very kind of you,' I replied. 'I really appreciate it, but please don't hurt him. Just keep him away from me, that's all I ask. If he tries to come into the club, you have my permission to throw him out.' I said this as a torrent of mixed emotions brewed inside of me. I was a little drunk with the power of knowing I could so easily get revenge. At the same time, I feared he'd know it was me who put out the contract on him. He might recover and come back to kill me. What finally won out was my conscience. Ordering such brutality, even if justified, was against my spiritual principles. I was content to think that his own karma would catch up with him. Better not dirty my soul with vengeance.

"I saw another side of my co-workers as they reacted to my trauma. They'd been helpful giving me advice and lending me stuff when I began dancing, but other than that kept to themselves. It wasn't an easy business. Trust had to be earned. When they saw how black and blue I was, and that I needed a few stiff drinks to kill the pain, they went out of their way to offer comfort and support. I'm sure they had all been through some tough times. I am also sure that because of the sweet, innocent way I looked they probably thought I had a soft life before I showed up there. None of them knew about the distress I had been under, until then. After seeing how I had been abused, I became part of the gang—as if I'd been through some kind of initiation.

"Kayleen was the kindest of them all, and surprised me by inviting me to share her apartment. We were instant buddies. My spirits began to lift with the prospect of a new home and new friends. We were both so excited that we went out for drinks after work to celebrate. Afterwards, she took me to her place. It was a cute little apartment in the upper level of a two-family house. It was on Revere Beach, less than a mile from work. Things were looking rosy, until we woke up the next morning.

"The landlord, who lived downstairs, came knocking on the door bright and early. Kay and I both had hangovers. With our heads pounding, we listened to the landlord ranting about the noise and destruction that had woken him up in the middle of the night. Kayleen's friend Ronnie had shown up before we got home. Drunk, and needing a place to crash, he busted the glass on the door to get in. It wasn't the first time the landlord was disturbed by Kayleen's rowdy friends, but he vowed it would be the last. We were ordered to vacate immediately. I was homeless once again.

"We got rooms next to each other at a local motel. It was pricey to spend a night, but they had better rates if you paid by the week or month. Before this, I had thought of a motel as a place to stop overnight on a family vacation, not a place to live. It was an eye-opener to discover that there were several other tenants who lived there on the pay-by-the-month plan. There was no kitchen or even a fridge in either of our rooms, so we ate all of our meals out. Between rent, restaurants, and cab fare to and from work, we were too broke to save up for another apartment. We got stuck there for a few months. It would have been depressing for most people, but I was so glad to be living anyplace where Eddie wasn't, that I didn't care." Eve grinned slightly, then reached for her coffee mug and took a sip. She paused, looking down at the mug and turning it slowly, as if to collect her thoughts.

"Did you ever see him again after the night he beat you, Eve?" I asked.

"Just a few times, and none were too pleasant." She replied. "He came in the club about a week after he pummeled me. He thought if he apologized I would come running back. *Unbelievable! – thought he could just say 'sorry, didn't mean it' after almost killing me AND my CAT, and all would be forgiven.* He must have been delusional!

"He was sweet as pecan pie trying to convince me. Once he understood it was going nowhere, he got belligerent. That dark cloud came over his face – the wild demon look in his eyes. The minute he grabbed my arm, Peter was right there at the table. 'This guy bothering you?' he asked. 'Yes, he is. I don't want to talk to him anymore,' I said. Peter gave him a look and motioned toward the door with his head. Eddie let go of my arm with a jerky motion that threw me off balance and stormed out. 'Is he the one that beat you up?' Peter asked me after he was gone. 'Yes, he's the asshole. I don't want him in here. I don't want to see him again.' 'Fine with me,' he replied. 'I don't want jerks coming in here upsetting my girls. I'll let the bouncers know.'

"I felt safe in the club, but every night when I left, I took a careful look around the parking lot to make sure he wasn't lurking. It was another two weeks before Eddie appeared again. I was sitting at a table having a drink with a customer, and he was suddenly standing above me. He said, 'I need to talk to you.' He was agitated. The customer I was with was ready to jump up and defend me. 'I don't think we have anything to talk about,' I answered, looking around for the bouncers. 'When are you coming to get your things—your clothes and your cat?' he demanded. It had been on my mind, but I didn't have a car, and I sure wasn't going there alone. I'd been worried about the cat too, so at least I knew she was still alive.

"The next instant there were three huge guys grabbing him. Peter noticed what was going on and had sent the bouncers. This time he didn't go peacefully. It took all three of them to subdue him. They dragged him, kicking and swearing, toward the door. I don't know if he was trying to assert his right to talk to me—to claim ownership—or to hurt me one last time. He yelled out, loud enough for every one in the club to hear, 'I fucked her over three hundred times!!!' I wanted to crawl under the table and vomit. I covered my face with my hands to hide the shame I felt at having let the sicko ever touch me.

"Peter asked me once again if I wanted him hurt. The guys who dragged him out were extremely pissed off, and wouldn't mind breaking a few ribs while they still had him in the parking lot. Again, I told Peter I just wanted him kept away, that's all—but I did need some help getting my things. That night, after work, he had those same guys accompany me to the apartment.

"Eddie was steamed when he opened the door and

saw the three goons with me. They were big as linebackers. He tried to slam the door in my face, but one of them shoved it open. They surrounded him while I ran around quickly gathering what I could, including my fluffy little cat. As I headed for the door, he lunged toward me. They all grabbed him at once, and while he was standing there, with his arms pinned behind him, he spat in my face. As I was wiping the slime off on my sleeve, I heard one of them say, 'You just say the word, sweetie, and we'll take care of this fucker once and for all—he'll never walk again.' 'No, let's just get out of here.' I replied. That's the second time I saved his knees.

"He was out of my life at last—*thank goodness!* I only saw him twice after that. One time was several months later. He showed up at another club I was working at. I was startled and a bit panicked. He let me know, with a haughty sneer, that he wasn't there to see me. Turned out he was dating another dancer. Her name was April. She didn't look a day over fourteen. She had just started working there, and mostly kept to herself.

"I tried to warn April about him, tell her what he'd done to me. She copped an attitude and said he told her I'd probably tell her a bunch of BS about him that wasn't true. I hoped she never found out the hard way that I wasn't lying. A few months later someone told me they saw her with some suspicious bruises on her. Maybe I should have let the wise guys take care of him, made sure he'd never hurt another woman.

"I had one last chance to be avenged. It was over a year since I'd seen him. I had another boyfriend by then. My friends and I called him Karate Jake, because he had a black belt. Jake and I were pulling into a shopping mall and I saw Eddie in another car. The second I saw him, my heart was pounding and I had that prickly feeling of panic from head to toe. I slumped down in the passenger seat, trying to hide while keeping my eye on him as our cars passed slowly. He drove by and didn't notice me.

"I knew Jake would have chased him down and beat the crap out of him, so I kept quiet. I did tell Jake, but not until an hour later. Jake was furious that I let him go by without saying a word—he would have welcomed the chance to pound on him. I'd had enough violence. Jake blamed our relationship troubles on Eddie, you see. As much as I loved Jake, I was going through post-traumatic stress, though I didn't understand it at the time. Any relationship I had following Eddie was doomed, no matter how good the guy was." Eve picked up the coffee mug and drained it, then set the mug down gently on the table. She paused to yawn and stretch a bit before she continued.

"Sorry Stella, I didn't mean to jump ahead in the story. I needed to get through all this Eddie bullshit so I can move on. After I got away from him, I thought I was done thinking about him. It wasn't so easy. I still have reminders—two patches on my legs of broken veins, scars from the deep bruises he caused. The worst of it though is the chronic back pain I had for years afterward. When I finally got to a chiropractor ten years later she said my back 'looked, felt, and reacted to treatment like someone who had severe trauma from a car accident.' For years I cursed him every time I suffered with my back.

"Eventually I came to forgive him. I had to, for my own sake. Holding on to the hatred was eroding my spirit. Whether he deserved to be forgiven or not was not the issue. I deserved the peace of letting go, of forgiving him. I saw that carrying the bitterness was weighing me down. Time to let the baggage go.

"My hatred for him turned to pity. I thought about how blessed I was, because I could go back anywhere I had ever been and find friends who would welcome me with open arms. Eddie could never go back, not anywhere, without risking his life. He burned too many people on the way. He'd have to keep running, looking over his shoulder, trying to stay ahead of his trail of enemies. His kind of 'lifestyle' was more like a 'death-style.'"

5. Banana Splits

"Good morning Stella!" Eve greeted me with a wide grin, looking quite refreshed. She had looked haggard the night before, after describing the brutality she had endured with Eddie. I had expected her to show up with dark circles and puffy eyes. Instead, she was all smiles and looked ten years younger.

"Hello, Eve," I said. "You look very perky this morning. I trust you slept well?"

"Better than I have in years!" Eve replied as she poured herself a cup of coffee. "It was very cathartic to get all that crap down on paper, or at least onto your tape recorder," she continued, as she settled down on the sofa. "Funny, I thought I had healed from it years ago. Going over it again with you, I feel like a huge weight has been lifted off my shoulders. I was still carrying around some of that old pain after all. I feel it has finally been purged! Are you ready to hear more?"

"By all means, please continue." I flipped the switch on the tape recorder. Eve drew a deep breath and closed her eyes briefly. When she opened them, she spoke slowly, almost in a whisper, as if waiting for words to flow from the depths of her memory.

"It's not so much that I *don't* remember, but *how* I remember that's frustrating," she began. "Maybe it's all the drinking and drugs I did. I don't recall my first few years dancing as one continuum, flowing like a long winding road. It's more a jumble of random events, like the scenic vistas and greasy-spoon diners you visit along the way. I'll do my best, but please bear with me."

"Not to worry, my dear. It's your story. Any way you tell it is fine," I reassured her.

"Thanks, Stella. Okay then. Kayleen and I were living in the motel. I don't know what I would have done without her! She knew where all of the clubs in the Boston suburbs were. She'd get hired at a club, then help me get in too. She knew people who were willing to help us with rides. We managed to get back and forth to work and then go out partying and neither one of us had a car. Kayleen knew enough of the other dancers to know who was cool and who to avoid—who you had to keep your eye on 'cause they'd steal from you the minute you looked the other way."

"Other dancers would steal things? Like what?" I asked.

"Money, jewelry, your weed, entire costumes if they could get away with it," she answered. "It was only a few who pulled that shit. Most of the girls I met were honorable, and very supportive of each other. There was a certain camaraderie amongst most of us. Nobody knows what it's like to be a dancer like another dancer. We knew we were living outside the social norm, so it created an *'us against the world'* kind of atmosphere. We shared our troubles, some good laughs, and our drugs. It helped us to bond with each other, especially the 'house girls.'

"There were 'house girls' and 'road girls' in most places I worked. The 'house girls' were employed by the club for an extended time, months or even years. To add some variety, the club would contract 'road girls' for a limited time, a couple weeks, a few months at most. It was hard for them to trust or be trusted. They weren't around long enough to bond with anyone. I had a lot of empathy for the 'road girls.' Even though most of them made more money, it had to be a lonely life, always moving from city to city, never having the chance to form any lasting friendships. I knew that life wasn't for me.

"Some of the 'road girls' were quite impressive. They influenced me, although I was unaware of it at the time."

"Impressive? In what way?" I asked.

"They seriously worked at putting shows together—music, costumes, props, professional choreography," Eve replied. "They had acts you'd expect to see at an upscale Vegas nightclub. I felt like my little 'show' was a scoop of vanilla ice cream, but they were banana splits.

"When I started dancing I threw anything on I could strip out of easily and played whatever jukebox tune appealed to me. After seeing 'road girls' with their Hedy-Jo ultra-beaded gowns, and the glamour and style they had, I began to develop more style of my own. It wasn't a competitive thing. Or, if it was, I was competing with myself, trying to be more polished so I'd be less embarrassed.

"I didn't put much effort into it at first, because I hated stripping. It had been my ticket to escape from Eddie. I didn't intend to make it a long-time career, and I certainly didn't want to 'make a name for myself' in the industry. But this was my livelihood and I thought I should try to do my best while I was in it.

"It's a philosophy I developed in my teens. I was working as a checkout clerk in a grocery store when it came to me. I looked at the other cashiers and noticed the different attitudes they had. Some looked weary and depressed while others were cheerful as they rang in the prices and packed groceries. I decided then that any job worth doing was worth doing your best at. So I greeted each customer with a big grin, and tried my best to be friendly, efficient, and upbeat. One day the store manager stopped at my station and gave me a thumb's up salute, saying, 'Class A, Eve!' I was stunned, because he usually was a sourpuss. His praise reinforced my commitment to excellence. Having a good outlook also made the day go by quicker, always a boon in a boring job.

"Well, I sure wasn't packing groceries anymore!" Eve chuckled. "Since I didn't know what else to do, I decided to do my best in the business I was in. I even started to have fun on stage after my attitude improved.

"I was working at a club north of Boston—there were several of them on Route One in Peabody. The first one I landed in was called the Checkmate. It was a cavernous, dark club with two separate rooms.

"The room on the left had a large stage on the far left side, with a red velvet curtain for a backdrop. It felt like a professional theatre. You could go backstage between songs.

"The right side of the building had a tiny stage— about eight feet by ten—smack dab in the middle of the room. It sucked, because you couldn't pop backstage during your show. It was awkward being out there for the silent pauses between songs. The worst part was if you had your period, you couldn't do a quick check to make sure you weren't bleeding through your tampon. It was the pits.

"I couldn't afford expensive costumes, so I spiffed up my act using small props and imagination. The first time I used a prop it was on that little stage in the middle. It rattled me to be totally surrounded by the guys. I used a water pistol and danced to 'Hey Joe — where you goin' with that gun in your hand?'—by Jimi Hendrix. The customers were shocked when I shot them with the water pistol. I had one that you could adjust the nozzle on. It would squirt in a different direction than it was pointing. That was the most fun! I'd aim it at my head, lean over, and some unsuspecting sucker would get it in the face. Most of my victims took it pretty well, while their buddies and other customers laughed their asses off.

"The other dancers got a big kick out of it too. They got some vicarious pleasure out of seeing me pull a prank on those dudes. Many of the girls didn't care too much for the customers. They'd refer to them as 'perverts.' In fact, the front row closest to the stage, in every club I was ever in, was called 'perverts row.' I knew some guys who stopped sitting there once they heard our pet name for it.

"That tiny stage I hated so much inspired me to improve my show. It was also a catalyst for getting me to quit smoking cigarettes."

"How so?" I asked Eve. I had been trying to drop the nasty habit myself, and was curious and eager to hear how a stage in the middle of a strip club had helped her to stop.

"This was many years before smoking was banned in bars," said Eve. "That stage had the worst second-hand smoke I ever breathed. Most places had draft fans that sucked the smoke out. This joint had a fan on either side of the stage that blew all the smoke right at the dancer. I already smoked two packs a day, but must have been doubling my intake when I had to work that stage.

"One night it got the best of me. After my show I went to the dressing room, as usual. Without warning, my lungs locked up. I couldn't breathe—not in or out. I passed out cold. One of the other girls came in just in time. I vaguely remember being loaded into an ambulance. The next thing I recall was 'coming to' in the emergency room. They had given me a shot of speed — amphetamine — to jumpstart my lungs. It was like a severe asthma attack, though I'd never had one before or since.

"So you quit smoking after that?" I asked.

"You'd think that would've done the trick, huh Stella?" Eve replied. "Fool that I was, I went back to it for two more weeks. Then it began to sink in, what a wake-up call I'd had. If I ignored it, I might not live to see my twenty-fifth birthday. I had quit once before, when I was eighteen, and managed to stay off them for three years. It wasn't easy. I used conscious willpower, and took up crocheting with string to help with the cravings. Every time I got the urge to light up, I took out my little ball of twine and hooked it until the obsession passed. My kid sisters were delighted. They kept getting little gifts from me — bracelets, belts, chokers, headbands. Making hippie accessories out of rainbow-colored string was my pacifier.

"This time I decided to try something different. Remember the mind control and meditation classes I told you about, that I took when I was nineteen and living in New York City? I had learned a self-hypnosis technique during that course for 'negative habit control.' Silly to learn such a valuable tool, and then not use it.

"Late one night after work, around two o'clock in the morning, I was in my motel room. I lit some candles, then sat on the floor in a lotus position. I went into a deep trance using the self-hypnosis method I had learned. I visualized myself smoking, and thought of all the bad aspects of it. Then I pictured painting a big 'X' across the scene. The mental exercise was complete. I began counting myself up, to come back into outer consciousness. I heard a noise that made me snap out of the alpha-state quickly. It was a faint 'hissing' sound. My gut told me something wasn't right and I shouldn't take my time 'counting up.' I turned toward the sound. My cat was standing on the dresser, near one of the candles. Her fluffy grey tail was *on fire!* In one quick motion I was out of the lotus pose, turning my body around as I got up. I grabbed her tail and pulled my hand across it swiftly, trying to smother the flame. In my panic, I grabbed her a little too hard and flung her off the dresser. She looked like Rocky the Flying Squirrel. She sailed through the air and landed with a thud on all fours. Luckily she was not hurt, only stunned. She looked up at me, bewildered, then sniffed at the rancid odor of her burnt fur. I had put the fire out before it reached her skin. *Phew!*

"I was fascinated by what I learned about that state of consciousness. I was able to go deep into my mind to a level where I could block out loud noises, like trucks shifting gears and kids setting off firecrackers. Yet, when there was danger, my mind was so alert in the alpha state that I could hear the sound of my cat's fur burning—a barely audible hiss. A sound I never would have noticed if I had been in ordinary consciousness.

"The other cool thing about the experience was that I didn't need to quit cigarettes—*they quit me!* I had programmed my subconscious to believe that cigarettes were repulsive to me. The next morning when I looked at my pack of Marlboros, I felt a wave of nausea. I threw the pack out of the window and never picked up the habit again. It was amazing how well it worked."

"Maybe you could teach me your technique sometime, Eve?"

"Sure Stella, I'd be glad to," she replied. "Just let me know when. You know, I don't think it works unless you truly want to quit."

"Maybe we should wait until the book is done." I said with a slight laugh.

"I understand." Eve nodded as her lips curved into a knowing grin. "I wouldn't want it to disrupt your creative process. Do you need a smoke break before I continue, Stella?"

"No, but thanks for asking," I replied. I had been stepping outside occasionally to have a cigarette. Eve had asked me not to smoke around her. It added to my guilt and frustration that I was still a slave to nicotine. "Let's work a little longer and then we'll break for lunch," I said.

"Sounds good," Eve replied, then continued with her story.

"Not long after that, Kayleen and I moved into a

house in the suburbs with another dancer. Mimi had just lost a couple of roommates, and we'd had our fill of motel living. After the misery of living in an abusive relationship, I felt blessed to be part of this new 'family.' Besides the girls I lived with, there was a small group of guys who usually hung around. They were mostly our buddies, not boyfriends. They'd give us rides, party with us, share drugs, that kind of thing.

"That's when I met Jake, whom I mentioned before. He was one of the regular visitors at our house. He was tall, very fit, with shoulder length dark hair. His deep-set hazel eyes quietly noticed everything. He was physically my type, though I wasn't attracted to him right away. I wasn't ready to be attracted to anyone yet. I was having the time of my life, coming and going as I pleased, partying all the time. The last thing on my mind was getting hooked up with a guy — *no way!*

"Jake had been hanging around the club and our house for a few months before I started to care for him as more than a friend. It was obvious he was hoping for more too. He had a depth and intelligence I had not found in most of the guys I knew back then.

"Kayleen copped an attitude when he began staying overnight with me. I knew she liked Jake, but I thought it was platonic. I wondered if she might have felt more for him than just friendship.

"One night, about 3:00 a.m., Jake and I were jolted out of a sound sleep by a loud ruckus coming from

Kayleen's room—her bedroom was next to mine. Kay was pounding on the wall, yelling, "... *fuckin' Eve* doesn't wanna come out and *fuckin'* party any *fuckin' more* ..." I went to see what all the commotion was about. I thought she'd put a fist through the wall if I didn't calm her down! She was blotto. She glared at me, struggling to keep her balance. She screamed, 'FUCK YOU BITCH!' with all the venom she could muster, then passed out cold on the bed. I took her shoes off and pulled the covers over her. I felt guilty, thinking she must have had a crush on Jake and was torn up that we had become lovers. Kay had done so much to help me out during the darkest days of my life. She was the last person I wanted to hurt.

"The next day, she made a confession. I wasn't off track that she was jealous—I just had it all backwards. It wasn't *Jake* she was in love with, it was *ME!* I didn't even know she was *gay!* I stood there blinking, mouth gaping. I was thinking we were the best of friends, while she was dreaming we'd become lovers. She admitted having fantasies one of us would get pregnant (the guy didn't matter—he'd just be stud service) and we would become a couple and raise kids together. I didn't know how to react to this. She couldn't believe I was so naive about her feelings for me. I didn't have a clue, not even after she'd kissed me one night."

"She kissed you?" I asked.

"It was a few months before this," said Eve. "We were out with a few other girls. We all got bombarded on tequila, doing shots at a little dive on Revere Beach. We stumbled out of the bar, and went across the street to the beach. Some guys were skinny-dipping in the ocean. One of the girls thought it would be funny to grab their clothes. Kayleen handed me a pair of pants, and yelled '*RUN!*' I looked towards the water and three guys were running at us. I took off as fast as my boozy brain and body could. When I reached the street, I was surrounded by three naked, pissed-off guys. My friends were nowhere in sight. I dropped the clothes that had been stuffed into my hands. One of the guys grabbed the pants. He was hopping and flopping, struggling to get into them. They were all as wasted as we were. Sudden terror wiped out the fog I was in. One of the guys was waving an empty beer bottle in the air, about to crack it over my head.

"I heard, 'Leave her alone—at least she stuck around to face the music.' The guy whose pants I had taken came to my defense. Luckily, his friend dropped the bottle. I had not 'stuck around' on purpose. I was just too drunk to know what was happening when my pals were already running up the beach. I scrambled away like a mouse before the guy waving the beer bottle could change his mind.

"I ran up a side street and heard '*psst.*' I turned to see Kayleen hiding in the shadows between a couple of buildings. 'Come here!' she said, pulling me into the narrow alley. 'You okay?' she asked. 'Yeah, a little shook up, but I'm fine,' I replied. 'Where's everyone else?' she asked. 'I have no idea. They all took off,' I said.

That's when Kay stretched up toward me and planted a kiss right on my lips. I was so drunk and unprepared for it, I just stood there, dumbfounded. For her, it must have felt like kissing a mannequin. She backed away and I said, 'What the hell did you do that for?' 'I just wanted to see ...' she started to answer, then stopped. 'See what?' I asked. I wasn't angry, just confused. 'Oh, *NEVERMIND!*' she said in a huff. 'Let's get outta here!'

"Kay talked about that night when she confessed her true feelings for me. She figured I wasn't gay after that incident, but wasn't sure until we had been in an orgy together.

"As long as I wasn't attached to anyone, she could dream that I might return her feelings someday. Hooking up with Jake had put an end to her hopes. Kay said she was sorry for causing such a scene the night before. I did truly love her, as a friend. She said she was coming to a place of accepting how things were with us. We made a pact not to let the whole thing wreck our friendship."

"Eve, do you mind telling me more about—you said you were in an orgy together?" I couldn't resist delving further into this.

"Oh, that—hmm—I guess you would want to know about *that*, Stella!" Eve laughed, shaking her head and looking upwards.

"Kayleen came with me on a visit 'home,' to New

York. We went out with a bunch of my old friends. Much the way I used to with that crowd, we went out drinking and dancing. I asked my friend Bob if we could crash at his place for the night. He had a full house, but he knew this nice couple, who'd probably put us up. After the clubs all closed, we went to Aimee and Andre's house. There were several other people there. Everyone was hanging out on a sectional sofa. It was red suede and swung around filling up the small living room. We were smoking a bowl—I thought it was weed, but it tasted funny. It was African Yohimbe Bark. I thought it was some kind of exotic pot or hash, didn't find out 'til later it was an aphrodisiac.

"I was in a haze from drinking, toking, and being up so late. I felt like I was in a weird dream—all at once everyone around me started stripping. Kayleen got naked too. She looked at me, standing there fully clothed, and said, 'Well—*come on!*' I felt like I was in a quirky Fellini flick, like there was something I was supposed to be doing, but they forgot to give me the script.

"I just stood there, clueless, while everyone around me acted out their roles confidently. The stuff we smoked made me feel all tingly, and I found myself peeling my clothes off. Next thing I knew I was in a pile of naked bodies. I was surrounded by flesh—skin everywhere I turned. It was like being in a live Picasso painting; hips here, thighs there, breasts, butts, cocks, all around, but I didn't know what parts belonged to whom. I was groping and being groped. I had no idea who was touching me or who or what I was touching. Kayleen cupped her hand around my breast and tried to kiss me.

"It all seemed so silly, I burst out laughing. I extracted myself from the heap of writhing bodies, grabbed my clothes, and headed into a bedroom. I didn't want to disrupt everyone's fun with my giggle fit. The lusty scene made me feel giddy. I wasn't repulsed, but I wasn't sexually aroused either. I realized I just wasn't an orgy type of gal.

"I was discovering who I was by finding out who I wasn't. I was trying on lifestyles like they were footwear. It's always been hard for me to find shoes that are just right. My various jobs and modes of living have been like that: too tight, too loose, too flashy, too boring. I wonder if I'll ever find a life that truly fits me. Maybe that doesn't happen until we die. Maybe that's what Heaven really is—finding the perfect pair of shoes!"

6. Self-Mantra

Eve told me she was ready for a break. I shut the tape recorder off and headed into the kitchen to make sandwiches.

"Anything I can do to help?" Eve asked.

"Thanks, no, I can manage. Tuna okay?" I called back to her across the room.

"Sure, it's my favorite!" This was often Eve's reply, no matter what I offered her: "Would you like iced tea?" "Yes, please, it's my favorite!" "Coffee?" "Sure, it's my favorite!" "A chocolate truffle?" "Yum, it's my favorite!"

I was tempted to offer her something gross and slimy—like goat's eyeballs, just to see what she'd say. Instead, I asked Eve if she realized how often she replied this way.

"Life is good today, Stella," she said. "Being here with you, gazing outside at your luscious garden, sipping peach iced tea. Today is bright and sunny. I have lived through many dark days. Even in the depths of despair, I usually tried to find something to be grateful for. It wasn't always easy. Sometimes I'd have to swim around in my misery for a while. Eventually I would grasp a thread of something, any little thing, I could be glad about. That spark of gratitude would be the first rung on a ladder I'd use to pull myself up.

"I'm sorry if it sounds corny, but saying 'it's my favorite' is one way I remember to appreciate the moment. I heard about a man who always said whatever he was eating was the best he'd ever had: 'This is the best pastrami I ever had,' or 'This is the best egg salad sandwich I ever had.' I began doing it after hearing about that man. I understand he lived to a ripe old age, smiled most of the time, and never complained. Do you think we could become immortal if we learned how to become totally positive about life? My Grandma lived to be a hundred, and she was one of the sweetest people I ever knew. Anyway, I can stop saying it, if it's annoying you."

"No, it's fine, Eve. More than fine. It's a lovely way to look at things," I said.

We took our sandwiches out to the terrace. I found myself drinking in my surroundings as if it were the first time I'd seen them. *How often had I looked past the azaleas and daylilies and just focused on the weeds?* My little piece of paradise had become just another chore. Not today — today I would revel in the beauty and even celebrate the weeds: the wild unplanned sprouts that push up through the red soil and mulch, struggling to survive against all odds.

I took a big bite, washed it down with some lemonade, grinned at Eve and said, "This is the best tunafish sandwich I ever had!" We both laughed and relaxed under the speckled shade of the old oak that dripped Spanish moss. Butterflies danced on the gentle breeze as we savored our lunch in my divine garden.

After our siesta we moved back to the parlor. I flipped the switch on the tape recorder. Eve kicked off her shoes, stretched out on the sofa, and said, "Every decision we make affects the direction of our lives in ways we can't predict. I am curious, more than regretful, about how different my life would have been if I had gone through *this* door instead of *that* one."

"Is there a particular door you are thinking about at the moment?" I asked.

"Uh huh," Eve replied. "I had been very content living with my roomies, Kayleen and Mimi. When I became lovers with Jake, I knew things would change, but didn't have any notion of leaving. Our three bedroom suburban ranch was like a stripper's sorority house. We partied a lot, but tried to keep it reasonable so the neighbors wouldn't complain.

"It was great having a kitchen again, after living in the motel. One time I made lasagna for our crowd. It was like my mom used to make. She got her recipe from an Italian butcher in the Bronx when she was a girl. It was the richest, goopiest, yummiest lasagna I'd ever made; layers of crushed meatballs with sweet and hot Italian sausage, heavy on the mozzarella. I simmered the sauce for hours the day before. It was a two-day project to do it right. The pan was so heavy we decided to weigh it. It weighed twenty-one pounds, and twenty people ate it all—more than a pound of lasagna apiece!

"Boy, we could *eat* back then. We all had that young metabolism going for us, but dancing really burned up the calories too. We did three or four twenty-minute sets per shift. We'd often work double shifts, and no weekends off, either. Sometimes I worked three weeks straight without a break. You danced no matter what: sprained ankles, colds, menstrual cramps—you just had to keep going. That's what army boot camp must feel like. You get up and do it every day, no matter how tired, or sick, or sick and tired you felt.

"Jake was part of the regular crowd we let into our secret world. We were very selective about who we invited over—*you had to be.* Some of the nicest guys I ever met were club patrons, but there were some real creeps lurking around there too. Bad enough they knew where you worked, but home was sacred ground. There was no formal screening process, no questionnaire to fill out before they could enter our private domain. We all relied on our instincts, which became sharper the longer you hung around those clubs.

"I still wasn't nuts about stripping for a living, but I loved the sense of freedom it gave me after the torturous confinement of being with Eddie. So when Jake pressured me to move in with him, we locked horns over it. He was spending a lot of time with me, and away from his widowed mother. His father had been killed in a car accident a few years before. Jake was a good man and felt responsible for the welfare of his aging mother and teenage sister. His guilt over spending so many nights with me was wilting our romance.

"It had been a struggle for me to commit to the relationship. I assumed he was only looking for a passing fling. When it became clear he wanted more, I had to take a hard look at my resistance. I did care for Jake, but was afraid of giving up my newfound freedom. I dreaded letting anyone have the kind of control over me that I allowed Eddie to have.

"In the process of figuring out what to do, I had a revelation: *I was afraid I wasn't good enough to be loved by a truly nice guy.* I looked back on my past relationships and it dawned on me what a streak of losers I had hooked up with, long before my dancing career. Alcoholics, heroin addicts, liars and cheaters — *boy, could I pick 'em!* I used to call it the 'Florence Nightingale Complex' — you see someone broken and you want to fix them. Psychologists now call it 'co-dependency.'

"I remember the exact spot in the Checkmate I was standing in when I had my epiphany — halfway between that tiny stage in the middle of the smokey chokey room and the dressing room in the corner. I suddenly understood it was low self-esteem that had gotten me into trouble time after time. There were plenty of nice guys I steered away from, always drawn to the bad boys. Well, not any more. I decided right then that I was a good woman, and *damn it, I deserved a good man!* It was one of the pivotal moments of my life.

"It wasn't all peachy from that moment on, but every relationship I was in after that was better than the one before it. There was genuine progress in my choices of men and in my behavior toward them and toward myself. It was the beginning of learning how to like myself. It got me thinking a lot about the self-esteem thing. My new self-mantra became, 'You're just as good as anyone else—not *better* than, or *worse* than, but *just as good.*'

"I repeated that phrase under my breath whenever I needed a boost of courage. It came in handy when I had to face a roomful of strangers. Instead of giving in to painful shyness, I would often scan the room for someone who had that scared-rabbit look. Then I would engage them in a conversation. It was rewarding to see the relief on their face—takes a wallflower to know a wallflower. Anyone who knows me now, or ever saw me onstage, would not believe that I was once so shy. I wonder if it's something one is born with or if it's an acquired trait." Eve looked toward the window, as if the answer was somewhere between the white lace curtains and the rose bush outside. She paused a moment and took a sip of water before continuing.

"I decided to give it a try with Jake. I didn't want to lose him and someday be looking back wondering if I made the right choice. Something weird happened, too, that put me over the edge about it.

"It was early in the morning—maybe five a.m.— first blush of dawn. Jake and I were sleeping in my room. I was half asleep and opened my eyes to see a man standing at the foot of the bed. He was looking down at me and Jake. I saw him as clearly as I am seeing you, Stella. I heard him clearly too. He said only two words—'Oh, beautiful!'—with a sarcastic tone and disapproving look. I was about to grab Jake to wake him up, but the man evaporated into thin air.

"My adrenaline kicked in. No way could I go back to sleep. I woke Jake to tell him. He bolted out of bed to check the house, but there was no sign of the man. I described him in all the detail I could recall: tall, middle aged, slightly heavy, balding, red plaid flannel shirt. As I went on with my description a strange look came over Jake's face. I understood his look a few days later.

"We were at Jake's house. He pulled out a photograph, asking me if the man in it was the one I saw. It was the spitting image of him, right down to the flannel shirt! I told Jake, yes, that was exactly who I saw and asked who he was. 'My father,' was all he said.

"We stared at each other's pale faces. I could almost hear the Twilight Zone theme, expecting Rod Serling's voice to break the heavy silence. His father had been dead for four years. I had never seen a picture of him until that moment. I was spooked, not just at seeing his father's ghost, but because it seemed his spirit was restless and unhappy. We figured he was upset because Jake was needed at home by his mother. I was afraid if Jake kept spending nights with me, and away from his house, the haunting would continue. So I moved in with Jake, his mother, and his eighteen-year-old sister. We never had any more ghostly visitations."

7. THE OLDEST PROFESSION

"I told Jake I'd move in with him as long as he didn't pressure me to quit dancing. He agreed, reluctantly. We kept my occupation a secret from his family and friends, told them I was a waitress.

"I was living a schizoid life. By day I played the dutiful housewife, by night I worked at playing the vamp. We lived in an old house on a dirt road in a rural suburban town north of Boston. It wasn't an official town road, which meant it was up to the residents to maintain it. After heavy spring rains, I was out with Jake shoveling mud and gravel to fill in the ruts and smooth out the road. I'd wash off the mud, head in to the club, and put on the greasepaint and tinsel.

"We made a garden in the backyard, which was more or less a swamp. The mosquitoes were thick and ravenous. They just laughed at insect repellent. I heard they couldn't bite through silk. So I put on silk pajamas and layered corduroys and a flannel shirt over them. It kept the buggers from biting, but I was tilling huge clumps of swamp grass in ninety-degree heat wearing multiple layers of clothes. I sweated in the garden all day, showered, then sweated on stage all night. I wondered what the customers would've thought if they saw me a few hours earlier, bundled up and toiling like a medieval peasant.

"Jake was a great lover of nature, and helped me reconnect with my own passion for the outdoors. We often went hiking in the state park nearby and in the mountains of New Hampshire. Once, we were hiking a steep trail with another couple Jake had known since high school, Andy and Jan. The three of them were much taller than me. One by one they jumped across a small stream using the river rocks as a bridge. Their long legs made it look easy. When I leapt across, my heel skidded on the slippery rock. I went straight into a split. Andy looked horrified. He had visions of splints and a makeshift litter to haul me down the mountain. I bounced right up, and Jake laughed to see his friend's mouth gape open. Andy didn't know I was a dancer, and that I practiced splits daily to stay limber enough to do them on stage, and to kick my leg as high as the ceiling. Jake knew the impromptu acrobatics on the mountain were just part of my everyday routine.

"One of the sweetest memories I have of our outdoor adventures took place across the street from Jake's house. It was state park wilderness, in midwinter. We sat under a tree, slid our legs into a sleeping bag, and covered the bag with snow. Then we scattered sunflower seeds all over it and waited quietly, snuggled up in the freezing cold. After about ten minutes, there was a flock of chickadees all over us — tweeting and pecking at the seeds. It was so dear to have them on my lap, singing their hearts out:

chicka-dee-dee-dee-dee-dee-dee-dee-dee. It was a peaceful respite from smoky barrooms.

"I didn't have a car. Jake usually took me to and from work. It was a long commute, so he asked if I could find work closer to home. I found a place in Lawrence, Mass. I wouldn't even call it a club. It was a divey little joint that had a small platform up behind the bar. I had to use songs from the jukebox, which hadn't been updated since 1955. After being used to playing my own tapes, and having a good-sized stage, I couldn't make the adjustment. I felt sick to my stomach every time I had to go to work. I didn't know until then how important it was to me to actually *dance*, and feel creative. I also realized how crucial it was to have the right music—music that resonated with my spirit, that helped me to express who I was.

"I felt more awkward in that place than in my whole ten-year career. The stage was so small it was like dancing on a shelf. I loved doing mad spins and twirling fabric around, but there I couldn't use my capes and negligees. There was hardly enough room for a leprechaun to do a jig. All I could do was writhe around like my feet were glued to the floor, shedding another piece of clothing with each lousy jukebox tune.

"I stuck it out for two miserable weeks. One night I was talking to a guy at the bar when this other dude starts vying for my attention. The guy I was talking to was a car mechanic, came in for a beer after work. He wore overalls streaked in black grease with his name embroidered on the pocket. The other guy felt insulted because I chose to talk to the grease monkey instead of him. He was fresh-scrubbed, tailored, and full of himself.

"I was sitting in the corner of the bar, with the mechanic on one side and the preppie on the other. Mr. Clean reached over and put his hand on my left breast while I was in the middle of a conversation with the mechanic. Without looking away from the mechanic, I grabbed the preppie's hand and tore it away from my boob. I was pissed, but when I turned to look at the jerk, I completely lost it. He had a smarmy smirk on his face—proud of what he got away with. I had a tight grip on his hand, especially his ring and middle fingers. I bent them backward, hard and fast. I heard a crack and felt the reverb from his finger breaking through my own bones. His eyes popped out of his head as he snapped his hand away from me. The mechanic and a few other guys jumped up, ready to pound him. I motioned for them to back off. They did, though I could see they were itching to teach him a lesson in strip-club etiquette. He mumbled something about having better things to do, and I said, 'Yeah, like having your fingers x-rayed.'

"It happened so fast. I didn't think first—it was pure reflex. My boyfriend Jake had a black belt in Karate. He had shown me that technique many times. I grabbed the guys fingers, spread them apart, and tore away, but not until I saw that arrogant look on his face. I bet he thought twice before he ever grabbed another dancer. Most of the clubs I worked in had bouncers who would be all over a guy for that crap.

"I told Jake about the incident, and how miserable I was working in that dive. We agreed I should leave, and stay away from Lawrence. It was a tough city, at least back in the seventies.

"Soon after that I got a call from Kayleen. She and Mimi were working at Jason's Place, near Seabrook, New Hampshire. Our favorite light man from the Checkmate, Jack, was there too. We called him Wolfman, as he announced us onstage with a raspy voice and colorful flair that reminded us of the famous DJ, Wolfman Jack.

"I wasn't crazy about the stage set-up. It was floor-level, with no railing around it. No barrier between us and the patrons—just a parquet floor with four large columns in the corners marking the perimeter. It was set up lounge-style, with small tables surrounding the stage to the left of the entrance, and a bar with stools to the right.

"Not the most elegant room I had worked in, but I was once again with my pals. That made it the happening place to be. The dance floor was big enough for me to use my double full-circle negligees, and Jack's talent with the lights helped give it a touch of Vegas-style class. I was happy to go to work again.

"As much as I loved Jake, I wasn't ready to settle down to a life of domestic bliss. I continued to help with the chores, living like an Amish housewife by day, and letting my alter-ego wild party girl out to play at night. We drank, smoked pot, snorted coke, swore, laughed, danced and stripped. Very un-Amish behavior." Eve laughed through her nose at this last remark. Shaking her head and lifting an eyebrow, she added, "That was another one of my puritanical fantasies—in my late teens. I wanted to run away from home and join the Amish, live a simple life: milk cows, bake bread, wear the same clothes every day. Meet some nice Amish boy who would drive me to church in a little surrey. I started to daydream about that life after falling in love with Gary Cooper in Friendly Persuasion.

"The owner of Jason's was so happy with the quality of our shows, and the crowd's response, that he gave Jack and his girlfriend Candy the job of managing the dancers. They hired who they wanted, making sure they were class acts and trustworthy ladies. It ended up being mostly girls I had gotten close to from other clubs, and created a cozy family-like feeling.

"Our biggest challenge was keeping the atmosphere from getting too gnarly. At the time, the Seabrook Nuclear Power Plant was being built. It was in the news a lot because of the demonstrations. There was a group called the Clamshell Alliance that was anti-nuclear. They held 'sit-ins' to disrupt the creation of the plant. They tried to keep it non-violent. There was a lot of hostility from the construction workers, who were just trying to feed their families and took the opposition very personally.

"Men from both sides of the controversy showed up at Jason's Place after five to kick back, have a beer with their buddies, and ogle naked women. The club was small. Crowds of guys from two sides of the fence were crammed in that tight little place, drinking. The tension hung in the room thicker than a cloud of smoke. You could choke on it.

"We did wacky comedy—reminiscent of Old Vaudeville—to lighten things up. We had artistic freedom because of the deal Jack and Candy set up with Jason. As long as we were packing the crowds in and selling drinks, he didn't care *what* we did on stage. We didn't have to stick to the standard twenty-minute formula: one dancer on stage, one less article of clothing each song until she was naked. Someone could pop onstage and do something ridiculous for one song, in between the regular shows.

"For instance, one of the girls would wrap a white feather boa across her butt and boobs and put on a pair of webbed rubber feet and duck's beak and dance around to 'Disco Duck.' The audience loved it. We'd get everyone laughing and forgetting about their cares. The nuclear power struggle they had earlier in the day dissolved, if only for a night.

"Every so often, we'd get a few who weren't into joining the fun. Nothing we did could wipe the belligerent look off their faces. They were drunk and ornery. We were right on the floor—arms length away from them. We didn't have any bouncers in that club. If someone became violent, they could do some serious damage.

"When it got too scary, Jack and I had a special routine. He'd wink at me and say, 'Pink Floyd, Lisa?' I'd give him a nod. We had a secret way to ward off doom.

"There's a bizarre Pink Floyd song called 'Careful With That Axe, Eugene.' It's not a typical stripper song, but I liked it. It was acid rock. Music you'd trip-out on, even without drugs—strange screechy guitar chords that twisted your mind like a pretzel.

"I wore my hot pink negligee, tons of fabric. It was studded all over with rhinestones, which gave it great weight for flaunting around. I'd spin around and around, fabric swirling all over the stage. Jack would sync the lights in rhythm with the music. The more intense and cacophonous it got, the wilder the lights flashed. Then he'd hit the strobes—quick bursts of bright white lightning. That would polish them off. Anyone who'd had too much to drink would fly out of the club, barely able to get to the parking lot before barfing their guts out.

"Simulated motion sickness, under the innocent guise of a striptease show. It cleared out the bad elements, leaving the club feeling light, like clean air after a rainstorm, all the pollen and pollution washed away.

"I remember seeing a twinkle in a customer's eye, and a cute little grin. I knew he was onto us—that he'd guessed about our crowd control method and was amused by it. We only did it when we felt it necessary, about six or seven times. It worked the same each time, like cranking the handle on a jack-in-the-box.

"It was during that phase I took *'Doolittle'* as my last name. Up until then I had just used 'Lisa.' Wolfman Jack insisted on doing fancy intros for all the girls. I never wanted to be a star in the industry, like some of the road girls I met. Many of them had pre-recorded special intros." Eve cupped her hands around her mouth, pantomiming a megaphone, and said with a deep voice:

"LIVE ... DIRECT FROM THE STAR-STUDDED WORLD OF LAS VEGAS, THE FABULOUS AND FAMOUS MISS SUZY SNOWLFLAKE!!!

"That just wasn't me," Eve continued. "As an antithesis to that style, and in keeping with the silliness we were so fond of at Jason's, I became *'Lisa Doolittle.'* It worked for me on several levels: My Fair Lady is my favorite musical, and the name was close to the heroine. It also has 'Little' from my last name of Littlepage. I had a few slogans that I had fun with. When a customer would ask me why my name was 'Doolittle,' I'd say, 'It means, say anything, do *nothing.'* It was clear to most of them, just from my name, that they could look, but don't touch, that I wasn't into doing anything more than dancing, that I wasn't going to 'DO' them."

Eve had a queer smirk on her face. It seemed to be a good time to ask her something that I had been burning to know. "So, Eve, are you saying you didn't engage in sexual relations with the customers, either in or out of the clubs? I'm sorry to ask so bluntly, but it's a common assumption that strippers are often prostitutes as well." I held my breath, hoping that she trusted me enough to answer honestly. She had been so open up until then; I didn't want to shut her down by hitting a raw nerve, and prying into a touchy subject. She grinned at me, and I let my breath go. I think of myself as an emancipated open-minded modern woman. It amazes me how the subject of sex can take me right back to my upright, uptight upbringing. I am still held captive by a sexually repressed societal mindset.

"Inquiring minds want to know ..." Eve giggled as she began her reply, with an impish sparkle in her eyes. Then she sat up, throwing her shoulders back. As if making a formal announcement, she proclaimed, "Prostitution is said to be the oldest profession, but I don't agree, Stella. I suspect the first lady who sold her favors did a sultry little dance first, as she shed whatever garments she wore—whether fig leaf or saber-toothed tiger fur. *Therefore, I propose, that strip-teasing is the oldest profession.* Let's not confuse the two—one is merely the promise of carnal pleasure, the other, its fulfillment. I make no judgment about either expression of human sexuality. I just want to make it clear that both professions are independent of one another, though they sometimes commingle.

"There are a lot of misconceptions about dancers,"

Eve continued. "They are like people everywhere though, as individual as snowflakes: some snowier, some flakier, but individual. I met bank tellers who were more promiscuous than many of the strippers I knew. Why do people try to pigeonhole everyone and think they can calculate someone's sexual behavior based on their occupation? What about all those priests who are diddling little boys? It just gets my Irish up when people want to stereotype anyone. That's why I want my identity kept a secret. I am not ashamed of how I lived back then, but I don't want the stigma that goes along with '*stripper*' to follow me all my life—people whispering under their breath, behind my back, making assumptions that I was hopping into bed with every Billy, Jim, and Bob out there.

"As far as my sexual activity, Stella, I was a product of my generation—love, peace, Woodstock— especially love—'free love'. It was before AIDS, and before I decided it was a mind-fuck to share that kind of intimacy with so many people. Too confusing emotionally: jumping into bed with someone first, then figuring out later if I actually liked them. A lot of people were into that back then, breaking down the old social mores. It ended up feeling empty, at least for me. I had already done enough sexual experimentation before my dancing days to know that I was happier having one partner at a time.

"A serial monogamist, that's what one of my friends called me. During most of my ten-year career,

I had one lover at a time. Many, but not all, I met in the clubs. Like most of the girls, I was cautious and usually had to know someone for a while before I would see them outside of the club. If you went out with someone you met there, and he turned out to be a creep, or even a nice guy that you just weren't into, well, *he knew where you worked.* It could be hard to get rid of someone if they decided to stalk you." Eve shivered a bit, as if to shake something *(or someone?)* off her shoulders, before adding, "Then again, a few drinks, a dash of drugs, and a spoonful of loneliness, and you've got the perfect recipe for common sense to take a hike—so, yeah, once in a while I'd wake up on the wrong side of the sheets.

"Most of the regulars knew that dancers were about the hardest women to pick up. We were getting hit on all day, every day. It became so routine, it wasn't even flattering. Promiscuity is relative. By some people's standards, I slept around a lot—more so before I was a dancer. But if you look at it in terms of percentage, how many guys I said 'Yes' to, versus how many opportunities I had, I would be considered almost abstinent.

"As far as charging for 'services rendered'—I didn't do it. It was a line I just couldn't, wouldn't cross. I'm glad I knew myself well enough, even back then, in the peak of my alcohol and drug consumption. I don't make any judgments about hookers; I just knew it wasn't for me. The best way to sum it up is to tell you what happened when my parents found out I was a dancer.

"For the first couple of years, I told them I was a waitress. It was easy to put on a facade—I lived in another state, and rarely went back home. They were getting suspicious, though. When I really was a waitress, I had stories about the restaurants—what my boss was like, my kooky co-workers, that kind of thing. So, it must have been odd that when they asked me about work I'd say, 'yeah, still waitressing.' Then I'd change the subject, didn't even say the name of the restaurant, or tell a colorful story about spilling soup on someone.

"Then I had a phone conversation with my older brother. He told me that Mom and Dad knew about me dancing. He denied being the one who clued them in, but I know it was him. His own life was a mess, but it was easier to focus on fixing mine. He said my parents were worried, afraid the Mafia had taken over my life and turned me into a hooker.

"I took a few days off work and went back to New York. I needed to talk to my parents about this in person, not just by phone. I'm not sure why that felt so important, since it would be scarier to see their faces when I told them. I was in my mid-twenties and had been out on my own for a few years by then. I didn't expect them to yell or carry on—we all knew I was not under their control anymore. I just didn't want them to fret.

"Dad was at work when I got there. That made it easier. I told my mother I knew they heard I was stripping for a living. There was no apology or shame in my voice or manner. Then I said, 'I know you and Dad suspect I'm turning tricks, but I want to assure you I am not, nor do I ever intend to. I don't think that makes me any better than the girls who do, but it's just not something I'm into. I can't separate love from sex, and I can't put a price tag on either.' I could see the relief in her face. All she ever said about it was, 'Well, dear, as long as you're happy ...' I knew she wasn't thrilled, but I think she was less worried after our conversation.

"It went unsaid, but my parents knew if I had started hooking it would indicate a fundamental shift in my character. I am a bona fide romantic — I meant what I said about not being able to charge for love or sex. I wouldn't have liked myself if I did something that went strongly against my nature.

"I was seriously tested one day. I was offered a thousand dollars to spend the night with someone. That was a lot of money in the mid-seventies. *Heck, that's a lot of money now!*" Eve paused a minute to sip some iced tea.

"No kidding? A thousand dollars? What do you think he wanted you to do for that?" I asked. I wondered what it would feel like to have someone offer me that much for a one-night stand. The most I was ever propositioned with was dinner and a few drinks, maybe a movie thrown in.

"I didn't want to find out, Stella. Probably some kinky shit," Eve replied. "Even if it was straight sex he wanted, I was only flattered for all of thirty seconds. I was working at the Checkmate at the time. Had just finished my act, and was heading back to the dressing room. I had a negligee draped around me, with the rest of my costume scooped up in my arms. I was sweaty, makeup dripping off my face, and was not inclined to stop and talk to anyone. This Latin-lover type in a ritzy suit jumped in front of me, blocking my way. 'I have a proposition for you,' he says, in a sexy Spanish accent.

"'I'm sure you do,' I answered, 'but I'd like to get by, please.' He ignored my request. He said he was sent to me by his boss, who was offering a thousand dollars to spend the night with me. I looked at him haughtily and asked why his boss didn't just ask me himself. 'Don't you *know* who he *is?* He's very famous — *one of thee greatest jockeys in all thee world!'* He announced this as if I should be so impressed that I would pay to sleep with *him.*

"I looked where he was pointing and saw the man he was referring to. He was small enough to be a jockey, but what he lacked in physical stature, he made up for with his giant ego. His beady eyes stared at me from that arrogant, angular face, as if he had just done me the biggest favor in the world, selecting me out of all the other girls in the club. *No way was I going to let his royal little majesty saddle me up and ride me all night!* Boy, he was ticked when his minion went back to him with news that I had rejected his offer. Strutted right out of the club with a half dozen of his peons trailing behind. Never saw him again. Never had any more offers like that, which was fine with me.

"Many years after I had quit dancing, I went to a past life regression workshop. Apparently, in one of my previous lives I was a *'Lady of the Evening'* in a New Orleans bordello in the mid-1800s. Maybe it wasn't my Catholic upbringing and romantic notions about love that gave me such an aversion to turning tricks. Maybe I just had enough of it from that lifetime." Eve shrugged, then grinned.

She swung her legs off the sofa, leaned forward, and said, "Speaking of Catholic upbringing, one day in the dressing room I overheard a couple of dancers talking about Catholic school. I chimed in that I'd gone until fifth grade. Another girl had gone all the way through high school. Out of about ten girls in the club that day, eight of them were raised Catholic. I remember laughing and saying, 'Wow, will ya take a look at all of these ex-future-nuns!'

"It got me wondering what the numbers would be if you could take a comprehensive poll. If you surveyed strippers coast to coast, how many would be former Catholic-school girls — sixty, seventy, eighty percent? It made me think about repressed sexuality, and how oftentimes a strict upbringing and rigid moral attitudes breed the opposite of what they intend." Eve leaned back, yawning and stretching. That was the signal she'd had enough strolling down Memory Lane for the day.

8. SWEPT AWAY

"Remember yesterday, Stella, when I was talking about promiscuity being relative? I did some calculations. I danced for ten years, and averaged about 250 days each year. A conservative estimate is that I got hit on at least four times a day. That's a bare minimum of ten thousand offers to have sex. I only did it with about twenty guys over the course of ten years. That's approximately one 'Yes' and four hundred ninety-nine 'No's' for every five hundred opportunities. Like I said — nearly abstinent!

"I told a friend I wanted to write a memoir of my dancing days. He said to 'make it spicy — very spicy and steamy.' This is the story of my striptease career, not my sex life. It's club patrons and the general public who think they are one and the same. I understand the confusion. A guy comes into a bar and sees a woman dancing naked. He thinks of sex. He assumes the stripper must be thinking about it too. It's more likely she's thinking about what to cook for dinner, or where to take her car for a tune-up.

"Maybe some women do get horny on stage, I never did. I did get turned on by the adrenaline rush, and I was a sucker for the applause. It wasn't a sexual high. I would have felt the same if I was in a Broadway play, fully clothed, with the audience praising me for reciting an exquisite monologue.

"I got a kick out of creating a persona that fit the strip club environment more than my natural self. It appealed to the inner actress that had retreated so many years before, after that conversation with my dad. I hated getting naked. That was the trade-off— not only to earn a paycheck, but also to live my childhood fantasy of being an actress. Many of my co-workers agreed that it was a lot like playing dress-up when we were kids: putting on Mom's ruby red lipstick; trying to walk in her high heels that were five sizes too big; tripping over her sky-blue silk dress with the crinoline petticoat. Little did we know what we were practicing for!" A wistful expression crossed Eve's face. She seemed lost in childhood memories for a moment before she continued.

"Sultry, sensuous, seductress—these are words that come to mind when one thinks of a striptease dancer. They did not describe my act. I was more the smiley, syrupy-sweet ingénue than sophisticated siren. Picture 'Rebecca of Sunnybrook Farm' in gaudy makeup and glitzy garb. 'The girl next door, with something extra'—that's what one of my fans once called me. I'd bop and twirl around the stage, spinning like I was on ice skates, trying to move lightning fast so that no one could actually see me. My bright-eyed grin was the mask I wore to cover my dismay at making my living that way."

"If you disliked it so much, Eve, why did you stay?" I asked.

"I've often wondered myself, Stella. It was a combination of things. I had a love/hate relationship with stripping. What would I do if I left? Go back to waitressing? No thanks! I had done a few other jobs prior to dancing. They were pretty boring — compared to getting paid to play dress-up and party all day. It was also the best money I could make without a college degree.

"I liked the autonomy too. I was basically self-employed. The club bosses generally left me alone. As long as I showed up and did my job, no one told me how to do it. I picked the music, costumes, and moves I liked. I hung out with whom I wanted to in between my sets.

"I tried quitting for a little while when I lived with Jake. I didn't have a car, and was totally dependent on Jake for money. I stayed home with his mother and sister, helping around the house and watching soap operas. I was lonely, bored, and depressed most of that time.

"Jake tried to help re-direct my career. He worked in a tannery and knew a lot about leather. He showed me how to make belts. It was something I could do from home, something to keep me occupied and out of trouble. I did enjoy it, for a bit. I loved the smell of the leather, and working with tools to carve patterns into the belt blanks. I would get lost for hours staining and finishing belts, waxing the edges, setting grommets and adding buckles. It was rewarding to do something creative, besides taking my clothes off. I made over three hundred belts during that time. We were going to sell them, eventually, but we broke up before we had the chance.

"Although he had promised not to push me to quit dancing, it was his hope all along. He was always trying to rein me in—to change me. His intentions were honorable. He saw the potential of what I could become, if only he could get me to stop drinking and partying, stop stripping, stop being a stubborn knucklehead.

"The more he tried to reform me, the more I rebelled. The more I rebelled, the less he trusted me. Our relationship was doomed from the start anyway. We were both on the rebound from hellacious affairs. Jake was the first boyfriend I had after I'd been beaten up. And he had been burned by a female version of Eddie right before he met me.

"Her name was Midnight. She hadn't physically abused him, like Eddie had with me. The mental torture she inflicted, and the delight she took in doing so, were damaging nonetheless. He never told me all the details, and I never pressed him about it. The dark expression that came over his face at the mention of her name spoke volumes. He just said she took him for everything she could, then dropped him cold. He said she was pure evil. I never quite believed that. It's easy to call someone evil for the crime of not fulfilling your expectations.

"Midnight was a dancer too, very petite, with a tall aura. She had long glossy black hair, large chocolate almond eyes. She had a powerful presence, on and off stage. Kayleen was friends with her, and introduced me to her in the dressing room of the Checkmate. Kayleen told me before I met her that Midnight was a Witch. She had a proud, aloof look on her face when she first saw me. When Kayleen told her I was born on Halloween, her whole demeanor changed. She stepped backward a bit, then bowed slightly, in a gesture of respect. I glared back at her with a look that said, 'That's right, *I am a Witch Queen — don't fuck with me.*' My instincts told me she could be dangerous. If she wanted to think I had some special power, why not play along? I found out later it wasn't a bad idea to put up a psychic shield when she was around.

"I didn't see her much after that meeting. She went out of town — for at least a year. Then, out of the blue, I had a dream about her. I woke up and said, 'Midnight's coming back and *she's going to cause trouble.*' Jake was jolted awake by my statement. He immediately replied, 'She wouldn't *dare* show her face around me.'

"I described my dream to Jake. No obvious indication she was going to do something bad, but it left a haunting feeling that she was going to stir things up. I saw her on stage, wearing a black netted veil across her face — the kind that ladies used to wear on their hats in the forties. She had never worn anything like that when I saw her perform. That was pretty much the whole dream. Within a few days I had confirmation that my dream was a premonition.

"I was working at a club next to the Checkmate called the Cabaret. I had been off for a few days. When I returned to work, my friend Sabrina was in a snit. Something happened the day before that had her in an uproar. We barely said hello when she started venting that this bitch, named Midnight, had been hired while I was away. Sabrina was ready to rip her eyes out the next time she stepped foot in the club.

"Jimmy, the club owner, came in the dressing room to calm Sabrina down. He reassured her that he had fired Midnight, and had told her not to come back—ever. Somehow, the little charmer had managed to piss off almost every woman in the place—dancers, waitresses, and barmaids all wanted to strangle her. Takes a lot of talent to get that many people ticked off at you in just two days.

"Apparently, Midnight had thrown herself onto Wayne's lap. She flung her arms around him, knowing full well he was Sabrina's husband, and ignored Wayne's rejection of her attentions. Then she taunted Sabrina while she was in the middle of her act. It was all my friend could do to keep from jumping off the stage and planting the spike of her high heel into Midnight's forehead. From the other reports I got, she showed a similar disrespect to everyone else in the club. I asked Sabrina what Midnight wore when she went on stage. She thought it was odd that I would ask, but said she had this weird black netted veil across her face — the kind that ladies used to wear on their hats in the forties.

"A couple days later Jake and I went to visit Kayleen and Mimi, in the house I used to share with them. Kayleen was distraught, her eyes all puffy and red from crying. Her fiancée, Johnny, was royally pissed off at her and was threatening to call off their wedding."

"Excuse me, Eve," I interrupted, "but I thought you told me Kayleen was a lesbian. Am I confusing her with someone else?"

"No, Stella, you are not confusing her — she's the same person who confessed she was in love with me about a year before this. She went back and forth about her sexual preferences — gay, then bi-sexual, then straight, then bi again. I couldn't keep track. I didn't care, either. I loved her as a friend, whether she liked boys better than girls or vice versa. It didn't surprise me that when she did fall in love with a guy, it was Johnny. It made some quirky kind of sense. He was a rocker — long hair, liked to dress flamboyantly, even wear a dash of makeup now and then. They seemed to fit well together.

"Anyway, Kayleen spelled out what happened to make Johnny so angry. She said Midnight came to the house and caused quite a scene. Right in front of Johnny, she shoved Kayleen down on the couch, jumped on top of her, and tried to make out with her, in spite of Kayleen pushing her away. Then the little bitch looks over at Johnny and says, 'Oh, sorry

Honey, does this bother you?' and lets out a wicked laugh. She seemed to get a sadistic kick out of emotional torture.

"Kayleen screamed for Midnight to get out—immediately. She did, seeming satisfied that she left a wake of heartache. Kayleen pleaded with Johnny to believe her that there was nothing going on between her and Midnight—they had fooled around a long time ago, but it was over. She was true to him now and had no idea why Midnight carried on like that. He wouldn't listen, just stormed out of the house. Poor Kay was a mess. She was pregnant with Johnny's baby, and fretting she would be a single mother.

"Jake looked at me differently after that. He was right that Midnight wouldn't dare come near him. But I was right that she was coming back and was going to cause trouble. A lot of people around me were freaked out by her within a few days of my dream. She didn't come near me and Jake, but we spent a lot of time consoling friends who were scorched by her.

"I didn't hear anything else about Midnight until a few years later. Someone told me she had gone down the tubes on coke, that her fit and agile little body had gotten fat. There were rumors she had stolen costumes from dancers—not an outfit or two, but someone's entire wardrobe. Can you imagine? A wardrobe is to a dancer what a toolbox is to a carpenter.

"She was still trying to con guys out of money,

drugs, or anything else she could. She no longer had the beauty and charisma to pull it off. She became a pathetic caricature of her former self. It's a classic case of abusing one's personal power. What a waste! Who knows where she could have gone if she had channeled her energy toward more positive pursuits?

"There's a line in the I Ching about evil — how it feeds on the energy of others until there's nothing left, and then it dies, like a fire that consumes all its fuel and then finally burns out. I noticed a copy of the I Ching on your bookshelf. If you don't mind, I'd like to look it up to see exactly what it said."

I nodded yes, but Eve was already heading over to retrieve it. She flipped through the book, which I hadn't cracked open in years. I was amazed how quickly she found the passage. "Here it is," she said. "Hexagram number thirty-six — titled *Ming I, The Darkening of The Light:*

> Here the climax of the darkening is reached. The dark power first held so high a place that it could wound all who were on the side of good and of the light. But in the end it perishes of its own darkness, for evil must itself fall at the very moment when it has wholly overcome the good, and thus consumed the energy to which it owed its duration.

"I don't agree with Jake that Midnight was *pure evil*, but certainly some of the things she did were. There's always more to a story—maybe something horrible happened to her that made her heartless. After I got beat up I understood how some women get very bitter after being abused. We can't always choose what happens to us, but we *can* choose how to react. I made a conscious choice not to become hateful. Perhaps Midnight didn't realize she had other options."

"Eve, you seem very familiar with the I Ching," I said. "I do recall discussing it at dinner when we met, many years ago. I nearly forgot I had that copy of it. I think for my friends and I it was just a passing whim. I'll have to look into it again—sounds like some real gems of wisdom there."

"It has been a big influence on my life, Stella," said Eve. "And the books your friend Carol wrote about it—A Guide to the I Ching and The Philosophy of the I Ching—were extremely helpful."

"In what way, Eve?" I asked. I had never read either one of Carol Anthony's commentaries. I never took the I Ching seriously. I suppose I put it in a category with reading crystal balls and Tarot cards—something fun for parlor games, but not to give any credence to.

"The language of the I Ching is very flowery and cryptic," Eve replied. "The answers it gave me always pertained to what I was asking about, but I had trouble understanding it sometimes. Carol's books explained it in terms of modern western psychology. Much of its guidance has to do with controlling your ego, instead of letting it call all the shots. It counsels restraint. We often make matters worse because our ego reacts quickly. Many situations would be better resolved if we contemplated the right course of action instead of doing the first thing that comes to mind.

"It teaches patience, humility, and perseverance. Almost every hexagram has the phrase *'Perseverance brings good fortune.'* I learned a lot from it, about hanging in during tough times, or knowing when to leave an untenable situation. I read it so much over the years that after awhile I would remember a phrase that would help me, without having to throw the coins and open the book.

"I read that Confucius wore out four copies of the I Ching in his lifetime, and said he had barely tapped the well of its wisdom." Eve looked serene as she explained her relationship with the mystical book. She drew a deep breath and let it out slowly as she meditated on the next phase of her story.

"I often consulted the I Ching if I couldn't make up my mind about something. Even when the answer it gave me seemed vague, it helped me get to a place where I was more in touch with my inner truth. The book was pivotal in my breakup with Jake, but not in a way I would've expected.

"We had our struggles, but things were good between us for the most part. I understood later that our compatibility was mainly due to working opposite shifts. For the first year and a half we were together, Jake was on days, I mostly worked nights.

Then they did a rotation at his factory and he began working second shift. We thought it would be great—having schedules that were more in sync. It had the opposite effect. We started fighting a lot.

"Much as I cared for Jake, I felt like I was being pushed into settling down. I was still riding high, sowing my wild oats. When I left home in my teens, I didn't want the white picket fence. That still hadn't changed in my mid-twenties. Jake thought it was just a matter of time—that after I grew up a little I'd be content to do the 'happily ever after' with him. But I had a serious aversion to mundanity, and that's all I thought marriage could ever be.

"After taking IQ tests in junior high, I remember the guidance counselor telling my parents, as if I wasn't sitting in that tiny room with all of them, that I had '... *a low tolerance for routine.*' His expression was very solemn, like it was a *grave secret* I should never forget, or my life could be at stake. Maybe I was afraid of getting stuck in the routine of married life, afraid it would kill me—or land me in a mental hospital.

"As if the tension between me and Jake wasn't bad enough, I discovered I was pregnant. We went through a torturous few weeks trying to decide what to do. Jake said he would stand by me, no matter what my decision. He kept his wishes from me, not wanting to influence me one way or another. It forced me to focus on what I truly wanted, regardless of how he or anyone else felt.

"When I told him I wanted an abortion, it was

through many tears—not an easy or casual choice. I loved him deeply, but the thought of having my life tied to him—or any man—so permanently, terrified me.

"I pictured myself living out my days in that house, hanging the clothes out to dry on the porch in the winter, just like his mother did. She still used an old wringer washer, the kind I had only seen in movies that people used before electricity. The laundry would freeze on the clothesline. We'd take the stiff clothes into the house and drape them all over the bathroom and anywhere else we could to thaw them out. Jake might have sprung for some modern conveniences, like a washer and dryer. I think his mom liked doing things the old way. She had lived through the Great Depression and was one of the most frugal people I ever met.

"Anyway, changing diapers on my younger siblings when I was still a mere child left a lasting impression on me. We didn't have disposables back then. I used to dunk the pooey diapers in the toilet to get most of the shit off of them before throwing them in the wash. I had no illusions about how hard it is to raise a child. Babies take a lot of work. Then they grow up to be teenagers, which scared me even more. God forbid I had one that turned out like me— drinking and staying out all night at fourteen. Love kids, just never wanted any of my own.

"Jake accompanied me to the doctor for the procedure. He was unusually quiet, on our way there, and afterwards during my recovery time. I knew then that he was hurt beyond words that I would deny his child coming into this world. It was tearing my heart out to look into his eyes.

"I'd had two other abortions when I was much younger, the first one when I was nineteen. I got knocked up by a man who literally made my skin crawl. I ended up, through a complex set of events, living with him for a few weeks in a remote farmhouse in upstate New York. I refused to sleep with him for the first couple of weeks. He badgered me daily, until I finally gave in. The whole time he screwed me, I couldn't wait for it to be over. I know he bathed every day, but he smelled bad to me. There was something oily and sinister about him.

"I found out I was pregnant a few weeks after I got away from him. All I could think about was Rosemary's Baby. I feared I had been impregnated by the Devil. The abortion was so incredibly painful that I hallucinated during the procedure. I saw two dark creatures flying over my head, making screeching noises. One looked like an owl/ bat and the other a black vulture/hawk. It was the most terrifying nightmare I'd ever had, but I was wide-awake.

"I found out later the doctor who did that abortion had his license suspended some time after my ordeal. He had delivered babies most of his career, and was teaching young ladies a lesson—by *not using anesthetic* for abortions. In spite of the physical agony, I never regretted that decision. I was able to make a complete break with Mr. Slime. A child would have bound us for life, married or not.

"I had another abortion two years later. That one was emotionally tougher. I was seeing two young men at the time. Both of them nice, sweet, guys. Both very handsome. It would have been a beautiful baby, but I was in a quandary not knowing who the father was—no DNA testing back then. Wasn't ready to be a single mother. I never told either of them, and stopped seeing both of them after I did it.

"I was still reeling from the pain and confusion of it when I met Eddie. It wasn't just the fight with my Mom, but a cascade of inner turmoil that made me leave New York with Eddie. I was running from my own fuck-ups.

"When I aborted Jake's child, I think it killed, or certainly diminished, his love for me. It was unbearable to live with him after that, but he was still too attached to let me go. I was more willing to part and start my life over again. It was my general way of doing things back then—to run, rather than reconcile.

"I wanted to make sure I was doing the right thing, so I consulted the I Ching. I got the hexagram titled 'Po' meaning 'Splitting Apart.' It seemed clear the best course of action was for us to break up. I showed the chapter to Jake. He couldn't get past the heading without losing his temper. He tore the book out of my hands and tossed it out the second story window— out into the cold, wet, New England-in-March weather.

"Instead of feeling anger, I went numb, completely dispassionate. I thought, Well, that's all the confirmation I need. Any man who could throw my I Ching out the window is certainly not the man I want to spend the rest of my life with. I walked calmly down the stairs and out of the house to retrieve my book. It was splayed out face down in the mud and snow. The pages were wet and ripply, the binding loosened by the impact. I knew our relationship was as beyond repair as my book.

"Within a few days I was packed and ready to go, waiting for my friend Sabrina to pick me up. She said I could stay with her and her husband and their two-year old girl, until I found another place.

"I didn't have much—a few pots and pans, my clothes, toiletries, and books. I had never seen Jake in such a state. He dragged my things out into the rain, flinging them into the driveway, screaming obscenities.

"His mother was hysterical, trying to get him to stop raging. May was a sweet woman. It hurt even more to see her so upset. She always showed me such kindness. There was something innocent and unsophisticated about her. She was loving, gentle, dutiful, and non-judgmental. She was one of the few women I met who lived her Christian principles—in Heaven now, no doubt. I often wondered how she was after I left. I would have called or visited, but the break-up with Jake got so ugly, it didn't seem a good idea.

"I was ragged out and wrung out by the time I got to Sabrina's. My eyes were so swollen from crying they were nearly shut. I smoked some weed and had a few drinks to calm myself down. She lived in a split-level in a semi-rural town in New Hampshire. She helped me get settled in to a small room in the basement and said good night. As I was drifting off to sleep, I was jolted awake by an unexpected visitor.

"It was Mimi's boyfriend Marco. He'd heard I'd been through a nasty break-up, and came to Sabrina's to comfort and console me. *What a nice guy!* I roused out of my drunken, stoned sleep to find him at the foot of my bed, offering me a joint. Next, he pulled out a vial of coke and I snorted a few lines with him.

"Before I could get a handle on what was happening, he started making out with me. I had been attracted to Marco, but never invited anything like that. He was Mimi's guy, and I wouldn't dream of betraying her. He was kissing and caressing me, and my body's natural instincts just took over. In the moment—in my half-asleep, half-drunk and drugged state—I didn't question what I was doing. I let him strip me down and make love to me without any resistance. Remember, too, I believed the quickest way to get over a guy is to do it with another one.

"The next morning I felt a wave of nausea when I woke up next to him. *I slept with one of my best friend's boyfriends!*

"As if I didn't feel bad enough, I had to face glaring condemnation from Sabrina. I asked her why she let him in the house in the first place. She said, 'He told me he wanted to cheer you up. I never would have let him in if I knew you were going to fuck him!' Then she made me swear I would tell Mimi, own up to it myself. Sabrina was so pissed off you'd think it was her husband I screwed. She was ready to toss my stuff out on the street. Instead she told me I could stay two weeks max, that Wayne was furious too and wanted me out of the house.

"I had always believed I had a lot of integrity. All of a sudden I was a person who couldn't be trusted. Whatever pleasure I had the night before was not worth feeling like the lowest slime on Earth the next day.

"It's one of the things I am most ashamed of doing in my whole life. Emotional trauma, combined with alcohol and drugs, equals moron—you do things that are against your own moral code, things you can't take back, no matter how much you wish you could.

"I told Mimi, but I could see from her expression that she already knew. I was teary, genuinely remorseful, begged her forgiveness. Her green eyes shot sparks and flames. Every muscle in her body and face locked, as if paralyzed with rage. I'd never seen Mimi angry before. She was one of the most ladylike, gentle, kind, and classy dancers I'd ever met. She was a loyal and true friend.

"I couldn't bear the shame I felt at betraying her. I told her I wouldn't blame her if she never spoke to me again. She told me she was mad, but not at me so much as Marco—that he had deliberately gone to Sabrina's to seduce me, knowing I was in a vulnerable state. Mimi was the one making excuses for my behavior—that I was distraught, and high on booze and drugs. Forgivable in her eyes, that I got swept away in the moment. Marco, on the other hand, had pre-meditated and manipulated the situation. Her understanding and kindness only increased my anguish. *How could I be such an asshole, to hurt someone I loved as much as her?* She forgave me, but I never forgave myself.

"My friends from Jason's place, Jack and Candy, heard about my break-up and said I could stay with them. Just me, not my cats. Candy was allergic, and their landlord said 'no pets.' I had two cats by then. I had left them at Jake's for the time being. My cat Bunny, the one who survived being dropped out the window by Eddie, had a litter while I lived with Mimi and Kayleen. They were all so adorable. We used to call them 'tuxedo cats.' All four of them had similar markings—mostly black, with white chests and tummies, and white paws. If you put a bow-tie on them they'd look like they were wearing tuxedoes. I kept one of them, the only one with long fur, and named him Frodo.

"Jake's mother and sister were cat lovers, and totally spoiled their own golden tabby, Tyrone. They assured me they would be delighted to take care of my kitties. It was especially hard to leave Bunny. She had been through so much with me. I was very attached to Frodo too, but he was only a few months old when I brought him to Jake's, so it's all he knew. He roamed the forest across the street by day, and had May and Susie to feed, cuddle, and fawn all over him by night. Not a bad life. I've often said if I was reincarnated, I'd want to be a cat in a cat-lover's home," Eve said with a sly grin.

My own fluffy companion, Cinnamon, who had been curled up napping near Eve on the sofa, awoke right on cue. She stretched, then tiptoed over to Eve, nudging her on the knee. Eve reached toward her, both of them purring as she stroked the little calico behind the ears. "Not a bad life at all, huh, Cinnamon? Purrrrrrr ... prrrrr," she said. I never could get the hang of it myself, but Eve made such convincing cat sounds that I wondered if she had been a feline in another life.

9. ONE-NIGHT UNDERSTANDING

"When you expose your body for a living, you expose yourself to unexpected hazards, said Eve. "I'd always wanted a life of excitement, but not danger. I got enough of an adrenaline rush going on stage. I never intended to flirt with death." She paused, biting her lower lip. She looked a bit sullen this morning. I wondered if she'd had a restless night after dredging up unpleasant events the previous day. Letting skeletons out of your closet to dance around in public can be an unsettling thing. Eve continued before I could ask her.

"Many days in the clubs were fairly routine, Stella. Once in a while something mind-blowing would happen—like the time I was working at the Checkmate, and a dancer pulled a gun on me," Eve was very matter-of-fact as she said this.

I, on the other hand, felt my eyes widen as I said, "Heavens Eve! That does sound mind-blowing! Why on earth did she do such a thing?"

"I had just finished my act, and headed for the dressing rooms, "Eve replied. "They were in the basement, down a long flight of stairs, far away from the hubbub of the club. The basement was a huge room, mostly used for storage, I think. It was so dark I couldn't tell for sure how big it was, or what they stored in it. A few small dressing rooms were scattered around the dimly lit perimeter.

"I strolled into one of them to dry off and change. There was one other dancer in the room, Cleo. She was a black girl who had just started working there. Her back was to me as I entered the room. I must have startled her. She whipped around with a wildcat look in her eyes. She was raving about some chick named Zina—crazy lunatic rambling about Zina and someone named Rico. Then I got it. There was another new girl, named Zina, whose boyfriend was Rico. Cleo had fooled around with Rico, and Zina found out. Zina was on the warpath. She threatened to come after Cleo with a knife and slice her face.

"Cleo was babbling, more to herself than me, 'She gonna come after me—says she gonna cut my face. But I got *this* ...' at which point she pulled out a small pistol and waved it around, spewing about how she would shoot Zina if she came near her. It was a pretty, dainty gun, with a pearl handle—the kind Miss Kitty might tuck in her boot to back up Marshall Dillon. Cleo ranted on for what felt like eternity, flailing that cute little derringer around as if it were only a toy. I could feel imaginary bullets hitting each place on my body she pointed to: my right thigh, left shoulder, my gut, my eyeball.

"Time slowed, like that first time I went on stage. I thought for sure the gun would go off. That would be the end of my short life: over at twenty-five, in a stuffy little dressing room, my half-naked body oozing red all over the liquor-stained carpet, my arm still clutching my rhinestoned costume.

"Once again, in the midst of panic, my cool-headed self came to the rescue. I began talking to Cleo—softly, gently, like you would talk to a small child who was frightened by thunder. I told her everything would be all right, that Zina didn't know she was there. She seemed to believe me. Then I told her, calmly and patiently, that she should put the gun away before Tony sees it.

"Tony was one of the club owners. The dressing room was the last place he would ever show up, but Cleo didn't know that. 'Tony, come *here?*' She asked. 'Yes, Cleo, I think he's coming now. If he sees you with a gun he'll fire you for sure. Now, we don't want that to happen, do we?' I said to her, in the most soothing manner I could. That, along with the protection of my guardian angel, worked. Cleo tucked the gun back into her handbag. My knees buckled. I collapsed into the nearest chair and let out a breath I had been holding for an hour.

"I hated ratting on anyone, but this wasn't just pilfering a bottle of liquor. Someone could get killed—maybe one of my friends. I couldn't live with that, so I had to tell Tony. I begged him not to confront Cleo or she'd know it was me who blew the whistle. He let her go shortly afterward. I felt terrible, but the girl was out of control. What else could I do?"

Eve sighed, her eyes misting. She was obviously sad about causing Cleo to lose her job. It surprised me that she could feel so much compassion for someone who had almost blown her head off. I wondered, as I often had listening to Eve, what I would have done. *Would I have been calm, trying to soothe this wild woman, if I was staring down the barrel of a gun?* I shuddered and hoped I would never be put to that test.

"Of course, there were plenty of funny things that happened," Eve continued, "like the time me and a couple of other girls got locked in the club after it closed."

"Hmm, that doesn't sound too humorous, Eve. Please—go on." I said.

"You're right, Stella. It wasn't funny at the time, but my friends and I have a good laugh about it now when we're reminiscing." Eve never seemed to dwell too long on the macabre. Her face brightened, as she moved to a lighter memory.

"As I said, the dressing rooms were a long way from the main part of the club, and Tony didn't usually venture downstairs. Most nights we hustled our bustles to get out at closing time. We lingered one night, primping and preening for some 'hot dates.'

"Earlier that day, I was heading into downtown Boston with two of my co-workers, Kayleen and Lee. We all needed new dancing shoes. You couldn't get those special spikes at the suburban malls.

"A stretch limo passes us and we notice the guys in it have long hair. Not business executive types coming in from the airport—these dudes were cool! They rolled the windows down, waving and catcalling. We flirted back. They hand-signaled we should follow them. We batted our eyelashes and acted like we would. Lee was driving. She hit the brakes and when the limo pulled ahead, she swerved quickly behind them and took the next exit off the highway. We were laughing our asses off. We got hit on all the time. We weren't about to let some strange guys pick us up on the highway like we were lovesick teenyboppers.

"We drove about two miles through a mangle of city streets. Then we came to a stop light, near Copley Square. *We couldn't believe our eyes!* The same limo was sitting right next to us, waiting for the green light.

"The guys waved at us again, inviting us to have a drink with them, pointing toward the posh hotel ahead. Lee starts to pull over behind them. Kayleen and I yelled, 'What the hell are you doing?' Then Lee said, 'Didn't you hear? They are in the band *America!*' Kay and I looked at each other and shrugged, saying something like, '... *what the hell, I've never been a groupie before – let's try it out.*'

"We went into the hotel bar for a few beers. They invited us to their gig at the Boston Garden—with backstage passes. We told them we were performers too, had to work that night and might not make it until the end of the show. They said come and party with them afterward.

"The three of us dutifully went to work. We talked about playing hooky. If all three of us called in sick the boss would know something was up and we'd all be canned. These guys were cute, and famous, but they weren't going to take care of us if we lost our jobs.

"I remember how excited we were when we finished our shows. I thought we freshened up and changed at the speed of lightning. Imagine our surprise when we bolted up that long staircase to the front door, only to find it was locked up tight—from the outside! No windows, no way to get out. *We couldn't fucking believe it!* Of all the nights for this to happen, why did it have to be when we had the hottest dates of our dancing careers? We laugh now, but at the time we weren't happy about spending the night in that stinking club instead of rubbing elbows, and maybe other parts, with rock 'n roll royalty.

"At least we were locked up with a large supply of booze to drown our sorrows. Before we hit the bar, we decided to dig around the boss's office and see if we could find a phone number for one of the owners. We managed to find Tony's number. We were amazed how fast he was there. He was probably more concerned we'd drain all the liquor from his bar than about our comfort and safety.

"By the time we got out, we knew we had missed the concert. Lee was tired and decided to go home, but Kayleen and I went downtown to see if we could meet up with our 'dates.' We found them in the bar at the Fairmont Hotel, unwinding after their gig. We made it just in time for last call. We had a choice of either leaving, or going upstairs to continue the party.

"Kay headed off to a room with the bass player. I spent the night with the drummer. He had a handsome, kind-looking face, and a tight bod—drummers are usually pretty fit—long reddish hair, very Anglo-Irish looking. He looked a little nervous, maybe shy. I was lonely, but not especially amorous.

"He leaned over to kiss me, but it felt awkward. I sensed he was reluctant, only going through the moves because it was expected. I didn't want to be just another notch on some musician's belt. When I asked him if it was okay if we just cuddled, and didn't do 'it,' he seemed relieved. Maybe neither one of us wanted to be a cliché: just another one-night stand between a musician and a groupie.

"We relaxed and had a nice long conversation. On a whim, I had brought along my I Ching. He'd never heard of it before, but was intrigued. I told him to hold a question in his mind while he threw the coins. I figured out the hexagram and read the chapter out loud. I don't know what his question was. From the look on his face, it seemed the answer helped him resolve something that was troubling him. Just a hunch, but I felt it had something to do with a relationship.

"I also felt he appreciated my company to ease the loneliness that is part of road life, but was glad he didn't have to feel guilty about cheating on his woman. I assumed he had one, back home, even though he didn't say so.

"We were strangers, but during our conversation, our eyes hooked into each other's souls. Instead of a one-night stand, we had a one-night understanding. We slept together, clothing on, cuddling sweetly in each other's arms. He looked at me next morning like I was some kind of mystical messenger: an angel sent to comfort and console him, and send him on his way wiser than before. It was a role I enjoyed far more than if I had played the 'free-love-let's-just-fuck-little-groupie.'

"Kayleen had a far different experience. She came pounding on the door as I was saying goodbye to my little drummer boy—pah-rump-pah-pah-pummm. Practically screaming, she tells him his buddy was really rude, just about tossed her out the door. Said she screwed him 'til she was sore, then he treats her like crap—'wham-bam-no-thank-you-ma'am.'

"I felt bad for her, but I wasn't surprised. The sixties did little to change the old double standard. When it comes to sleeping around, men are seen as heroes, women as whores. The inequality is reflected in the names we use. *Don Juan, playboy,* and *ladies' man* are not demeaning the way *slut, tramp,* and *floozy* are. It irks the shit out of me, but seems the way the world works. Maybe it'll change before the next millennium.

"It's a real mind-fuck, this Madonna/Magdalene complex. People want to put a woman into one category or another, instead of understanding there are many facets to most of us. You can be pure of heart, fundamentally a good person, but branded a tramp if you also have a healthy libido.

"I believe the repression of people's natural urges to express their sexuality is at the root of a lot of perverse behavior. By perverse, I am not referring to what two (or more) consenting adults may do together, no matter how kinky it may seem to some. I'm talking about people inflicting harm on others: rape, kiddie porn, sexual homicide. I wonder if these things are prevalent in societies with more accepting attitudes toward the natural expression of hormonal drives." Eve reached for her glass of water, took a long sip, and plunked the glass down hard on the coffee table. "But I digress, Stella. This is a subject for a whole other book—I'm sure there's one out there, written by someone with a PhD.

"It's just that I had to deal with the schizophrenic attitudes about sex on a daily basis. It could make a girl crazy. I had to become resolute and not let the opinions of club patrons determine how I felt about myself. There'd be a guy out in the audience gazing at me all dewy-eyed, like I was a goddess. The guy next to him is spitting venom with his eyes, like I'm dirt under his shoe. I was not comfortable with being put on a pedestal, but I'd be damned if I was going to let some sucker think I was just something to wipe his feet on. Somewhere in between those extremes was a place I could settle into, where I could just be my little ol' multi-dimensional self.

"After the breakup with Jake, I went through a period of alternating between depression and exhilaration. I was determined not to settle down any time soon. I liked the feeling of being footloose again, but at the same time I was lonely. Not that I didn't have plenty of offers for company. But a one-night stand with the wrong person can leave you wishing you cuddled up with a good book instead."

10. SHADES OF GREY

"Speaking of books," continued Eve, "I had always liked to read—probably got the reading bug from my Mom. She had an antique mahogany bookcase so full you couldn't squeeze another book into it. I sometimes wondered if she'd read them all. I tried to read them all, even the encyclopedias. Partly so I could be as smart as her some day, but mostly because I loved learning new things. Reading was also an escape from the chaotic racket of my large family and the somber routine of parochial school.

"Through my childhood, teens, and young adulthood, I always had a book going. When I fell into dancing, I fell out of the habit. After work I was too stoned, too tired, or both. A common expression for drinking and smoking pot is 'getting wasted.' I used to think that sounded cool. Now I understand what 'getting wasted' truly means—it's a waste of money, time, and your mind. I was so caught up in it, I convinced myself I was having fun.

"Ironically, part of the appeal of moving to Boston was that it had so many great schools. When I left New York with Eddie I thought I might get an education. I was getting one all right, but not in anything with fancy initials after it, like BS, or MBA. Then again, 'ecdysiast' does sound impressive, if you don't know what it means—could be some kind of scientist, maybe one who studies snakes," Eve said with a smile. I wondered if she was using humor to mask a deep disappointment.

"So why didn't you go to school, Eve?" I asked.

"Nothing about my life was very stable after my breakup with Jake—not me, my home base, or my job," she replied. "I never knew when a club would decide it was time for a new face. If they liked you, they'd tell you to come back in a few weeks, or a couple months, that they just needed to mix it up and give the guys some new bodies to look at. I bounced from the Checkmate, the Cabaret, and the Golden Banana—all in Peabody, to the Surf and the Butterfly—in Revere. I didn't have a car, and never had much money. I couldn't fathom going to school— surviving day to day was all I could handle." Eve shrugged. She set her gaze across the room on my massive collection of books, lost in a daydream.

"Tell me about the Golden Banana and the Butterfly. You hadn't mentioned them before," I asked, breaking her reverie.

"I worked at the Butterfly only for a few weeks," Eve began. "It was a small club, near the Wonderland Dog Track. That was the only place I danced where the boss blatantly came on to me. Billy, the manager, called me into the office for a 'chat.' I can't recall his exact words, but he seemed to imply that if I wanted job security I would have to 'put out.' Just to make sure I wasn't misinterpreting, I said something like,

'You mean to tell me, that if I want to enjoy the privilege of taking my clothes off in front of drunken perverts, that I have to sleep with you?' He said, 'I wouldn't have put it like that, but, yeah, that's pretty much the gist of it.'

"I felt a wave of nausea as I digested his unsavory proposal. Everything about this guy repulsed me. It wasn't just his homely face with those huge bug eyes. His shady aura told me he was a cold-blooded creep. No way would I let his slimy paws touch me. It'd be like screwing the Creature from the Black Lagoon.

"I began to chuckle—a muffled, amused snicker at first. It became louder and louder until I threw my head backwards, forcing a barrage of phony ha-ha-has that were meant to sound defiant and mocking. His face turned beet-red and he shouted, 'Okay! Okay! I get the point! Just forget I mentioned it!'

"After that day, he never approached me again. I still felt his eyes following me around the club and on stage. It gave me the heebie-jeebies. I was canned soon afterward. I wasn't sad to leave. About a year later I heard someone had put a bullet through him. No one was surprised, or sad, about it. No tears for Billy T.

"As for the Golden Banana, I was there a couple of months. It was a notch above the other clubs for atmosphere and professional shows. They booked some of the more famous acts in the biz. I don't remember dancing there as well as I recall seeing the shows they imported from Vegas.

"One of the acts I was privileged to see there was Dusty Summers, known as 'Las Vegas' Only Nude Magician.' She seemed to float on air across the stage. She pulled a couple of doves out of nowhere, wearing only a sheer negligee. My jaw dropped and I almost fell off my chair. I was fascinated, but at the same time it was a bit intimidating. I wondered if I could ever develop my show to such a professional level, or if I even wanted to try. She seemed so far out of my league.

"I also saw Chesty Morgan at the Banana. No way could she actually dance with the size of those mammaries. Just walking must have been a chore. She strolled onto the stage like a regal monarch, preceded by two midgets who hoisted her breasts over their heads on silver trays. It was a great gimmick.

"I wonder how many of those who ogled her thought about what a relief it must have been for her to have those enormous breasts feel weightless for a few minutes. I know women with boobs half that size who complain of backaches and permanent grooves in their shoulders from double-D bra straps. Ms. Morgan was a legend. I'm glad I got to see her, but sad that I never got to know her. Like many of the big acts, she had the VIP dressing room and tended to stay away from the house girls.

"Another feature of the Banana that set it apart was 'Ladies Night.' We never had to work on Thursday night—it was reserved for male striptease shows. I had zero interest in going to the club on my night off. I finally went when a group of co-workers invited me to tag along. One of the women in our gang was married to one of the male dancers. She thought it would be fun for us to harass her husband and his buddies.

"The mostly-male audiences I danced for were fairly tame, especially on the day shifts. Guys would show up — alone, or in small groups — dressed in their work duds: white collar, blue collar, no collar. Strip clubs are a great equalizer. Men from opposite ends of the economic scale and various backgrounds, who normally wouldn't mix socially, are brought together by the common denominator of watching beautiful women get naked. They'd stare and glare, commenting to each other, or lost in their individual fantasies, but generally quiet during the show. In between each song, and at the end of the show, they'd clap. The applause varied from polite acknowledgment to wildly enthusiastic thunder mixed with hooting and howling.

"I was amazed at the uproarious behavior of the 'ladies' on 'Ladies Night.' I could hardly hear the blasting music over the screaming cacophony. Women tossed various articles of clothing onto the stage — mostly bras and panties. If I had to work in front of a crowd as loud and unruly, I wouldn't have lasted a day.

"The only way to get through the night was to join the fun. We parked our fannies in perverts row and taunted every one of those brave young men as they bared their butts. We hollered every insult that had ever been tossed at us onstage, and relished every rowdy minute of it. It was not about getting aroused, or fantasizing we'd end up between the sheets with the Chippendale wannabees.

"The unifying factor I shared with all of my sisters in the club that night—the strippers I came with, the secretaries, nurses, mothers, and maids—was *revenge*. After centuries of standing by, silently tolerating this exclusively male pastime, women were coming out in droves to enjoy one of the silliest fruits of our emancipation. Silly, but nonetheless fun!

"I found out later the male strippers said it was the hardest night they'd ever had. The catcalling and chaos didn't faze them. They were intimidated by us. They knew the front row was full of strippers. It mattered to them to be good, and not look amateurish in front of their peers. Knowing how hard it is to get up there myself, I felt bad that we made them so uncomfortable. It was the first and last time I went to see male striptease artists.

"The Banana was a hot spot for upscale shows, but it left me cold as far as working there. Maybe it was because they rotated their shows more often than the other clubs, so it was hard to build friendships.

"The first five years I was like a ping-pong ball—bouncing from one club to the next, then rebounding to my three home bases: the Surf, the Checkmate, and the Cabaret.

"I was at the Cabaret when I split up with Jake. I was sad the relationship ended on such a bad note, but relieved that I didn't have to keep living up to Jake's expectations. There was something uncomfortably familiar about the way Jake tried to straighten me out. His stern expression and disapproving glare reminded me too much of my father. I could never do anything right in his eyes either." Eve turned toward the window, her lips pursed in an angry scowl.

"Eve, you mentioned having low self-esteem. Did your relationship with your father have something to do with that?" I asked. I wondered if she might feel more open to discussing her upbringing. I knew there was something else, something profound, that she wasn't ready to divulge earlier.

"Dad had been an only child," Eve replied. "I don't think he ever got used to having eight children—the constant chaos, noise and fighting that was just us being kids. He yelled a lot, and was very critical, but never raised a hand to us. I know he loved us, but I always wondered if he was genuinely happy with having so many of us. Maybe his short fuse and hypercritical attitude dented my fragile self-esteem, but five years of Catholic school did nothing to build it up.

"I have scattered but happy recollections of kindergarten, which was a public school. First grade was a radical shift: uniforms, stern-faced nuns shrouded in mysterious robes, and endless repetition of lessons. They enforced military-like discipline. Your brown oxfords had better be shined, or you'd have to say ten 'Hail Marys' and sit in the corner wearing a 'dunce cap'. They were masters of humiliation — not all of the nuns, but enough of them to keep you in mortal fear of doing anything that would incur their wrath.

"I was a quiet student. I did my homework, polished my shoes, and tried not to get noticed. I was almost invisible. Then one day in third grade I screwed up. I was running on the playground with my friends. We weren't allowed to play on the grassy fields that surrounded the parking lot. God forbid we should ruin their acres of green! We were confined to the asphalt for our lunchtime breaks.

"I tripped and fell face-down on the blacktop. Not over the initial shock of it, I felt myself being pulled up by my collar and set hard on my feet. It was Sister Justine. She had come to my rescue, and stuffed her white cotton hanky under my nose to stop the bleeding. My gratitude fizzled in an instant. She laced into me, scolding me with a voice so shrill it was like a flock of blue jays screaming at me.

"My crime: I was a stupid idiot because I had fallen down, scraped my hands, bloodied my nose. Her handkerchief was ruined and she was further inconvenienced, as she had to take me to the school nurse. She had me by the collar the whole time, screeching and scolding as she dragged me along. I was sobbing my eight-year-old heart out. I was shaken up with having the first bloody nose of my short life, but her sadistic reprimand was far more traumatic. All the kind, sweet, and truly Christian Dominicans I met, before or after, could not erase the emotional scars left by 'Sister Psycho.'

"I told you I wanted to be a saint, but knew I could never be good enough. We were reminded every day that we were sinners. Our sins were so terrible that even a newborn baby couldn't escape purgatory unless it was baptized and cleansed of 'original sin.' We all were so evil that Christ had to suffer inconceivable pain and hardship so we might be saved.

"I didn't question any of it in my tender years. If my parents, the ultimate authority figures in my life, chose that school for me, then it must all be true. *They* would *never* lie to me." Eve said this with a sarcastic lilt in her voice. She swung her feet off the sofa, stood up, and paced around the room. I refrained from asking her anything. She seemed to be struggling with her thoughts and memories. I wanted to give her space to sort out whatever was making her restless. After a moment she continued.

"God, Stella, this is hard. I wish I could skip this, but it's too significant to skirt around. It finally dawned on me that low self-esteem caused my self-destructive behavior and bad choices about men. I had to do some soul-searching to figure out how my ego became so damaged in the first place." Eve paced back and forth, looking down at the floor, her arms folded in front of her. She plopped down on the sofa and took a long drink. She put the glass down gently, drew a long breath, and released it with a huff. She leaned over a bit, facing me squarely. Her elbows rested on her knees, hands clasped with fingers interlaced in front of her. I thought back to that first day she began her story, and the moment she looked away, fighting tears, when she talked about her mother.

After a long pause, Eve continued, "As I said before, my mom was hitting bottom on alcohol when I was reaching puberty. That had a lot to do with our tumultuous relationship, but there was something else, something that took me a long time to understand.

"I thought my mother hated me. I'm the only one of my siblings she ever cracked across the face. She only did it three times, but the physical sting didn't compare with how it burned my heart. She'd scream, 'DON'T LOOK AT ME LIKE THAT!' each time she did it. I never understood what facial expression I wore that provoked her so. Every time she yelled at me for *anything*, I was terrified I'd have some look on my face she didn't like, and dreaded her slapping me again. I'd look down at the floor. Then she'd yell, 'Look at me when I'm talking to you!' It was a no-win situation.

"We all got spanked from time to time. When it got to be too much for her—the constant fighting and general mayhem of eight wild kids—she would line us up and take us into the bathroom one at a time and wallop our bottoms. She'd grab whatever was most convenient: a leather belt, a wooden spoon, or the back side of a hairbrush and give us half a dozen paddles each. It was never a pleasant experience, but at least we were all getting the same treatment. It's important to kids that they get an equal share of what the other kids are getting.

"It bothered me that half of us hadn't done anything wrong. But that never hurt as much as feeling singled out and being the only one she ever smacked across the face. I was also the only one she ever threw out of the house. It wounded and baffled me for years. I wondered what I had done that caused my mother to hate me.

"I was a few years into my dancing career, in my mid-twenties, when a repressed memory surfaced. I recalled, in great detail, an incident that happened when I was about thirteen.

"I was in seventh grade. In the middle of my school day, I came down with a nasty stomachache. I went to the school nurse. She tried to call my mother, but didn't get an answer. The nurse said she was on her way out and would be going near my house, so she would drive me home. She dropped me off in front of the house. I climbed the steep driveway, went into the house and called out, but my Mom wasn't there. I went upstairs and noticed her door was ajar. I thought she might be napping, so I pushed it open gently. She was there—and somebody else too. An eerie prickly feeling washed over me, as if I had done something very wrong. I had. I wasn't supposed to be home and wasn't supposed to have seen what I just saw.

"My mother was sitting sideways on the edge of her bed. Someone was laying on their back, feet on the floor, stretched out across the width of the bed. It was a man. His pants were unzipped. My mother was rubbing his belly in slow circular motions. They were talking softly, smiling at each other.

"Suddenly they noticed me standing there. My mother was on her feet quickly as I dashed out of the room. I was overwhelmed with a feeling of guilt—guilt that I had witnessed something I was never meant to see—*but what had I seen?*

"My mother put her arm around my shoulder gently, and explained, 'Father Murray had a stomachache, and I was trying to help him feel better.'

"I nodded, agreeing that it sounded better than my wild assumption that my mother was about to make love to a Catholic priest. I accepted her explanation, then blocked the incident from my mind for the next twelve years.

"When the recollection of that day snapped back into my consciousness, I questioned it at first. *Had I simply dreamed it? Was this a real memory? If so, why had I been unaware of it for so many years?*

"I'd like to think it was merely a warped dream, but there are too many details, from the nurse picking up that heavy 1950s telephone, to Father Murray's polished black oxfords. The time expanse made it seem real too—reporting to the nurse's office, riding home with her, walking up the stairs, opening the door. It was all too fluid, not choppy and vaporous like a typical dream sequence.

"If it hadn't happened, then I had no hope of knowing why my mother cracked me across the face and threw me out into the world before I was ready. If it *was* real, then many pieces of the puzzle fell into place—like why she yelled at me to *'stop looking at her like that.'* She must have seen a reflection of her own guilt in my eyes.

"It would explain why I felt that my mother, who was supposed to love me unconditionally, seemed to hate me instead. I was the only one who knew her secret, or so she thought. She had no idea my mind had buried her secret so deep that it wouldn't surface for years.

"It helped me to understand why I had become disillusioned with the Church, and organized religion. It probably had a little to do with why I started drinking, smoking cigarettes, and staying out all night when I was only fourteen.

"It would also account for why I couldn't stand Father Murray, who was a frequent visitor to our house all through my teens. He was a 'friend of the family.' Everyone in my household—Mom and Dad, all of my younger siblings—adored him.

"My one older brother and I couldn't stand him. We would greet him politely, then play practical jokes on him. It was one of the brattiest things I ever did—I wasn't usually cruel. We knew he had a habit of throwing his head back when he laughed. One of our favorite tricks was to take him by the hand upon his arrival, and lead him to a certain spot on the couch in front of the windowsill. After he was seated, we'd say something like, 'Hey, Father, what's an Irish seven-course meal?' 'I don't know—what?' he'd reply. 'A boiled potato and a six-pack,' we'd answer. He'd throw his head back in a boisterous laugh. CRACK—the back of his head would smash against the windowsill. We could get away with two or three more jokes before he'd get up and move to another seat. I'm not very proud of that behavior now, but at the time my brother and I would bust a gut trying not to laugh at our sadistic prank.

"My young impressionable mind had its belief in the sanctity of marriage, and the holiness of the Catholic Church, shattered in that few seconds of witnessing a scene I shouldn't have seen. It was too much to assimilate, so I conveniently 'forgot' the incident until years later. The incident was forgotten, but the damage was done. I no longer believed in Santa Claus, the Easter Bunny, or anything my parents or any 'authority figure' told me.

"When you're a kid, you see things as either black or white, good or evil. With maturity you see that although we live in a world of polar opposites, there are many shades of grey, and many ways to judge, or misjudge people.

"It may sound scandalous that I suspect my mother had an affair with a Catholic priest. But when I reflect on it now, I see my mother's extreme loneliness. She was a very bright woman, marooned in the suburbs with a houseful of needy kids and surrounded by ditzy neighbors for company—nice enough people, but not her intellectual equals. Dad was away all day at work, or out of town for weeks at a time on business trips. Then this new priest shows up in town, whom she happened to know from the city when they were kids, before either of them had taken their respective vows. He's handsome, personable, intelligent, and *safe*—what other man could have hung around my mom all that time without Dad getting suspicious? I believe they were actually in love. What a heartbreak it must have been, to find your soul mate and not be able to be with him 'cause you're married with eight kids, and he's married to the Church.

"When I got into my thirties, my relationship with Mom had healed considerably. We had both worked on ourselves—she through AA and I mostly through the I Ching and reflection. I wanted to hear her perspective on what made me feel like she hated me back then. When I tried to find out, all I said was, 'Mom, there's something I've always wanted to ask you ...' She cut me off sharply before I could finish my question. She raised her voice in a terse manner she hadn't used with me in years. She said, 'Eve-Marie, sometimes it's best to let the past stay in the past.'

And that was it—no further discussion. Her reaction validated my suspicions. I'll never know the whole truth of it though—she passed away in 2001.

"This part of my story, Stella, more than anything else, is why I want to keep my identity a secret. It would be too painful for my family. None of them know what I saw that day. My dad is still alive. He believes to this day that their friendship was innocent. I'd rather let him and my siblings keep their fond feelings for Father Murray. I don't want to disrespect my mother's memory, either. I could fill a few chapters talking about her good qualities. If it wasn't for some of the things I inherited from her, like creativity, patience, kindness, and resilience, I would never have survived this long.

"The realization there was another reason for my self-destructive behavior—that I was a victim of circumstances and not just a defective human being— was the beginning of my path to healing. I didn't want to get stuck in blame. Both of my parents were alcoholics and both of them made mistakes that helped screw me up. *So what?* That probably describes half the population. I didn't want to live in a pity-party, whining 'Poor Me,' and acting out forever. Those kinds of revelations come swiftly, but changing habits you've been stuck in for years takes time—first the 'Revolution,' then the 'Evolution.'" Eve stood up, yawned and stretched.

My head was spinning trying to take it all in, seeing how a chain of events can be triggered by a singular moment in time. I wondered what path Eve's life might have taken if her discovery of her mother's affair hadn't set up the difficulties between them. She wouldn't have been thrown out of the house, driven into the arms of a psychotic stranger, and probably wouldn't have become a stripper. I never would have met her and she wouldn't be telling me her story.

"I imagine you've had it for the day, Eve?" I said.

"Definitely," she replied. "Let's continue tomorrow. I hope this explains a little more about my 'low self-esteem,' Stella."

"Yes, indeed," I replied, reaching toward the coffee table to press the 'off' button on the tape-recorder.

11. BETTER ON THE OTHER SIDE

Eve fixed a cup of coffee and settled down in her usual spot on the sofa, opposite my easy chair. "Ready?" she asked.

"If you are," I replied. She nodded and I reached over to the coffee table to start the tape recorder.

"Hmm, where was I, Stella?" she began. "Oh, yes, I was telling you what happened after I broke up with Jake, but I guess I got a little distracted." Her playful grin underscored the irony of her words. Revisiting childhood trauma was more than a slight distraction from the chronology of her story. We had talked about it more after we shut the recorder off the previous day. Eve said she was grateful she'd never been molested as a child. She knew many women, in and out of 'the business' who spent years struggling with the scars left by such abuse.

She had not been physically abused, but seeing her mother in bed with a priest was disturbing enough for her mind to block the memory. The incident itself wasn't as scarring as the tension that ensued between Eve and her mother as a result of her discovery.

Repressed memories are a queer phenomenon. They can cause a person to act out in response to a traumatic event, without any clue as to why they are driven to certain moods or behaviors. Only after the damaging incident is called back into consciousness can the person begin to understand and, hopefully, heal.

"You told me you were dancing at the Cabaret during your break-up with Jake," I said, to help Eve reconnect with her story line.

"Right, Stella," she continued. "For the next few weeks I settled into a comfortable routine—dancing, drinking, and smoking pot all day. Sometimes the party continued into the night, but often I would just go back to Jack and Candy's. They rented a small house in Malden, a densely populated suburb of Boston. It was an older house with one main floor and a large attic, in a quiet neighborhood. I had a room to myself on the first floor. Jack and Candy had no problem with me staying as long as I wished, but I was not to bring guys over to spend the night. That was fine with me. I wasn't keen on spending the night with *anyone* at that point.

"The Cabaret was not very big. When you walked in the door, the stage was immediately on the right, the bar to the left. On the other side of the bar there were some pool tables. There was the usual row of chairs rimming the stage, and a scattering of tables filling the rest of the room. The place didn't get much action, especially during the day. I would have gone stir crazy if it wasn't for my friends. Sabrina and I had been close, until I screwed up and slept with Marco. But she took her cues from Mimi, who was willing to forgive and forget. Neither one of them seemed to hold a grudge about it. I was frosty toward Marco when he came in the club, so everybody was clear it was a one-night mistake I was not going to repeat.

"Maybe because I was feeling the blues about breaking up with Jake, I began to notice how somber many of the customers were, particularly the ones that came in alone. When guys came with a buddy, it was all about having a good time—a few beers, a few laughs, a few wolf whistles at a naked chick. But day after day I would do my routine in front of some of the saddest looking faces I've seen anywhere. I wondered why they were so depressed, but not enough to come out of the dressing room and talk to any of them. I struggled between my claustrophobia and my crowd-a-phobia: hide in the dressing room, or mingle with drunk, depressed perverts. My solution was usually to light up another joint, get a beer, and hang with the other strippers in that closet-sized cubbyhole where we changed and put on our make-up.

"I saw a face one day that pulled me out of my seclusion. He was young, slim build, with thick sable hair styled like the early Beatles 'mop top.' His eyes were round, and as dark as French-roast coffee. But it was his smile—a broad, luminous, adorable grin— that made me think, *I'm gonna talk to that guy after my show, and I'm gonna have a good time.*

"His name was Luke. Turned out he was a guitar player—I always had a thing for guitar players. He was a delight to hang out with, after all the gloomy types I usually ran into at the 'Cab.' I ended up going out with him after work. We went to Kelly's in Revere. He had a roast beef sandwich, which Kelly's was famous for. I ordered a lobster roll—big chunks of fresh lobster, on a toasted roll, light on the mayo—best I've ever had. We ended up walking, talking, and hanging out on the beach until the sun came up.

"I enjoyed his company, but wasn't thinking of anything more than a passing fling. There was something about the way he unexpectedly kissed me while we were sitting in the sand, the way he looked deep into my eyes afterward, that told me he was hoping for more. My heart was racing and my hormones were running amok. The last thing I thought I would be doing, so soon after my break-up, was falling in love, but that's just what happened. There is no drug I know of that can match the euphoria of fresh romance. We were smitten, and there was nothing for it but to spend as much time together as possible. My ecstasy lasted for all of a week before life blind-sided me once again.

"All week long there had been an extra bounce to my step. I felt like my face would crack from smiling so much. Luke dropped me off at the Cabaret one morning and headed off to his job. I went to work eager to see Sabrina, as I had scored some very tasty weed. We always split our bags of grass with each other, and this stuff was high-test, from Thailand. I knew she would be thrilled. I stepped into the dressing room and knew right away something was terribly wrong. There were three other dancers in that tiny room—all with the same hollow look in their eyes—no spark of life, just dark emptiness. It felt like the air had been sucked out of the room and nobody cared 'cause their lungs felt too heavy to breathe anyway.

"I scanned the room, searching for the dear friend I looked so forward to seeing. 'Where's Sabrina?' I asked. One of the girls turned toward Mimi and said, 'I can't tell her—can you do it?' Mimi looked at me, the hollowness in her eyes melting into deep compassion. She quietly told me, 'Sabrina's dead. She was killed last night in a car accident on her way home from work.'

"My mouth dropped, eyes flooding. I barely had time to react, when we were interrupted by Jimmy, the club owner. He barged into the dressing room. With a voice that cut through the silence like a crack of thunder, he barked, *'You – get on stage,'* to Mimi. He pointed to the other two dancers and said, 'You and you—get out there and mingle. Then he pointed to me and said, 'And you—you can go home.' Jimmy knew Sabrina and I had a bond that sisters would envy, some magic between us that is hard to explain. He knew there would be no 'getting over it' and getting on stage for me that day. I took a cab to Jack and Candy's. I spent the next several hours crying until my eyes couldn't make tears anymore.

"What a week—to have my heart soar to the sky, riding the wings of newfound love, only to plummet into a chasm of devastating grief. It was the first time I ever dealt with losing a loved one.

"People were speculating about whether she was drunk. She may have had a few drinks, but exhaustion was the key factor. Sabrina was pulling the whole load to support her husband and their daughter. They had recently bought a new house — the one in New Hampshire she let me stay in when I broke up with Jake. She was doing all the things a normal housewife and young mother does — laundry, shopping, cooking, cleaning, and childcare. On top of it, she was grabbing all the double shifts she could to keep up with the bills. Wayne was supposed to be helping out with their two-year old, Tanya. Half the time he got a babysitter so he could hang around the club shooting pool. I knew that aggravated her, but she told me she didn't want to confront him about it. She could keep an eye on him while he was there. If she bitched about it, he'd just go to another club.

"Sabrina was getting burnt out keeping up with it all. She was taking speed (amphetamines) to get through those long days. It was a gradual decline. I hadn't noticed she was getting very thin, and had dark circles around her eyes. I only became aware of the signs when it was too late.

"I'll never know how it happened, whether she fell asleep at the wheel, or swerved to avoid an animal. She had worked a double shift that day. That's about a fourteen-hour day, with eight shows. A few pills, a few drinks to keep going, then a ninety-minute ride through winding country roads at two a.m. — maybe it was only a matter of time before something like that would happen.

"My mind and heart were so overwhelmed that my emotions shut down. I went numb. I smoked about ten cigarettes to get through the wake and funeral. They made me dizzy — like the first time I ever smoked. There was no danger of getting hooked on them again. Every one of them tasted repulsive thanks to the self-hypnosis. I had a few beers, but there was nothing that could ease my pain.

"There were quite a few people at her funeral, all dressed in bright colorful clothing. Sabrina had said to me, a few weeks before this, 'When I die, I don't want anyone wearing black and getting all morbid ... I'd want them to be dressed in colorful clothes, celebrating and being happy for me. After all, it's supposed to be *better* on the other side, *isn't it?*' All the people who came to bury her knew her well enough to dress as she would like, but nobody seemed joyful about losing her. Sorry Sabrina, that was too much to ask of us.

"I went back to her house after the funeral with some of the other dancers. Her family had all traveled from Kentucky and were staying with Wayne. An eerie feeling crept over me as I looked around the room at her relatives — *they all had her eyes.* I was looking into Sabrina's soul through each set of those bewitching dark-brown eyes. Beautiful eyes, all staring back at me, knowing from the look on my face that I mourned her loss as much as family did.

"One of her brothers approached me. He was about fifteen. Almost in a whisper he said, 'You loved her too, didn't you?' I nodded—I couldn't manage anything else. Then he stunned me by asking, 'What was she *like?*' When he saw the puzzled look on my face, he added, 'I was so young when she left home, I never really got to know her.'

"His grief had an extra dimension to it. He also mourned the lost opportunity of knowing who his sister was. What could I possibly tell this sensitive young man about Sabrina that would explain why I loved her so much? We reached our hands toward each other. Our fingers clasped like a yin and yang symbol. I looked into those large Sabrina eyes, and words just flowed, without pre-thought. I said to him, 'She was one of the most down-to-earth and real people I ever met—nothing phony about her. If she liked you, half of anything she had was yours, but if she didn't like you, well, she didn't make any bones about it. You always knew where you stood with her.' We both grinned through glistening eyes. She could have a temper, we both knew, but her wrath was just and fair. 'Yeah, that's how I remember her,' he said, as his face brightened. 'I'm so glad she had a friend like you, who really loved her—she was so far from home.'

"Luke tried his best to offer comfort. I told him not to come to the funeral. He didn't know Sabrina, and I didn't want to burden him with my heavy emotions, especially so soon after we had started seeing each other. I wanted to be with my fellow dancers. We had all lost a sister, and we needed each other.

"I couldn't take too much time off if I wanted to keep my job. Besides, I thought it would be better to keep busy, instead of sitting around all day dwelling on my sadness. I went back to work at the Cabaret. Dancing on the same stage she had danced on and missing our girl-talks in the dressing room didn't do much to take my mind off her death.

"There were rumors her husband Wayne had been fooling around with one of the barmaids, Charlene. It was odd that he kept coming back in there as often as he did. That was too much for me—to be looking at the two of them, wondering if it was true, wondering if Sabrina had known, and wondering if—in a jealous, exhausted rage—she had jerked the steering wheel hard to the left, crossing the road and smashing into a tree to put an end to her pain.

"I was still in love with Luke, but grief made it hard to get back to the state of exhilaration I felt with him before Sabrina's accident. A couple of weeks after she died, I had an intense dream that brought relief from my sorrow. Luke and I had been spending some nights at his house. He lived with his father, and his father's second wife. I was glad he was there so I could share my dream with him as soon as I awoke.

"I told him Sabrina had come to visit me. I honestly believed that's what my dream was—a visitation. It had a different feeling about it than most dreams. I saw Sabrina more clearly than I ever saw her in real life. She was surrounded by beautiful light, but more than that, the light was coming from her and through her. She was wearing one of her dance negligees—wispy silk fabric swirling around her. Her face was glowing. She looked ten years younger—no trace of the dark circles and weariness she wore before her death. She flashed me a broad smile, her lips curled a little more on one side, just like I remembered. It was an endearing trait she had, always a touch of mischief in that grin. Her eyes were penetrating right into my heart. She didn't say anything, yet I was getting a clear message from her: PEACE. That was the overpowering feeling she was sharing with me. She looked happier and more serene than I had ever seen her in life. I was convinced she came back to let me know she was at peace, that I shouldn't be sad—it really *was* better on the other side. I woke up feeling like a fifty-pound rock had been lifted off my chest.

"Whether my dream was her spirit reaching out to me from beyond, or an invention of my own psyche, that vision helped me get back to living and enjoying my own precious life once again. That majestic apparition of Sabrina is what I chose to hold in my heart and my mind, and what I've carried with me to remember her by." Eve closed her eyes, perhaps to envision her friend's spirit once again, dancing in the ethereal light. I remained silent, so as not to disturb her trance.

She opened her eyes a moment later. "Hey Stella,

how about going out for lunch? I could use a stretch and a change of atmosphere. Rehashing old sorrows has worked up my appetite. My treat—you've been so generous making us sandwiches almost every day since we started this."

"Sounds lovely. I could use a stroll, and a day away from the kitchen, myself," I replied. I was pleased at the suggestion. Eve's story of her friend's tragic death had stirred up memories of my own losses. Perhaps a walk downtown and lunch at a sunny bistro would lighten our hearts.

12. House Girl

Eve hadn't been to Savannah before her visit with me. She asked me to choose a place for lunch. I had been writing reviews of local eateries for a few years, and knew just the spot. It was an easy and pleasant walk from my house. I thought the vibrant colors of the Soho South Cafe would provide a merry atmosphere for our break.

Eve's face reflected childlike joy as she took in the artsy décor of the cafe. Now in her fifties, she still had a youthful look about her. I often find that youthful quality in people who possess great enthusiasm for life, who seem to appreciate the ordinary as much as the extraordinary. Could the secret behind the mythical 'Fountain of Youth' be a positive attitude? *If so*, I thought, *maybe I could bottle it and become the exclusive worldwide distributor.* I fantasized about making millions from an optimism potion that would make the world a better place, one youthful person at a time.

Eve disrupted my daydream. Settling into a turquoise chair, she said, "Stella, this place is awesome! Every inch of it is so cheery. Why don't they make strip clubs colorful and artistic like this? Maybe they do now, but the ones I worked in favored black walls, grey carpet, and boring brown chairs.

Maybe that's why the customers looked so depressed half the time. It was all up to us, the dancers, to brighten things up. Would've been nice if the bosses helped out by creating a cheerier atmosphere to begin with." She raised her eyebrows and waved her hand in a dismissive gesture, then reached for the menu.

Eve and I had agreed not to discuss her striptease days when we were on lunch breaks. I wanted to confine her memoirs to my parlor, with the benefit of my little black box to record them. Sometimes we couldn't avoid the topic on our 'time off.'

"I know we said we wouldn't talk about my story on our breaks, Stella, but there was one thing I wanted to add, about what I told you this morning, if that's okay." This wasn't the first time I'd wondered if Eve was reading my mind.

Before I could answer her, a young woman interrupted.

"Are you ladies ready to order?" she asked.

Eve ordered the grilled salmon BLT—hold the bacon. I asked for the quiche of the day, crab and artichoke. The spunky young lady hopped off to get our food as we resumed our conversation.

"Go ahead Eve—you were saying?"

"It's about Sabrina's death," Eve began. "I told you it was the first time I had to deal with a loved one passing away, but that wasn't quite true. There was a neighbor when I was a little girl. His name was Herbie. He and his wife, Andrea, were very kind to all the kids in my family. Andrea would give us treats, and Herbie loved to do card tricks and other stunts—like that disappearing quarter prank where he 'finds' it behind your ear.

"Herbie had a heart attack when I was about ten years old. I was sad, but understood it to be a fact of life, that old people die. He seemed old to me then, though he was only in his fifties. My whole family went to the funeral. It was open-casket. I saw his wax-like face laid out in white satin. I wished I never saw him like that. I would rather have remembered him full of life, laughing and telling us stories, not like a plaster statue.

"When I was about to walk into Sabrina's wake, that image of Herbie came to mind. I couldn't bear the thought of seeing Sabrina's corpse. My knees buckled. I would have collapsed, but my friend Toni grabbed my arm to steady me. As if Toni read my mind, she said, 'It's okay, it's closed.' I heaved a sigh of relief that I wouldn't be haunted with visions of Sabrina laid out and lifeless like Herbie.

"I told you my dream about Sabrina gave me a joyful image to cling to, that helped heal my grief. There was something else, that thread of something to be grateful for, like I mentioned before. I was twenty-seven when Sabrina died. In the midst of my agony, I realized I had gotten pretty far in life without feeling the pain of losing someone close to me. I was grateful I had never experienced the loss of a family member, like my friend Raven had. Raven was only eight years old when she lost her mother to a brain tumor—so young to go through that. I was lucky indeed. Through the heartache of losing Sabrina, I kept coming back to that thought.

"I hadn't been aware of how I've used gratitude to pull myself out of the pits, time after time, until I began regurgitating my life. Hmm ... maybe regurgitating is a poor choice of words when we're about to eat." Eve snorted a little laugh. We enjoyed a relaxing and delicious lunch, without further conversation about her life, until we were back in my cozy parlor a couple of hours later.

Eve and I resettled into our comfortable spots at my house. I pressed the tape recorder on and asked, "You said you were having a difficult time going to work at the Cabaret, with so many reminders of Sabrina. How long did you stay after she died?"

"I think it was only a couple of weeks before I heard that a club in Revere was looking for dancers," Eve replied. "I went to the Squire to check it out. I was told to ask for Norma, the woman who managed it. She was half a foot taller than me, not fat, but sturdy-looking. Her jet-black hair was swept back into a fifties-style bun. She wore no make-up, and had a stern look about her—a very imposing presence. She said they'd try me out, and let me know they didn't tolerate troublemakers. She reminded me of the most intimidating nuns from Catholic school. I could picture her wearing a habit, and swatting your hands with a ruler for speaking out of turn.

"The entrance to the Squire was to the far left of the

building. The bar was the first thing you encountered when you walked in. It was to the immediate right, and stretched the entire length of the building along the front wall. The stage wasn't quite centered in the room—about two thirds of the room was on the left, where you walk in, making the stage a little distant from the front door. There was no 'perverts row'—no chairs rimming the stage. There were rectangular tables with chairs on either side, but an aisle kept them from abutting the stage. It was like having a moat around the stage. It made me feel a bit safer than having strange men at arm's length when I was flashing my naked body around.

"The stage was huge—maybe twenty-foot square, raised two feet above the main floor level. There was a cast-iron rail on each side. The front that faced the bar was open, with wide stairs, the length of the stage. If you walked down the stairs you'd end up on the lap of some guy sitting at the bar. I never understood why those stairs were there. No one ever used them. Only once—some guy in a drunken daze was heading for the exit sign he saw in the corner. He stumbled up onto the stage while I was dancing. He looked very confused. It was obvious he didn't intend any harm. Two huge bouncers came out of the woodwork as fast as you could snap your fingers and helped him find the exit.

"In the front corners on each side, there were small elevated platforms that were lit from inside. They reminded me of the old go-go dancer light boxes.

And, big surprise—a floor to ceiling sumptuous red velvet curtain lined the back wall of the stage. It must be standard decor. Almost every club I worked in had red velvet curtains. It was like a uniform. I wonder if there's a 'How to Decorate a Strip Club' manual out there. If there is, it's a very small book.

"That stage was twice as big as any I had been on. I was thrilled to have so much space, but it was challenging. I felt I needed to be more creative to fill such a large stage. I had room to move, and to twirl fabric like a madwoman. Consciously and unconsciously I had picked up moves from other dancers and put them together to develop a style of my own. I never considered myself a great dancer. Someone complimented me on my dancing in front of my old boyfriend, Jake. He said, 'She's not really a dancer, but she carries herself well on stage.' That statement resonated with me. I learned from watching other strippers what moves looked graceful, and what looked awkward. I danced differently in the beginning of my set, fully clothed, than I did when I was topless and only wearing a G-string. I generally started with a fast song or two, then slowed it down toward the middle when I was half-clothed. I might do something upbeat again for the last song, when I would wear a negligee or cape to ditch my G-string.

"Becoming more polished on stage and comfortable in my dancing shoes was a gradual process. By the time I had arrived at the Squire, I had been a striptease dancer for five years. I had a good idea of what music and moves I liked, and had a little variety in my costumes. But my style and stage presence evolved to another level at the Squire. It was a combination of things: time and experience, that roomy stage, and the quality of shows the other girls did.

"Norma encouraged us to invest in our wardrobe. She favored the glitzy Burlesque Queen look, like the costume designer Hedy Jo Starr was renowned for. I wasn't inclined to spend three grand on a gown to strip out of, but Norma's preference for lady-like acts and Vegas-style costumes created an atmosphere more in sync with my fantasies of being a modern Gypsy Rose Lee.

"A few weeks after I started, Norma called me into the office. I felt like I was being called into the principal's office in grade school. I was sure I'd done something wrong, but had no idea what. Norma's voice was always a bit screechy, and her face had a permanent scowl. No matter what she was saying, you thought she was pissed off. So when she said, 'I want to make you a house girl,' I didn't get it at first. 'Excuse me?' I replied, with a puzzled look. Norma raised her voice a screechy notch higher and said, 'A house girl—a house girl—I want you to be a house girl. It's a good thing—it means you have a steady job. Would you prefer to be on the day shift or the night shift?'

"I was flattered she thought that much of me. After jumping from club to club for years, I was delighted to have some job security. I picked the day shift. It was a calmer atmosphere. Guys who came in the middle of the day had to go back to work. If they came right after work, they had to go home to wives. Not good to get skunked in either case. The nighttime crowds were different—seriously out to party. More guys came in groups, and consumed larger amounts of alcohol.

"The day shift would also allow me to spend my evenings with Luke. Our relationship was blossoming, and I wanted to be on a schedule more in sync with his. I was still living at Jack and Candy's. They could see Luke was a nice guy, and that we were serious about each other. They lifted the rule about having no guys over, and said it was fine if he stayed with me.

"I was always closer to Jack than Candy. He and I could hang out for hours shooting the breeze. He loved to talk about UFOs and metaphysical things. Candy was too spooked by that stuff to participate in our bull sessions. Jack also had a warped and wonderful sense of humor.

"One day I came home and heard him laughing all by himself in the attic. He had a deep gravely voice. His laugh was audible through the whole house. I went up to see what was going on. He was shining a laser out of the attic window. A thin beam of bright red light was streaming down through the trees and suspended in the middle of the road. He'd wait until a car approached close enough to see the light, then shut it off. After the car passed, he'd switch it back on so the red beam would be visible if they looked in their rear-view mirror. Jack was thoroughly amused that people might think this light was coming from a space ship.

"I stayed with Jack and Candy for a couple of months. Luke slept over several nights a week. It was a happy arrangement—for a while. Jack and Candy were working at a club further north, called Mac's Two. He worked the lights, she was a dancer. I can't remember how I found out Candy was having an affair with the owner of the club. Jack must have known, but never talked about it. The atmosphere at the house became morbid. When they were together, a thick silence hung between them. They went about their routines as if everything were normal. But you could feel a rubber band was being stretched so tight it would snap any minute.

"Candy became a manager at Mac's. She was working long days and decided it was too far to commute home all the time. She got an apartment close to the club. Jack went to work at another club, after Mac's Two decided they didn't need special light shows.

"Maybe Candy felt less guilty leaving Jack at home, assuming he had me and Luke for company. We actually saw him less and less. He was so despondent over losing her that he became reclusive. He'd hover in his bedroom until we left and was back there again when we got home.

"Once, when Jack was out of the house, I had to go into his room to look for something of mine. I was floored by what I saw. The room looked like it hadn't been cleaned in a year, but it was worse than just clutter. Empty booze bottles were strewn everywhere, among heaps of dirty clothes. Ashtrays were overflowing. Jack hadn't been a smoker or drinker before Candy's infidelity. Everything Jack was hiding from me about his state of mind was revealed in that foul-smelling shambles.

"Luke and I decided to get a place of our own. We found an apartment in a two-family house in the next town over, Everett. I was sad to leave Jack, but he had shut me out of his private hell. I tried to reach out to him after we had moved out. He wouldn't answer the phone or return my calls. I went to the house and knocked on the door. I knew he was there, but he ignored my pleas to speak with him.

"A couple of weeks later, I was rocked by news that Jack had committed suicide.

"I suppose I shouldn't have been shocked. The signs were all there. The excessive drinking, the chaotic bedroom, the reclusiveness—they were not characteristic of 'Jolly Old Jack' who had been my buddy. There was another layer to my grief, that I think is common to people who lose a loved one to suicide—guilt. I kept turning it over it my mind—*Could I have done something to prevent this? Did I give up on him too easily? Should I have called someone, tried to intervene?*

"A couple of weeks after he was laid to rest, I had a dream. I am convinced it was a visitation from Jack. This dream had a lot more detail than the one that helped ease my mind about Sabrina: I was back in the bedroom I stayed in at Jack and Candy's house. I was looking at a portrait of Jack, a large sepia-tone photo. He was dressed up like Pancho Via — wearing a sombrero, with straps of bullets crisscrossed over his chest. It was an actual photo that was in his house. As I was staring at it, he came alive. The photo was no longer sepia, but full, vivid colors. Jack looked wonderful — smiling, radiant, younger than before. No trace of the drawn, stressed, face I had last seen him wearing.

"Then I heard his laugh, that deep, robust, belly laugh that was uniquely Jack's. I ran into the kitchen, where the laugh seemed to come from. He wasn't there. I noticed a bottle of tequila on the counter. I heard a cat 'meow' and turned around to look. No cat in sight. I heard his laugh again. I turned quickly and looked toward the sink. The bottle of tequila was now in the sink, with less booze in it. I heard his laugh, turned — nothing. Spun around again to find the tequila bottle moved to the other counter, with still less tequila in it. Then his laughter filled the whole room. I smiled, as a feeling of peace came over me.

"I woke up from that dream shaking my head and giggling. I thought, *if Jack could come back to haunt someone, that's how he'd do it. He'd pull a practical joke — lighthearted and harmless.* The dream, much like the one about Sabrina, gave me a feeling he was okay—free from pain, and at peace. It also helped me let go of the guilt. Jack had sent me a clear message from the other side. He didn't want me to blame myself—there was nothing I could have done.

"Poor Luke. He'd only been with me for a few months and already had to hold my hand through two tragic losses. His love and my 'visitation' dreams helped me to heal. And always, through these ups and downs, the show had to go on. After getting over being naked, which I never really did, the next hardest thing was to light up the stage with smiles when your heart feels like it's been through a paper shredder." Eve sighed and reached across the table to shut the recorder, ending our session for the day.

13. Shiny New Land

"I have more memories of the Squire than the other clubs I worked in," Eve began, shifting around carefully on the sofa, trying not to spill her coffee. "Partly because I worked there the longest—five years, but also because I cut back on drinking. It's easier to remember when you're not clouding your mind with booze.

"I hadn't thought much about my alcohol intake until Luke mentioned it. Luke had a beer now and then, but he was fairly tame when it came to partying—especially for a rock 'n roll musician. He liked to smoke weed, but had an aversion to overdoing alcohol. His father liked to drink, a little more than Luke cared for. He was wary that he, too, might have 'alcoholic tendencies.'

"He knew better than to insist I stop drinking. I was too much of a rebel—it would've had the opposite effect. After letting Eddie push me around, I was determined not to let any guy control me.

"When Luke asked me not to drink so much, he did a clever thing—he appealed to my vanity. He said to me, '... it's just that you're so much prettier when your eyes aren't all red and glazed over, Eve.' It wasn't my vanity that responded. I was touched by the gentle way he talked to me about it. I knew he was concerned about me. I didn't want to lose him for such a foolish thing as drinking. I made a 'rule' for myself that I wouldn't drink more than two beers a day at work.

"I still needed to smoke a joint before I went on stage. Getting stoned created a veil that I needed between me and the audience. One day no one had any grass. I had to go on stage cold sober. It was the most naked I ever felt—even with my full costume on! My childhood shyness came flooding back. I wished I could wrap myself in that red velvet curtain and hide until the crowd went away. I made sure I never ran out of weed again." Eve had finished her coffee and was shuffling around to get more comfortable.

"Where did you smoke, Eve? Did the managers allow you to smoke marijuana in the club?" I asked.

"Not exactly, Stella," she answered. "I'm sure they knew about it, but looked the other way. Some of my bosses were probably into more severe crimes than possession of small amounts of marijuana. Whatever they did besides run the club, I didn't want to know. I came in, did my shows, and stayed clear of the club owners, or any regulars who hung out with them.

"Many, but not all, of the dancers smoked dope. We shared with each other. Someone always had some; it was rare the day I had to go on stage straight. We smoked in the dressing room, and tried to keep the aroma from drifting into the club. Between spraying perfume and lighting up cigarettes, I think we did okay covering it up.

"There was a closet-sized powder room in the dressing room, with a toilet and a small sink. One day we were smoking in there, to keep the smell from wafting out into the club. It was extra potent stuff—Thai stick. We didn't know the vent was connected to the small office that Norma used to count her millions.

"Norma barged into the dressing room, raising her screechy, nasally voice and said, 'I don't know what you girls are smoking in here, but I'm sitting in the office, trying to do the books, and I'M HIGH!' She was trying to reprimand us, but I could tell by her glassy eyes that Norma was, indeed, stoned, and therefore too mellow to really give a rat's ass. 'Here, have some more,' I said, passing the joint toward her. She waved her hands at me, trying to suppress a smile, and yelled, 'Get rid of that shit!' and stormed out. We got rid of it alright—by smoking it up. So, yeah, they knew, but as long as we weren't too blatant about it, they left us alone.

"Most of the management stayed clear of the dressing room. Peter was the owner of the Squire—another Peter, not the same one who owned the Surf. His son Joey and his brother JF helped Norma manage the place. I don't think Joey or JF were comfortable backstage. It's one thing to see dancers onstage, taking their clothes off to music, it's quite another to see them behind the velvet curtain. I've read that three feet of personal space is the average most people need before they feel encroached upon. It was a small room, and difficult to keep three feet away from anyone. So they usually sent their minion, Ernie, if they needed to relay a message to any of us.

"Ernie was a midget. That's what everyone called him. I don't know what the politically correct term would be now — vertically challenged? Whatever you call a grown man who is waist high to the rest of us, he added to the carnival-like atmosphere. I remember sitting at the dressing table, light bulbs rimming the mirror, caking make-up on as thick and gaudy as a clown, about to don my flaming pink rhinestoned gown. Ernie — all four feet of him — entered the dressing room, and I thought, I finally fulfilled my childhood fantasy — *I've run away to join the circus!*

"That little guy was a good sport. Every year on his birthday we would get him loaded — it only took two beers. Then we'd haul him onto the stage. There was a strict rule about one person on the stage at a time, but an exception was made for birthdays. Once, we tied Ernie to a chair and hit him with whipped-cream pies. Another time, we stripped him down to his underwear and tossed him up and down in a blanket. He'd scream obscenities and pretend to protest, but I believed he loved the limelight. Those riotous birthday celebrations had a vaudevillian spirit about them. They broke up the monotony that sets in when you're stripping every day for a living."

"I never thought of striptease dancing as being monotonous, Eve. What made it feel that way to you?" I asked.

"I loved music, and I loved to dance, but doing *anything* over and over can become ho-hum after a while," Eve replied. "If I was bored with my routine, it was hard to get customers excited. If the customers weren't excited, they weren't coming in as much and the club wasn't selling drinks. The managers might start looking for new talent. So I had some incentive to keep it interesting. New costumes could be expensive. I didn't want to invest a lot of money into wardrobe—I still thought dancing was just temporary. Getting new music was one of the quickest and cheapest ways to freshen up my act.

"A guy named Richie made cassette tapes for dancers for twenty bucks each. He had a huge library of music and good recording equipment. His tapes played loud and clear through the Squire's sound system. If the music was too low, it was hard to get inspired. Music is what carried me out there. It was an invisible force that fed my spirit and charged my body with intense energy.

"Luke introduced me to a style of music that resonated with me—Southern rock, and rhythm and blues. That's the kind of music his band played. I was familiar with many of the songs, but never considered it as a genre to dance to until I was living with Luke.

"Whenever I heard a song I liked, I added it to a special notebook. I created huge lists of songs. Every so often I'd spend hours planning new tapes from them. I'd group songs together that had a common theme or style. I shuffled them around until I had a formula that worked—picturing what phase of my show, how much or little I would have on, for each song. It was tricky to fit songs into the twenty-minute formula. The club was strict about that, or it would throw the schedule off.

"It always perked me up to have new music. Once I got into Southern rock, I noticed many customers were fans of it also. I wasn't the only dancer who developed a following partly based on her choice of music. It was fun to see their enthusiasm when I played some of their favorite tunes—tunes you didn't often hear in strip clubs. Jazz, soul, and disco might have offered sexier music, but I didn't care. Ultimately I danced for myself, so it had to be music that moved me. I felt more connected to the audience when they were as enthused about my music as they were about me getting naked. Some fans brought me tapes they compiled themselves, with tunes they thought I'd like. It was very touching.

"The change in music inspired me to have a costume custom-made. Up until then, I bought bargain-basement frocks and jazzed them up, or bought costumes second-hand from other dancers. I wanted a costume that fit the mood of the Southern rock. I designed it, but had it made by a professional seamstress named Pat, who specialized in clothes for performers. I sketched out my ideas before I met with her. It brought me back to my childhood, when I spent hours doodling and designing clothes for my

Barbie doll.

"The finished pantsuit was more beautiful than I had imagined. It was made of bright sapphire-blue stretch satin. The jacket was fitted tightly around my torso, with a silver lightning bolt of glittering crystals streaking from shoulder to hip. At the elbows, the fabric flared into bell sleeves. The pants were tight around my hips and thighs, and flared into wide bells from the knees down. The excess fabric around the arms and lower legs added fluid movement and heightened the energy of the whole look. The under-pieces were bejeweled with diamond and sapphire rhinestones, and had stars and a crescent moon to create a celestial mood. I felt electrified when I danced in that costume.

"I unzipped the jacket, unzipped the pants, and whipped them all over the place before I tossed them across the floor toward the velvet curtain. Same thing with the bra, jock, and G-string. I never took something off and ditched it right away. Playing with my clothes gave me something else to do on stage. I spun them all around my body, like Bruce Lee wielding nunchucks. With all the abuse I gave that outfit, I never lost a rhinestone or had a seam split. Pat had sewn it to perfection. I wished I could afford to order five more outfits from her.

"Having new tapes and a new costume opened me up to a higher level of creativity. I created shows with different themes. I couldn't sustain the high-energy rock 'n roll sets all the time. I made a few softer, easier shows to vary things. To contrast my blue lightning bolt outfit, I had a white gown. It was 1940s Hollywood glam, with sequins glittering like ice crystals all over the bust and torso. I wore a white lace cape over it, that had a hood edged with snowy feathers. The lace caught the blacklights and glowed as if lit from within. Customers with moon-pie eyes would gaze at me with their mouths gaping, sighing as I floated by, an angel in a cloud of white lace, twirling gracefully to a gentle ballad. It was pure romance.

"Luke helped me evolve to another level with my dancing, by connecting me with music that inspired me. So it was ironic that he had to stop coming into the club." Eve said. She looked ready for a break, but I wanted to understand what she meant before I headed off to make lunch.

"What was ironic, Eve? Was he not allowed in the club because he was your boyfriend?" I asked.

"Oh, nothing like that, Stella. He didn't show up often, but it always brightened my mood when he did. One day he said, 'I can't come in the club to see you anymore, Eve.' 'Is it because you can't stand seeing me strip?' I asked. I was feeling blue, wondering if he was getting tired of dating a stripper after all. Luke said, 'No, that's not it. I love to watch you. You're beautiful up there—it's just that I can't stand to watch all of those other guys watching you. It bothers me, what they're probably thinking. They have no idea what you're really like, how classy you are.' I nodded my head that I'd understand if he stopped coming in. I felt reassured that he genuinely cared. I'd rather see him at home anyway, without all those curious eyes upon us," said Eve. Then we broke for lunch.

After lunch I began our session with a question that had been popping into my mind between bites of my egg salad sandwich. "Eve, why do you suppose you still thought of it as temporary, after you had been dancing for five years?"

"For a few reasons, Stella," she replied. "One was my schizophrenic relationship with dancing: loving it one moment, despising it the next. Another was the inescapable reality of aging—no one can do it forever. I did see women who pushed it well into middle age. Some were inspiring—that they could still look good enough to pull it off. But in order to do that, your looks had to become a full-time obsession. I didn't want to go the surgery route, do the 'mirror, mirror on the wall' routine, freaking out over my fading youth.

"Once again, I knew what I didn't want, but wasn't sure what I did want, except for Luke. I was so happy in my private life, I just dealt with how I had to make my living as best I could. He didn't seem to mind too much. He never indicated that it bothered him, as long as he didn't have to watch me being watched.

"He knew what it was like to do something you're not crazy about to earn your bread. He worked for his father, who owned a casket company. It was a lot of physical work—carpentry, and loading trucks with the 'boxes,' as they called them. His father was flexible with his schedule. He could take time off for band practice, or if he needed to travel on Fridays to do a weekend gig. So he stuck it out even though it wasn't his cup of tea.

"He was devoted to his music, played his guitar every day. I did everything I could to be supportive. I saw other band members' girlfriends giving their guys a hard time, whining that they weren't spending enough time with them. I wanted Luke to have every chance of making it, so I was patient and understanding. I admired the passion he had for his art, and perhaps envied it. I wished I had talent that I could pour myself into, something that would consume my energy and feed my soul.

"I bought him a guitar, a sexy little Fender Stratocaster. He'd been talking about a 'Strat' since I'd met him. He was blown away when I told him I wanted to do that for him. We went to 'Daddy's Junky Music' on Route One to pick it out. I had never spent a whole week's pay on myself, but had no qualms about doing that for my Luke. I knew he'd use it well.

"I also knew I'd need a hobby. Because of Luke's band practice and gigs, I went home to an empty house several nights a week. I began selling Avon— partly to keep busy and partly to get my own products for free. I didn't go door to door, just sold it at the club. Without trying too hard, I did pretty well — enough to get invited to one of the 'President's Club' luncheons. I was recognized in front of a hundred other Avon reps for selling the most lipstick in the division. I was sitting in the midst of these respectable ladies — housewives and office workers — wondering what they would have thought if they knew *who* I was selling all that ruby red lipstick *to*. Luke was amused by my sideline and grateful I had a hobby that would keep me out of trouble. He dubbed me 'The Avon Stripper.' I called him 'The Rock 'n Roll Casket Maker.'

"Luke hadn't come into the club for months. One day I saw him in the crowd while I was on stage. He had a look on his face like his dog just died, only he didn't have a dog. It was torturous to finish my set, wondering why he looked so freaked out. When I finished dancing, I was out of the dressing room in record time.

"Luke said, 'There was a fire last night, Eve.' He spoke mechanically, with a blank stare, as if he didn't believe the words coming out of his own mouth. He continued, 'Our practice studio, it burnt to the ground. Everything is gone — everything except my guitars. Thank God I always brought them home ... but everything else: Jay's drum set, Tim's bass, Randy's keyboard, all our amps. Drew's saxophone was melted to a blob of brass.'

"No one was hurt, but that did little to console Luke and the other members of his band. It was a crushing blow. They had been hard at work for months, practicing, and finally felt they were tight enough to get some gigs. None of them had money for new equipment. Without equipment, they couldn't get paying gigs to buy new instruments—a real 'Catch 22.'

"I did my best to comfort Luke. My heart went out to all of them. I had gotten to know those guys pretty well. Feeling their pain had me down in the dumps too. I turned to my I Ching, as I often had in times of crisis.

"Luke was never interested in what I was doing with this book you threw coins to read, but he never questioned my need to delve into metaphysical matters. When I asked the I Ching for some advice on how to handle the catastrophe, I was stunned at the hexagram it guided me to. I told Luke I needed to read it to him. He shrugged as if to say 'I guess it can't hurt.' His eyes widened as I read a section from the hexagram titled 'Chen / The Arousing (Shock, Thunder)':

> Shock comes bringing danger.
> A hundred thousand times
> You lose your treasures
> And must climb the nine hills.
> Do not go in pursuit of them.
> After seven days
> you will get them back again.

This pictures a situation in which a shock

endangers a man and he suffers great losses ...
He must accept his loss of property without
worrying too much about it. When the time of
shock and upheaval that has robbed him of his
possessions has passed, he will get them back
again without going in pursuit of them.

"I read more of the passage to Luke. Its wise words
offered consolation and advice on how to deal with
catastrophic loss. Then I said quietly, 'I know you
might feel embarrassed about the guys in the band
knowing I'm into weird stuff like this, but I feel this
message is meant for more than just the two of us.'
Luke gave me no argument.

"I went with him to the next band meeting and read
the passage. All of the guys had that same stunned
look. They had a hard time digesting the fact that the
mystical book seemed to 'know' just what they were
going through.

"Tim remarked, 'A hundred thousand times you
lose your treasures and must climb the nine hills—
God, that's just what it feels like!' None of them
doubted the wisdom they heard, or rejected the
encouragement it offered. The leaden atmosphere
began to lighten. They started coming up with ideas
about how to keep the band together and move
forward.

"Other musicians heard about the disaster and
offered help—equipment loans, fundraisers, and
moral support. They pulled themselves together and

were doing gigs again in a few months. Luke was back to his happy-go-lucky self. We were back to enjoying our life together.

"He asked me to marry him after we were living together for a year and half. All of my previous aversion to the idea melted away. I said 'Yes!' without hesitation.

"Norma insisted on throwing me a wedding shower. She needed her stern persona to run a strip club, but could be surprisingly sentimental about 'her girls.' She had no children—maybe we served as an outlet for her maternal instincts. My shower took place in the Squire.

"One of the most generous things she did was to let all the dancers sit together the whole day, without having to mingle with customers. There were a dozen of us gathered at a long table—drinking champagne, eating a sumptuous buffet, and laughing 'til our faces cracked. Presents were piled high, all for me and my Luke. A large sheet-cake smothered in whipped cream had 'Congratulations Lisa' written in pink icing. My stage name was also spelled out with pimentos atop a platter of potato salad. I sat at the end of the table, under a large white tissue-paper bell. They pulled a string on it and 'showered' me with rose-petal confetti, the cue that it was time to cut cake and open gifts.

"One by one we excused ourselves from the festivities when it was our turn to go onstage, and returned to the revelry once we were done. Everyone was more tipsy than usual, tottering around the stage, trying, and not always succeeding, to keep their balance on spiked heels.

"When it was my turn to do a show, the uproar was so loud I couldn't hear my music. My co-workers started the hoopla. The customers joined in, going overboard with wolf-whistles and applause for this bride-to-be. Even with champagne bubbling-up my brain, I was aware of the ironic surrealism of it all. It was such a cliché for bachelor parties to come to strip clubs, or hire strippers to surprise a groom-to-be. I wondered if I was the only bride in history to do a striptease for a crowd of raucous men at her own wedding shower.

"Norma provided quite a spread. My fellow dancers showered me with gifts and joyful well-wishes. I was high on gratitude for all the love and kindness as they celebrated with me. One of the dancers, June, gave me a set of pearls wrapped in a poem she wrote:

> Three cheers for one of the prettiest girls
> With soft blonde hair and soft blonde curls
> She's getting married for the rest of her life
> Without a doubt she'll be a wonderful wife
> She's charming and witty and always happy
> Since she's known she's getting married
> She's even been zappy
> So three cheers for one of the prettiest girls
> When the happy moment happens

I hope she'll wear these pearls.

- Love, June

"I had never felt such camaraderie before. I've always been a bit of a loner, and had a hard time getting close to other women. That changed for me when I went into that business. I found a sisterhood I was privileged to be part of. Camaraderie wasn't enough to make me want to stay, but my friends made it a tolerable stopover on the way to the rest of my life.

"After the trauma I'd been through with Eddie, the yo-yo rebound relationship with Jake, and the grief of losing two dear friends, I was moving into a new phase. I gorged myself on optimism like one who hadn't eaten in a year. I was going to marry Luke! Cinderella had met her Prince. No more strippin' for a livin'—it wasn't the thing a dignified married lady would do. I had no immediate plan as to how I would quit. Luke couldn't support us at the time, but I was sure a way out would show itself.

"I called my mother and told her we were getting married. My whole family had taken to Luke. He was an easy guy to like. I asked Mom for help—something I hadn't done in ages. We wanted a casual wedding and were hoping to do it at my parent's house in Maryland. They had moved there from the house I grew up in, in New York, a few years before this. Without hesitation she said, 'Don't worry, just leave everything to us. You and Luke just show up. Your father and I will take care of it all.' It was the happiest conversation I'd ever had with my mother. She was glad I was getting married, and delighted I'd asked her for help. We were both ready to heal our bruised relationship. The wedding was the perfect instrument to begin the process. I was back in the good graces of my family after being the 'black sheep' for years.

"The ceremony took place in my parents' backyard. The azaleas were in bloom and the weather was glorious. It was my idea of a perfect wedding—a ten-minute ceremony and a three-day party. I was pretty relaxed beforehand, upstairs in my parents' room doing a final primp. All three of my sisters were with me. They reminded me of the three fairy godmothers from Sleeping Beauty—fawning all over me, sticking baby's breath in my hair, straightening folds in my white satin dress. They said my whole body stiffened like an ironing board and my eyes got as big as saucers when someone yelled, 'The preacher's here!' *Oh my God, I'm really going to do this,* I thought. I was grateful we opted for a short service, or my nerves might have been frayed to pieces by the time we said 'I do.'

"My parents had been used to feeding a crowd for years, having raised eight children who could all eat like lumberjacks. But I was bowled over by the way they kept fifty of us fed that weekend. People arrived Friday night and my folks had cold cuts on hand for everyone. They provided a feast Henry the Eighth would envy for the reception on Saturday. Mom made a scrumptious and elegant cake, iced with her signature buttercream frosting and a heavy smathering of love. The hearty brunch they set out on Sunday was the perfect cure for wedding hangovers. When Luke and I left Sunday afternoon, Dad was barbecuing a turkey for any stragglers.

"I was hundreds of miles from the club and from anyone who called me Lisa. It was comforting to be Eve-Marie again. I had a week off after the wedding before I had to put on the 'Lisa Doolittle' act again. Luke and I headed back home, but spent a few honeymoon days in Provincetown first.

"I felt like I'd been lost at sea for years, caught in a whirlpool of stripping, drugs, and lost love. Now a new course was set. I'd chart my way straight and true, with Luke by my side, to a shiny new land called 'Marital Bliss.'" Eve gazed past me, her eyes fixed on some distant point, as if she could see the utopian shore she spoke of through my parlor window. She was so transfixed, I had to turn to see what she was staring at. Lace curtains and the rose bush beyond were the only things in my view.

14. BUZZY'S ROAST BEEF

After a short break, Eve continued telling me about her marriage to Luke. "I didn't expect 'cloud nine' to last forever," she began, "but when we returned from our honeymoon Luke's attitude changed so fast it gave me whiplash. Almost the minute we dropped our luggage on the floor, I felt a chill coming from his side of the room. I avoided asking him about it—afraid to give him the chance to admit he had regrets, felt trapped. I wanted to believe it was just my imagination. *No one's feelings could switch that quickly, could they?* I thought. *Maybe he's just tired after all the commotion and traveling.* I let it go and hoped the warmth would return.

"I went back to work, and had a little post-wedding depression myself when I realized nothing had really changed. The main difference was that I was expected to behave like a happily married lady. We never discussed it after we were hitched, we didn't need to. I knew the quickest way to sabotage our marriage would be to carry on partying the way I used to.

"I was home every night, even if Luke was out at band practice. I did all the things I thought a good little wifey should—cooked and cleaned, sewed curtains, jumped his bones anytime he looked at me 'that way.' I ignored the fact that he wasn't looking at me 'that way' as often as he used to. I thought people waited until well beyond their twenties for their libido to drop.

"My profession hadn't bothered him while we were living together, but maybe now that I was his wife, he was ashamed I was a stripper. My fantasy was that his band would make it big, eventually. Then I could finally quit my 'day job' and be the respectable wife of a rock 'n roll star. Smoking grass day and night can give you all kinds of delusions.

"A few months after we were married he lost his job. His father's business wasn't doing well. People weren't buying wooden caskets like they used to. His father had to let him go. Luke was totally bummed. I told him not to worry—I was making enough to cover both of us until he found another job.

"I got so caught up in the grind of everyday life, it took a while to see what was happening. Luke didn't even look for another job. He said it would be hard to find an employer who would let him have time off for band practice and gigs. I bought it for a while, and didn't mind towing the line. I would help him make it to the top in his music career, and he would reward me once he was a rock 'n roll millionaire. I grabbed all the double shifts I could. I made just enough to cover rent, bills, and food, and buy a steady supply of weed to get through the drudgery.

"It was tough enough being the breadwinner, but Luke didn't lift a finger around the house. He'd be on the couch with his guitar and a joint when I left for work. I'd strip and sweat all day, stop for groceries, and come home to cook. The dishes from yesterday would still be in the sink. I'd have to clean up before I could cook. When we sat down to eat, Luke wolfed his food down in two minutes. He hardly spoke to me, then excused himself to get back on the couch with his guitar. The only company I had was exhaustion.

"I'd ask him what was wrong. He'd shrug and say, 'Nothing.' We went on like that for months. He only spoke to me when he needed something, like a new pair of sneakers. It was wearing me out physically. Emotionally I wasn't doing so hot either.

"Luke had abandoned me, without having the decency to actually leave.

"I was tied to him through sacred vows, and still loved him deeply. I wouldn't dream of cheating on him, no matter how rejected and dejected I felt. The loneliness was a whole new kind of hell.

"I made futile attempts to get him to open up. He refused to see a marriage counselor. When I said I couldn't hang on forever carrying the load for both of us, he snapped, 'What do you expect me to do—*pump gas?*' It couldn't have stung worse if he slapped me across the face. He was too good to get his hands dirty earning an honest day's pay, yet I was stripping in front of strangers to support us.

"During those dark months I went to work acting like everything was fine. I even fooled myself for a while. I'd put on my Lisa face, take a few tokes, and shed my clothes wearing a big goofy grin. No one knew my heart was cracking like a mudflat in the desert. I thought my marriage would be a refuge from my depressing job, but it was the other way around. I was relieved to go to the club. At least people there would talk to me.

"I had my dancer sisters for company. I also had my 'regulars.' Most of us had certain guys we didn't mind hanging out with when we were offstage. We didn't have to 'mix,' but Norma insisted we come out of the dressing room in between shows. We could sit at the bar by ourselves if we wanted. She knew if we were out there, some dude would offer to buy us a drink. He'd order another for himself, and stay longer than he might have otherwise. To my boss, it was all about selling drinks." Eve paused to take a long sip of lemonade.

"What did you mean when you said you 'didn't have to mix'?" I asked.

"Sorry, Stella. I thought I talked about that already," Eve replied. "'Mixing' was a common practice in the downtown Boston bars—in the Combat Zone. The dancers were expected to get customers to buy them drinks—preferably bottles of Champagne, if they could weasel it out of some poor sucker. Newcomers were caught off guard—the dancer's drink would cost triple what he paid for his. Some clubs had a quota. There was a lot of pressure on girls to hustle drinks or they could lose their jobs. Not a pleasant situation. Most of those guys expected premium treatment if they were paying premium drink prices. Dancers had to put up with being manhandled and God knows what else. I didn't know, and never wanted to know, what went on in the 'back rooms' of those places.

"After my brief journey into the Zone, when I high-tailed it out before my audition, I never went back. The vibes felt creepier than walking through a graveyard at midnight. I met a few dancers who worked down there. Most of them had an extra-thick coat of armor. I don't know if it was hard knocks, or the degradation of working in the Zone, but they seemed more prone to getting hooked on hard drugs. My heart went out to them, but I locked up my money and dope when I had to work with Combat Zone refugees. I hate making generalizations, but that was my experience with the few I met.

"Compared to the Zone, the Squire was like Disney World—almost a 'family friendly' place. No pressure to hustle drinks—if a guy bought you a beer, it cost the same price as his. I didn't want to come out of the dressing room most of the time. I'd stall as much as I could after my shows to avoid facing the crowd. I didn't want guys to think they had a chance with me, especially after I was married. It was a relief when I could sit with 'regulars.' They knew how rare it was for a customer to make it with a stripper. They didn't give you the old 'come on'—not if they wanted you to stop back at their table when they dropped in. Some were amusing to talk to, or at least tolerable.

"Norma didn't like us sitting with other dancers.

Two together were okay, but more than that and she'd break it up. That's why I said it was generous when she let us all sit together at my wedding shower. There was one exception—a customer named Tom.

"Norma had no problem with all the dancers sitting at Tom's table. He was a wheelchair-bound Vietnam Vet. He looked like a college professor, with his slight build, thinning hair, and horn-rimmed glasses. He usually wore a tweed jacket, with suede patches on the elbows. Not a likely candidate to attract a horde of strippers, but when Tom came in, it was PARTY TIME. We'd all sit with him, while the other customers looked on, wondering what charm this guy had. Maybe sympathy was a factor, but a minor one. He loved to surround himself with beautiful women. He ran up a healthy tab supplying all of us with food and drinks every time he came in. Norma loved him for that. We loved him for his warmth and wit, and for giving the sisterhood a chance to hang together.

"The management frowned on you refusing to sit with someone—bad for business. If I didn't see any regulars, I'd head to the back of the bar and try to sit alone, or with another dancer. I made sure not to make eye contact as I left the dressing room. If I didn't see them, they couldn't ask. I'm sure a lot of guys thought I was a snob. Truth was, I was still pretty shy. I was also tired of going through the same script over and over again. Some guys didn't get that I was just there to make a living, not trying to get laid like they were. So maybe it was cliché-a-phobia too. You wouldn't believe how many times I heard, *'What's a nice girl like you doing in a place like this?'*

"It was refreshing to meet Corey. I was sitting at the bar with him when he looked down at my spiked heels and said, 'I bet you're a good swimmer.' I said, 'I love to swim. I don't consider myself good at it, but what made you say that?' 'Your feet are like paddles,' he answered. *'What did you say?!'* I shrieked and laughed at the same time. He was right—my feet were double-wides. I just hadn't expected him to point it out. He said, 'I figured you get tired of hearing what beautiful eyes you have, and what a good dancer you are. I knew I'd have to say something different to get your attention.' It worked. I sat with him any time he popped in. I wasn't ready to leave my Luke for him, or anyone else. I just enjoyed his company. He liked jazz and poetry. It made the day go by faster to talk to someone who sparked my imagination.

"Another club buddy was Vince. He was slim, not tall, with thick brown hair, a Cheshire cat grin, and seductive green eyes. I was drawn to him, but made sure he understood that I was married. As long as he didn't come on to me, we could be friends. He'd show up every couple of weeks. He was one of the guys I was glad to see from the stage. I knew I'd have a buddy to sit with after my show—someone who respected me and wouldn't ask tiresome questions.

"For months I kept up the facade, pretending I was

happily married. All day at work I had men admiring and desiring me, thrilled if I turned my attention their way. Then I'd go home to my estranged husband and crushing loneliness. I floated on appreciation all day, and suffered alienation all night. It was the most alone I ever felt in my life. I was with someone who didn't want me, but not free to seek other company. The hardest part was, I didn't want anyone else. I wanted Luke. I wanted him to look at me the way he used to—like I was the most beautiful thing he'd ever seen. I felt like I had become invisible to him—like a faceless servant who graciously disappears once the floor is swept and the dishes are done.

"One morning, he called to me from his usual perch on the living room couch as I was leaving for work. I thought he might want to kiss me goodbye, or at least wish me a good day—neither of which he had done in months. 'Yes, Luke?' I said, eager for a shred of sweetness—a sign that he still cared. He said, 'Can you bring me a roast beef sandwich when you come home?' 'Sure, Luke—no problem.' I answered, feeling my shoulders drop, along with my chin, my grin, and my heart. I hadn't married a husband, I had adopted a little boy—one who didn't want my love and affection—just feed 'em and leave 'em alone.

"I struggled through the day, wearing the fakey Lisa Doolittle smile on stage, and hiding out in the dressing room between shows. Vince came in. I was grateful for the distraction. He had no clue I was so unhappy. Nobody knew. I stuffed my misery into a little box labeled 'Denial' and put on an Oscar-caliber performance titled 'I'm a Happily Married Stripper.'

"I talked and laughed with Vince all afternoon. He offered me a ride home. It was the first time I had been with him outside of the club. He was all grins when we got into his car. I don't know what he was expecting—it was just a ride home, but we were both stunned by what happened next.

"We hadn't even pulled out of the parking lot when my eyes flooded and I crumbled into a sobbing mess. Tears, blackened with mascara, were streaming down my face as I blurted out how miserable I was. A lot of guys would have felt awkward watching a woman fall apart like that. Vince pulled me gently toward him and offered his shoulder to sponge up my river of self-pity. Once I pulled myself together, he suggested we go somewhere to talk. He offered dinner, but I was in no shape to eat. My stomach was churning like a washing machine, agitated by emotions I could no longer repress. God, yes, I needed someone to talk to—to tell the truth of the torment I had been going through. If I tried to push it back down it would poison me until I rotted from the inside out.

"Vince and I talked and listened to each other for hours. No kisses, no flirting—just wholesome, healing companionship. I was more starved for that than hot 'n heavy sex. If he was hoping for more, he didn't let on. I don't know where the time went, but it was 3:00 a.m. when I finally noticed a clock. Luke would have expected me home by 9:00 p.m. Vince offered to get us a room if I was worried about going home, promising it would just be to sleep. 'No, thanks, I'm not worried he'd hit me,' I said, 'but before you take me home—do you know where to get a roast beef sandwich at this time of night?' He drove me to Buzzy's, a twenty-four hour sandwich shop in Boston, then back to my apartment in Everett.

"By the time Vince dropped me off it was 4:00 a.m. I opened the door as quietly as I could. As I tiptoed through the hallway, I was startled to see Luke in the living room. He was on his feet, with an angry scowl on his face. His voice was raised, his delivery slow and even. *'Where have you been?'* he asked. Luke had never shown his temper to me before. At last he showed some emotion—anger was better than apathy. I was trembling, my knees ready to give out. A nauseating guilt crept through me. I searched for words to beg forgiveness. Before I could squeak out a feeble apology, a wave of indignation swept away my fear. *How dare he?* I thought. *His total indifference is what drove me to this. He has no right to put me on trial.*

"I didn't raise my voice. I wasn't angry. I didn't feel anything—just blank. I stretched my arm toward him and handed him a small red and white bag. With a matter-of-fact tone, I said, 'Here's your roast beef sandwich—I can't be your wife anymore.'

"My words threw a bucket of water on his rage. I saw the fire in his eyes turn to ash. His shoulders slumped, his chin dropped to his chest. He nodded slowly. A nod that said, *'You're right ... I've been a real shit. What did I expect? Who am I to play the indignant husband when I haven't been a husband to you at all?'*

"I was as startled as he was to hear me call it quits. I hadn't planned it. I hadn't planned to stay out all night either. I had planned to stay married when I took vows. Now I knew that just wasn't possible, not if he was willing to let it go without flinching.

"I think when those words slipped out, I was hoping he'd say, 'Let's talk about it, Eve.' instead of, 'Well, I don't really have anywhere else to go.' My cracked heart finally shattered, splintering like a hundred shards of glass."

Eve had been staring at the tape recorder. She looked up at me, her mouth curling into a wry grin. Her eyes looked glazed, but not teary. "I'm running out of steam," she said. "Let's quit in a few minutes, Stella."

"We can stop now if you want," I answered.

"No—just a little more, then we'll pick it up tomorrow." She leaned back on the sofa, stretching her arms over her head, yawning before she continued.

"Luke stayed with me for a couple of months after that. I didn't want to throw him out on the street. I gave him up to three months to find another place. We didn't file any legal papers right away, but considered ourselves separated. He moved out of the bedroom to sleep on the couch. We were both free to see other people, but there were rules. We agreed not to bring anyone home—that would have been too much for either of us. I would continue to pay the rent and other bills, but he was on his own for food, gas money, and anything else. He would have to clean up after himself—I was through playing mommy.

"We were very civil to each other during that time. There was only one day when our turbulent emotions bubbled to the surface at the same time. In the three years we had been together, we never had a yelling match before. I don't remember what trivial thing triggered it.

"We were in the kitchen and the heat just turned up. We were screaming, swearing, and throwing word daggers at each other. In the middle of it, I stopped and looked at him tenderly, from the core of my being. I lowered my voice, almost to a whisper and said, 'This is *not* what we mean to each other.' His anger dissolved in a flash. 'You're right, Eve,' he said, 'I'm sorry.' 'I'm sorry too.' I said. We reached out to each other with forgiveness. We dropped our defenses and hugged, opening our hearts to each other's pain.

"Then I said to him, 'I know there is no going back—what's done is done. But I've always felt that if you've lived with someone, whether you're married or not, you've adopted them as family. Even if it doesn't work out, it's worth trying to preserve the friendship rather than become enemies, unless there is a good reason not to. I would hope, after all the

love we've shared, we could at least part as friends.'
He said that's what he hoped for too.

"It was an odd time we went through. Without the pressure of having to play roles of 'husband' and 'wife' we were able to talk openly, in a way we never had—not even in the euphoric beginning of our relationship. I finally understood the meaning of the word 'bittersweet.' I relished the sweetness of the talks we had, but with the bitter realization that Luke would soon be out of my life."

15. THE UNKNOWN STRIPPER

"Luke was finally gone." Eve paused to sip her morning coffee before she continued. "Thank God he let me keep the cat. At least I had her to come home to. There was no doubt Spooky was mine, she was always curled up on me or next to me. The only time she ever went to Luke was when he was eating green olives. She liked them so much I taught her tricks using them as a bribe. She sat up, rolled over, gave me her paw, and played fetch. No big deal for a dog, but anyone who knows cats would be impressed.

"Spooky was born in a horse barn behind Luke's father's house. I was afraid he might want to claim her on that account. I picked her out of the litter when she was no bigger than the palm of my hand. I couldn't take her home until she was weaned. Every time we visited his father I'd pop down to the barn to check her progress. She always tried to follow me — she knew I was her human, just like I knew she was my cat. Her fur was half black, half white, and longer than the other kittens'. The black markings around her eyes looked like a mask. Luke's stepmother said she looked like a Witch's cat, so we named her Spooky. If he had taken her, I'm not sure who I would have missed more.

"I don't know how couples with kids and property

to fight over survive divorce. We had neither, but it was still one of the most painful things I ever went through. In many ways I hurt worse than when Eddie had beaten me. You can take medication for physical pain. The only relief from heartache is being comatose. I fell into a black hole so deep that for the first time in my life I understood how someone could commit suicide. I wasn't considering it, but I was far enough down the rabbit hole to grasp *why* you could be so desperate to stop hurting that you'd end your life.

"Still, I had to go to work, don the Lisa face, and smile, smile, smile as I whipped off my costume one piece at a time. I couldn't stand playing the happy-go-lucky stripper while my insides were ripped to shreds. I made some new tapes so I could express myself more truthfully on stage. For customers who had seen the always-smiling Lisa Doolittle for years, it must have been a shock to see me tear out on the stage dancing to Loggins and Messina's 'Angry Eyes.' I'd whip around faster than ever—pouring hostility out through music and frantic motion—eyes narrowed and spewing sparks that said, *'Don't Fuck With Me!'*

"Some of the regulars looked scared. Others looked concerned. I wasn't out to torture them. I usually did one or two songs that let me be real, then I'd segue back into 'sweet-little-Lisa,' always ending my set on a positive note. I needed part of my show to be for me—to throw off the excess anguish. But I didn't need to take everyone down in the pits with me. Some guys went to strip joints to forget their own troubles—they didn't deserve a healthy dose of mine.

"I was able to pull myself together and get through those days with a little help from my friends, and increased doses of beer and weed. There was no one at home to tell me how pretty I looked when my eyes were clear, so I didn't care. I let my eyes and mind get as fogged as possible. I wasn't into hard liquor when I was working. Even after years of practice, I had to be careful in those spiked heels. The rubber sole would get worn down after a while—especially the inside front of the shoe—from pushing off to do spins, and sliding my leg out sideways doing sultry moves. Getting drunk and having worn shoes could be dangerous.

"I had a few close calls, even without being drunk. Once, I was on one of the light-boxes on the side of the stage. I was spinning around, twirling neon pink fabric all around me. My kneecap dislocated in the middle of a spin. My leg gave out and I nearly went flying off the stage. I reached for my knee and pushed it down and sideways. It clicked back into place. I caught my balance before I careened off and landed on a table full of guys. My knee was sore for a couple of weeks—I had strained it badly. No insurance, and not much money for a doctor, so I danced with a knee brace for the next few weeks.

"Another time I did go flying. I was wearing a wrap-around black dress with a zigzag hemline. It was an old favorite. I sewed bands of green sequins around the bottom to jazz it up. When I undid the belt, I'd turn the dress into a cape, so I could stay partially dressed for a while more. The sequins glowed in the blacklight and added to the 'kinetic art' effect.

"It was Christmas time and the place was jammed—large groups of guys coming in for holiday parties. They were very appreciative. Their enthusiastic applause put an extra spring in my step. As soon as I got on the stage, I kicked my right leg backward and caught the hem of my dress with the spike of my heel. When I brought my foot down, I pulled the dress—and myself—along with it. Square on my ass I fell, in front of a packed house. The only thing truly hurt was my pride. I picked myself up, checked my rear end for bruises, and made a 'thumbs up' sign to indicate no harm was done. I continued the set to thunderous applause.

"I had enough close calls without being soused. I was careful how much I drank at work. After work was a different story. In the months following my break-up with Luke, moderation was not in my vocabulary. If any of my co-workers were up for a party after work, I went along. The alternative was to go home and weep myself to sleep. I cried every night for months. I cried enough to fill a dolphin tank at Sea World. Usually, I could limit the tears to my time off, but not always.

"Most days, I would 'put on my face' once—when I

first got into work—and do a quick touch-up before each show. Makeup had to be strong and exaggerated to offset the stage lights—otherwise you'd look washed out, almost featureless. I used bright blue eye shadow, three coats of mascara, and the reddest lipstick I could find—every day was like Halloween.

"Maybe my break-up blues had a head-on collision with PMS. Whatever it was, one day I spent my entire shift, between my shows, in the dressing room. I was unable to pull myself together—except when it was time to go onstage. The floodgates opened and I cried the makeup completely off my face. I reapplied it, did my show, got back to the dressing room and cried it all off again. After the third time I went through this bizarre ritual, I thought to myself, *'I guess I am truly an actress after all, because the show must go on.'*

"Another day I fell into a heaving sobbing mess, but something different happened. I was backstage after a show. I hadn't finished drying the sweat off my naked body, and the faucet turned on again. I was shedding a waterfall. One of the other dancers patted me on the back saying, 'Calm down, sweetie. He's not worth it—no guy is worth it.' I didn't say anything. I didn't think she'd understand—I hardly did. I wasn't crying over Luke. It was bigger than that.

"My consciousness had expanded far beyond the dressing room and my little corner of the universe. I became aware of man's inhumanity to man in a way that is difficult to translate. All of the horrors and atrocities throughout history and all over the world came streaming into my mind at once. All the wars, murders, rapes, tortures, mental and physical cruelties flooded me with their unholy agonies. Beyond seeing these things, I was overwhelmed with compassion for the suffering of mankind. In that moment I understood why Christ thought the only way to save us was to sacrifice his life.

"How could I possibly explain that to my co-worker, who thought I was teary over a guy? And what was I to do with that epiphany? I dried myself off and got on with my life.

"In between bouts of boozing and bawling, in fleeting moments of sobriety, I did some soul-searching. I had to figure out why I was such a basket case about this—he *was* just a guy, after all. I'd been through break-ups before—from both sides: dump-er and dump-ee, *so what was so different that it had me falling off an emotional cliff?* It wasn't just about losing Luke. It had to do with my belief in marriage. Like so many Cinderellas out there, I bought the 'Happily Ever After' fairy-tale. I truly believed that once I got married it would be forever. Now that 'forever' was over, *what could I believe in?*

"My heart was shattered, yes, but so was my faith, and with it my hope. As misty a dream as it was, the road I saw ahead with Luke led me out of the gloomy world of strip clubs into a bright future. *Now what?* I cringed when I looked into the crystal ball. *What if I had to keep doing this for the next ten years?* I saw a haggard aging beauty trying to squeeze out one more year, and then another, of playing the vamp—the applause thinning with each sad show. Maybe one of the clubs would take me on as a cocktail waitress when I was finally too decrepit, when instead of hearing cheers of 'Take it off,' I'd hear jeers of 'Keep it on!' Maybe I'd wait on customers who would ask, 'Didn't you used to be Lisa Doolittle?' as they reached out to pat my sagging butt.

"My anchor dragged on the sandy bottom of the strip club scene, and now it was stuck until the tide would turn. The realization that I was more mired in it than ever sent me spiraling downward into deeper depression. I put a brick wall around my heart, and hung out a sign that said, 'Yes: Unmarried, but No: Not Available.'

"What is it about a woman who is unattainable that is so irresistible to men? As soon as I decided not to get involved, I had suitors gathering around me like Scarlett on the porch at Twelve Oaks. I had been lonely long enough to welcome some company, but I pity any guy who fell in love with me during that time. Even ones I shared my body with didn't stand a chance of having my heart. By then I was convinced I would never have a decent relationship until I wasn't a stripper any more. That might take some time, however. I saw no point in being celibate, as long as they understood no one was going to put a brand on my ass.

"One of my suitors was Charles. He was from England, so he had that charming accent going for him. He had gorgeous cat-like eyes, loved to laugh, and was loaded. His business required him to spend half the year in the states. He had a girlfriend back in England, and wasn't looking for a serious relationship. According to him, they had a 'don't ask, don't tell' arrangement when they were apart. Charles was fond of saying to me, 'I want to spoil you.' After supporting Luke for the past year, I relished having a man shower me with gifts and treat me to expensive dinners, especially one who didn't want to put a lasso around me.

"Charles bought me some of the most beautiful clothes I ever owned and took me to posh restaurants to show me off. He spared no expense on lavish meals, and was known as 'Champagne Charlie' for buying up all the Dom Perignon a place could stock. He was generous with his money, but not with his heart. He had zero tolerance for my bouts of melancholia over my marriage break-up. I tried to keep a lid on it, but I had a tendency to get weepy when I drank too much. And I often drank too much back then. I would cry, Charles would yell, and our date would end with me storming off to finish my crying jag alone.

"Since Charles had another honey across the Atlantic, I saw no reason for being exclusive with him. He came in the club one day to see me. We had been dating about six weeks at the time. He gave me a bracelet, a sweet little rope chain of glittering gold — the real thing, not plated. Then he announced he had made a dinner reservation for Saturday night for the two of us and a couple visiting from England. I told him I already had plans for Saturday night. I was a bit put-off that he made plans without asking me first.

"Charles justified it by explaining that he worked so hard during the week, he liked to 'let his hair down' on the weekends. He didn't care who I saw Monday through Thursday, but he expected me to reserve my weekends for him. I told him I didn't like anyone thinking they could 'reserve me' — if he wanted a date, he needed to ask, not demand. I'd never seen a line of red move up someone's neck until it covered their whole face like that. I expected steam to shoot out of his ears. He glared at me, gritted his teeth, and said, 'YOU DON'T MAKE THE RULES, I MAKE THE RULES!'

"I felt a line moving up my neck and turning my face the same shade of deep red as his. I was so steamed, I couldn't even talk. I jumped up from the table, stomped my way through the club, and landed in the dressing room, pacing frantically. I wrestled with the clasp on the bracelet, so agitated I could barely unhook it. I heard one of the girls saying, 'Keep the bracelet, honey! Dump the guy, okay, but don't give it back to him, it's yours. Even if you don't want it, you can always sell it!' I didn't even look at her. I wasn't in the mood to listen to advice.

"I marched out of the dressing room and back to the table where I had left Charles minutes before. I thrust my hand out and tossed the gold trinket on the table saying, 'Here's your slave bracelet. I don't want it, or you, any more. And, NEWSFLASH—we already fought the War for Independence, and guess what? WE WON!'

"He was stunned. He assumed he could boss me around because of his money. I had a ton of fun and good times with Charles during our brief fling, but we also butted heads a lot. In the 1980s women's lib hadn't taken hold in England the way it had in the U.S. Charles wasn't prepared to deal with an independent American female. I wasn't willing to go back to the 1950s and play 'the little woman.' We saw each other for six weeks, and had a major fight each week. Six weeks, six fights—it could only get worse.

"I knew women who could play a guy like Charles—manipulate and sweet-talk their way around his macho ways, cashing in on his material generosity. That wasn't my style. I never got the knack of playing games with love, romance, and friendship. I walked away with my independence, my integrity, *and* my empty bank account.

"I never got why they call it 'on the rebound' when it's more like ricochet. Rebounding is bouncing off a surface once. After my divorce I was like the little silver ball in a pinball machine that bounces and rolls over and over again, randomly bumping into things that sometimes light up and other times don't. Except it was men I was bumping into, not pinball gizmos.

"Without the safety net of being married, I was vulnerable to their attention, even if I kept them at arm's length. I was too caught up in the wild-child lifestyle to see that playing the party girl was my way of keeping the constant dull ache from turning into stabbing pain. Every time I was alone, I'd end up bawling my eyes out. So I filled my free time with sex, drugs, drinking, and partying.

"I resigned myself to the fact that I would be in the stripper business for a while. I put more time and money into my shows. I thought, *If this is what life is dishing out for me, I will make the best of it.* Being creative always lifted my spirits, so I designed another costume.

"I went back to Pat, seamstress extraordinaire, and commissioned a knockout 'New Orleans dance-hall girl' get-up. It was my favorite outfit—very 'saloon-girl of the Wild West.' It had a corset—black lace over scarlet satin, black lace arm gauntlets, and black lace leggings with zippers on the inside seam. Everything was made to come off easily and gracefully.

"I had Pat make two wrap-around skirts. When I took off the black satin one, there was a shiny red petticoat to remove before I was down to the bustier and black lace arms and legs. The longer I could postpone being naked, the more I liked it. That outfit had so many pieces I almost needed an extra twenty minutes to strip out of it. It was the teasingest costume I ever wore, and unwore. I felt sexier and flirtier in it than anything else I ever danced in.

"I also found ways to expand my repertoire that weren't so costly. The most fun for me was my

'Unknown Stripper' show. I got the idea from a character called 'The Unknown Comic' on the old Gong Show that ran on TV in the '70s and '80s. The guy would pop onto the show wearing a paper bag over his head and crack corny jokes.

"I discovered that if I dampened paper bags they became pliable enough to sew. I made brown paper pants and cut 'fringe' on the bottom. I was skinny enough back then for a standard grocery bag to fit the trunk of my body. I turned the bag upside down, cut armholes and a hole for my head, and voila—instant top. I painted a question mark on the front, and made bands of brown paper 'fringe' for my arms. I used a smaller bag to cover my head.

"My co-workers thought it was so hilarious that several of them helped me finish my 'mask.' We painted green glitter eyes, and red glitter lips, and glued strips of white paper towels on top for 'hair.' The girls were using pencils to roll the paper towel 'hair' to curl it. We were laughing so hard backstage I almost couldn't pull myself together when my music started.

"The music made the show work. The first song in the set was 'Who Are You?' by The Who. All the dancers were sitting together at the bar cheering me on. The customers' reactions varied from amused to confused. Then I started tearing the pants into little chunks and throwing them into the audience. Grown men turned into five year olds, falling over each other to grab a piece of my shredded paper costume. As the set progressed, I tore the armbands and the top that covered my torso into pieces and hurled them into the crowd, leaving the bag 'mask' on my head. I had sparkly red under-pieces, which I tossed backstage when I stripped out of them, leaving the 'mask' for last. I put on a red negligee before taking off my G-string, then played a song by Todd Rundgren that starts with the line, 'Hello, it's me ...' as I finally lifted the mask.

"The crowd roared, my co-workers laughed hysterically, but Norma walked by the stage with a peculiar look on her face, as if to say, 'What the hell ...?' Then she looked around, saw that guys were enjoying themselves, and most importantly, ordering drinks. She shrugged and moved along. The outfit was the opposite of what she considered suitable wardrobe, but the club was cashing in, so she let it go.

"I didn't do that show often. The comedy and surprise element would have worn out quickly. I also had to make most of the outfit again. I kept the 'mask,' but the pants and the rest had to be re-made every time. I got a thrill seeing the reaction of the other girls when I'd walk into work and announce I was doing my 'Unknown Stripper' show again. They were so enthused they acted like kids at Christmastime. And the guys rumbling for a little scrap of brown paper debris — I couldn't get over that. A guy I met two years later told me he had a piece of brown paper from my costume dangling from his rear-view mirror.

"I got a kick out of seeing guys wrestling over my discarded bits of costume. Maybe I enjoyed seeing them act in such an undignified way because I had to throw my dignity out the window on a daily basis. Whatever it was, I came up with a few more shows where I threw stuff into the crowd for laughs. I had a 'Valentine' show where I'd pull candy kisses out of my bra to songs like 'Kiss on My List' by Hall and Oates.

"In another show, I danced to 'What Do You Want From Life?' by The Tubes. At the end of the song, the singer blurts out a 'list' of material objects at lightning speed. I'd toss out small toys, and candy bars with names like: 'Mounds/Bite Size,' 'Baby Ruth/Fun Size,' and 'Bit-O-Honey,' The guys grabbed for that stuff, but not with the same kind of mayhem as pieces of my 'Unknown Stripper' costume. Must have been some magic in those paper bags, or perhaps getting a shred of paper that had touched my naked body made them crazy.

"They were novelty shows and I didn't want to overplay them. I also couldn't afford to buy out the candy store. But they did help break up the monotony, not just for me, but also for club patrons and my co-workers.

"One day a guy named Nicky came in. I was hanging out at the bar and we started talking, or more like bantering. We had a strange chemistry I hadn't experienced with anyone else. He and I just played off each other. It was easy to wisecrack with him. We got everyone around us laughing too. He moved quickly to the top of my 'Best Club Buddies' list. Whenever I saw him from the stage, I hurried out of the dressing room after my show.

"Nicky was in construction—loved big trucks. He was built like a linebacker, with expressive round eyes set in a square German-Italian face, and a broad, easy grin. He was handsome, but it wasn't a sexual attraction. I just had fun hanging out with him. He livened things up and made the day zip by. The energy crackled around the two of us, and we usually gathered a crowd.

"I commented to one of my friends that I didn't know what it was about the two of us that made everyone want to join the party. She exclaimed, 'I do! I know what it is! When you and Nicky are together, it's like the captain of the football team and the head of the cheerleading squad!'

"I was floored by her analogy, and tickled by it too. I was never popular in school. I was shy. I hated cliques. I befriended the social outcasts 'cause I felt bad about the way they were treated by the 'in crowd.' The last thing I expected to be compared to was the head of the cheerleading squad.

"This thing between me and Nicky was total fun. We picked on each other like crazy, but not on anyone else. Our verbal tennis matches were a great antidote to my underlying misery over my break-up with Luke.

"We kept things on the light side when we hung

out, but Nicky knew I was going through a tough time. He offered to take me to Hawaii, to help heal my blues. I'd always wanted to see the Pacific paradise, and hadn't gone on a real vacation in years. We weren't lovers, just friends. As long as he didn't expect that to change by taking me halfway around the world, I was up for it.

"In the weeks prior to the trip I should have been bubbling with excitement, but every time I was alone, I still cried buckets missing Luke. I gave myself one of those in-the-mirror pep talks, something like: 'You're going to Hawaii with Nicky, and *damn it*, you're going to have a good time! No crying for two weeks. You're not going to ruin his vacation, and yours, with a ridiculous stream of tears over a guy who doesn't deserve it anyway.' I couldn't tell myself never to cry over my divorce again, so I added, 'If you need to cry when you get home, okay, but not while you're in Hawaii.'

"My self-coaching worked. Nicky and I spent a couple days on Oahu chilling at a four-star hotel to get over jet lag. I hadn't shed a tear, or even thought about Luke. Then we flew to Maui, where we would be staying for the remainder of our trip. We were so relaxed, settling in to the 'island time' spirit, we didn't even get upset when the airline sent our luggage to the wrong island. They assured us they would have it back in a couple of hours, and shuttled us to the Maui Surf at no charge to compensate for the inconvenience. We arrived at the hotel and were told our room wouldn't be available for two more hours. We shrugged it off and decided to wander around and take in the superb tropical atmosphere. We were still in the U.S., but it was so exotic and different from New England I felt like I was in a foreign country.

"Nicky and I walked down the beach to an open-air restaurant with a stunning view of an aqua-blue bay. We got a bite to eat and each had one of those drinks that come in a coconut shell. Afterwards, we still had an hour before our room would be ready.

"We wandered through a complex of hotels, checking out little shops, scouting future places for drinks and meals. Nicky got a little ahead of me, making his way around an open-air cafe. I decided to cut through, taking a diagonal path through the tables to catch up with him. Out of the corner of my eye I saw a face that burned in my mind after I passed a table on my left. I stopped short, turned toward the familiar face, and said, 'Oh my God! Casey Owens! I haven't seen you since my wedding!'

"It was Luke's best friend, a guy who grew up next door to him in Massachusetts. Fate must have been sitting in the corner having a Mai Tai and a hardy laugh. I traveled 5,000 miles to forget about my ex-husband, only to bump into his 'best man.' The only thing that could have been more ironic would be Luke himself sitting there.

"Casey's look of astonished disbelief must have been a mirror of my own expression. I knew Casey and his brother Jeff had moved to Hawaii right after they came to our wedding, but they were on the Big Island. I had not expected to run into them.

"Nicky walked into the cafe just in time to see me and Casey greeting each other with hugs. It must have been a shock for him. He turns around and I'm not behind him. The next minute he sees me hugging some guy. He seemed relieved that it wasn't an old lover I was embracing. Though it felt a bit awkward when he found out it was Luke's best friend.

"Casey knew about the divorce—Luke had written to him. I would have loved to see that letter—or maybe not. He introduced us to the young lady at his table, his sister Dana. Turned out she lived on Maui. Casey was visiting her for a week or so. I decided not to let it throw me into hysterics, but just relax and enjoy. This was a message from the universe—no use trying to run from your problems, there's nowhere to hide from them anyway.

"It turned out to be a lucky twist to our vacation plans. We hung out with Casey, Dana, and some of their friends every other day for the entire trip. They knew all the ins and outs of island life. They told us where to buy groceries so we wouldn't pay tourist prices and took us to deserted beaches that only the locals were privy to. We all got along great and had plenty of laughs. I stuck to my promise and didn't shed a single tear over Luke. Nicky stuck to his promise and didn't try to change the platonic nature of our relationship.

"The last day we were there, Nicky wandered up

the beach and I was alone, drinking in the beauty of the surf, sand, and sky. A skinny weather-beaten man, who looked older than his years, approached me. He had rugged but tolerable looks and kind eyes that matched the blue of the ocean. He seemed like an interesting character. We sat and talked for a while. He told me he wove sunhats from palm leaves and sold them to tourists to earn money. He pointed to a sailboat just offshore and said it was his—he lived on it. He had made a killing selling kilos of marijuana, got out of the business, and invested his fortune in the boat.

"He made enough money from weaving hats for food and supplies, and spent his time sailing from island to island doing as he pleased. He said his life was perfect, except for one thing—he needed a woman to complete his paradise. When he saw me sitting there, he hoped I would be the one. He said he would do everything in his power to make me happy, and promised he'd bring me back to shore anytime I wanted out.

"I entertained the outrageous notion for at least twenty minutes. How deliciously insane it would be—to ditch everything I owned, which wasn't all that much, and take up with this vagabond sailor. I was feeling blue about going home, back to my smoky barroom job and my lonely apartment. I was seriously tempted.

"Then I thought of my cat, Spooky. I couldn't abandon her. She and I had imprinted on each other, like we shared a piece of our souls. I'd miss my closest friends. My family would be too far away for comfort. I may not have seen them much, but knowing they were only a day's drive was reassuring. I thought, *What if I got stuck here, with no money for a plane ticket, and never saw them again?*

"I've often wondered if my free-spirited Captain ever found his First Mate. I've wondered what my life would have been like if I had let it be me."

16. Fan Mail

"The year following my divorce was spent drowning my sorrows in a sea of drugs and booze, pretending to have a good time 'partying.' I didn't have the coping mechanisms I have now for dealing with disappointment." Eve began our recording session in her usual way: she kicked off her shoes, moved the cushions around to support her back, and stretched her legs out across the length of the sofa.

"What do you mean by 'coping mechanisms,' Eve?" I asked.

"Faith is at the top of the list, Stella. My belief in a power greater than myself, whatever name you want to give it. I'm fond of 'The Spirit That Moves Through All Things'—a Native American expression. After suspecting my mother was in love with a priest, I distanced myself from organized religion. I've heard people say they thought God had abandoned them. I don't know if I felt that way, but he seemed to be taking a long lunch break.

"It was so simple when I was a child to buy into the Catholic dogma. Between my personal experiences, and the social upheaval of the '60s, I couldn't accept it any longer. 'Question Authority' and 'Question

Everything' were the banner-waving slogans of my generation. I yearned for spiritual connection, but 'blind faith' wasn't cutting it. I wanted 'eyes-opened faith,' and that is more complex, more challenging, than just parroting, 'Well the Bible says ...' The Bible does say a lot, but much of it is open to interpretation. It was written over two-thousand years ago, for a population that was largely illiterate and dependent upon priests and popes to dictate its meaning. There is much wisdom and sacred guidance within it. Unfortunately, it has been abused by manipulative, power-hungry, unholy humans often disguised as clergy. I don't want to digress—suffice it to say that my estrangement from Catholicism left a spiritual black hole in my life.

"The I Ching had been helpful in many situations, but in the wake of my marriage break-up I was too buzzed to bother with it. You need to be grounded, and sober, to throw the coins. Double vision makes it hard to read the answers it guides you to.

"When I first got to the Squire, I moderated my intake of booze. After the break-up with Luke, the safety valve let loose. I was back to drinking the way I had in my early dancing career, and spiraling down a path that could only lead to one place—Oblivion City. That's where the broken people end up—the ones with broken hearts, broken dreams, broken spirits.

"A tiny shaft of light broke through one day. I went on stage, smile on my face, screaming inside because I couldn't stand it anymore. I couldn't stand the smoke, the leering guys, my habitual drunkenness—the going nowhere dead-ended-ness of it all. As I danced across the stage, a thought danced across my mind— *Be grateful you have legs, and that you can dance, and that you bring joy to people.* I found the simple grace of gratitude once again—that rung on the ladder I could pull myself out of the ditch with. Gratitude led to hope, hope led to faith—faith that there was a way out, and faith that I could find it if I stopped the merry-go-round long enough to look inside.

"That split-second crack-of-lightning thought was the beginning of turning my life around. I had been floating and drifting wherever my stream-of-consciousness life took me. I decided it was time to take the oars, and at least *try* to steer my destiny. I wanted out of that life, but I needed a plan.

"I had seen many women quit stripping in a fit of frustration, only to bounce back into it after a taste of working at K-Mart. Then they would sink into a pit of despair so deep, some of them didn't make it out. After making decent money for partying all day, it was tough getting minimum wage and having some power-junkie manager bossing you around. Most of the strippers I knew were used to calling the shots. We were rebels, who enjoyed living an unconventional life. Transitioning back into mainstream society could be a bumpy ride, especially when your resume has nothing on it but 'Waitress' followed by 'Stripper.'

"The first step I took to re-set my course was to stop

drinking. I knew I wasn't going to make any progress until I got my head clear — or almost clear. I had no alcohol, either during work or after, for three months. I still smoked weed — I couldn't get on stage without it — but I didn't smoke as voraciously. I didn't do a twelve-step program or get any other help. I was afraid to admit I had a problem. The fact that I could just stop reassured me I hadn't become a 'real' alcoholic. I had no doubt I *would* become one if I didn't get a handle on it. After three months, I allowed myself a drink now and then, but was moderate. I had it under control. I recognized my 'trigger point' and stopped myself before blowing my head off. That meant limiting to two drinks. If I had three glasses of wine, I could drink a bottle, then another one, and keep going until I landed on the moon. I couldn't keep taking trips to outer space if I was going to redirect my life on earth.

"I thought about my childhood fantasy of acting. Conventional wisdom told me it was silly to delve into it, at the ripe old age of thirty-one. But I decided I didn't want to be an eighty-year-old lady, smoking a joint in her rocking chair, wondering, *'What would've happened If ...'* I signed up for an acting workshop at an adult education center in Cambridge.

"There were a dozen students, some older, some younger. We sat in a circle and began with introductions — just our name, and a sentence about why we were there. I was wringing a handkerchief so tightly I choked the poor thing to death. When one speaks, one is supposed to exhale, letting the burst of air project one's voice outward. I inhaled my name, and could barely squeak out three or four words to greet my fellow students. I hadn't felt that shy since the third grade spelling bee where I was the last one standing in front of the whole class.

"I thought about how confident I was on the stage. I could whip around dancing, shedding my clothes for strangers, with just a little toke to help. My childhood insecurities came flooding back as soon as I had to open my mouth. I'm amazed I lasted through the workshop, but I did better than that. I signed up for more classes. They were held at the teacher's brownstone apartment near Copley Square in Boston."

"Those weekly acting classes lifted my spirits more than any drink or drug ever had. My coach, Eleanor, was seventy. Her hair, the color of orange flames, fit her fiery persona. I learned much more from her than acting techniques. She urged us to live with passion— that it was the key to vitality and true happiness. She loved to teach, and, because she loved it, it kept her young. She taught us to be truly present in the moment—that giving rapt attention to a person was honoring life itself. She was a true mentor, who helped me to believe in myself, in my dreams, and my abilities.

"One day she said to me, 'I try to encourage anyone who attempts to do this, but I am careful about giving false hope. You have what it takes to make it in this business. You have the right combination of being hard working, as well as talented. You need both to be an actor. I've seen people with more talent than you, but they are lazy; they think success will just come to them. It doesn't work that way—you need to pursue it. If you're lucky, it may meet you halfway, but it will never just show up on your doorstep. There are others who are heartbreaking to watch, because they will work harder than you, me, and everyone else, but they just don't have the talent. But you have buckets full of talent, and aren't afraid to do what it takes to get out there and make it happen. So, DO IT!' I've replayed her speech many times, like a film I re-run when I need a boost of inspiration or self-confidence.

"Having an exciting new life outside of the club made work more bearable. I met new people, who didn't know I was a stripper—and I wanted to keep it that way. If someone knew as soon as they met me, it colored their impression of me. They'd see me through the filter of whatever stereotype they thought a stripper was. If someone got to know me without that label, and found out later, they often questioned their perception of what they thought a striptease dancer was.

"I heard, 'Wow, you don't look/act/seem/walk or talk like a stripper' dozens of times. And dozens of times I'd ask, 'What do you think a stripper is supposed to look/act/seem/walk or talk like?' Most of them were dumbfounded. They may have had a picture in their mind, and didn't want to insult me, or couldn't articulate it. Or else they realized how stupid it was to define hundreds of thousands of individuals with one poorly drawn portrait. If you passed most of my co-workers on the street, you'd never pick them out as strippers, not unless they happened to be in a flamboyant mood.

"Occasionally we dancers were in a mood to take our particular form of flamboyancy out for the evening. I still went out partying, but it had more purpose for me than just having a good ol' time. I wanted to network, to meet people in Boston outside of the limited world I had been living in. I used my ability to put on a glamour to get noticed. The nightclubs on Lansdowne Street were trying to emulate Studio 54 in New York, especially the Metro, as it was called in the early '80s. They catered to the rich and famous, or at least beautiful and glamorous, and shunned those who didn't fit the image they were striving for. There were long lines to get in on Saturday night. Pack a picnic dinner—you could wait for hours—unless you knew someone, or dressed the right way.

"I had met Patrick, the owner of the Metro, but you would hardly say I knew him. I may have talked to him for all of five minutes. I knew he had a brother named John, but I had never laid eyes on him.

"One night I strutted past the endless line on Lansdowne Street with a couple of other dancers, dressed in skin-tight glitz. I approached the hulking bouncer, who guarded the door like it was the entrance to the Emerald City, and announced that I was a friend of Patrick's and his brother John. The bouncer had a bemused grin, scanned me from head to toe, and replied, 'Well, *I* am Patrick's brother *John*. You may be a friend of Patrick's, but I have never seen you before—I'd certainly remember you if I had!'

"*Damn,* I thought, mortified that I had been caught like a fish in a net trying to bluff my way in. I leaned toward him and whispered, 'Well, I *have met* Patrick, and me and my friends, we didn't want to wait in this line.' He swept his hand to gesture toward my attire, and said, 'Well, dressed like *that,* you wouldn't *need to,'* as he waved us in. My purple mini-dress, with the sequined palm tree and glittery purple leggings were in high style in the disco-frantic era. I probably wouldn't have had the guts to wear such a bold and skimpy outfit if I had never become a stripper. I'd still be waiting at the back of the line.

"I was in short supply of academic achievement or intellectual brilliance. What I had was an abundance of good looks and gumption. I used them to pry open any doors I thought might lead me to a new and improved life. I was in an expansive phase, having an adventure. I wasn't sure it would lead me where I wanted to go, but the journey was exhilarating.

"It was during that phase I met Doug, and consequently met you, Stella. I met Doug at the Squire, and at first I was infatuated. He was supportive of my struggle to find a new career, and also appreciated my interest in alternative spirituality.

"He brought me to dinner at his father's house, not just to show me off to you and Max. He knew Art, your playwright friend, would be there and thought he might help somehow with my acting career.

Doug was sweet, and thoughtful, and loved his Harley. Bikers have to live with stereotyping too. Doug wasn't like a typical biker—I don't believe such a thing exists. Bikers, like strippers, are rugged individualists. I liked his looks: deep-set hazel eyes, sandy-blond hair and wiry build. He seemed out of place on the East Coast. I pictured him belonging to the vast landscape of the Wild West, a cowboy with a cultural bent.

"I've had my heart broken and never wanted to inflict that pain on anyone, but sometimes it can't be helped. I warned Doug when we met that I wasn't looking to settle down, that my life was in transition and I needed to be free to pursue my dreams. He wanted more than I could give. He had such a yearning in his eyes. He may have won me over at another time, but he had the misfortune of meeting me when I was hell-bent on spreading my wings. The needier he got, the more I retreated.

"After I told him I didn't want to see him anymore, he left me a gift. It was a hardcover edition of the complete works of e.e. cummings. Doug knew he was my favorite poet. It would have been a lovely gesture, except that he left it in my car while it was parked in front of my apartment overnight. The idea that this guy, who I had asked to stay away from me, was sneaking around outside my apartment while I was sleeping creeped me out. I had been trying to let him down easy, but I lost it after that. I was freaked out that he was stalking me and I laid into him the next time he came in the club. That was about the last I saw of him, except once more when he dropped off a 'good-bye' poem he had written."

"I never knew Doug wrote poetry." I said. "That was a side he didn't share with me, or his father."

"There's something I want show you, Stella. I've been waiting until it was in sync with the timeline of my story. I'll be right back," said Eve, as she stood up. Then she headed up the stairs toward the guest room she had been staying in. She returned a couple of minutes later with a blue file folder. She flopped down on the sofa and began shuffling through an assortment of papers.

"Here's the farewell poem Doug wrote. Would you like to hear it?" Eve asked.

"If you want to read it, please do," I replied. Eve had already shared so much of her life with me. Yet I felt myself squirm a little as she read from the yellow lined paper in her hands. Maybe I was uneasy because I knew Doug, or perhaps reading other people's love letters seemed a bit like rifling through their lingerie drawer.

"He wrote some sweeter things to me before this, but this one was after I dumped him," she said, then began reading:

> This is someone you once knew,
>   with a message for you.
> Since you like to rhyme,
>   I'll no longer waste my time.
> By now you should know how I feel.
>   Which to you is no big deal.
> I hope you won't shed a tear.
>   I really want to hold you near.
> I wish to be your friend and lover,
>   a man for you like no other.
> But when you come crashing down
>   from oh so high
> The love I have for you will never die.
> And when you fall you might call.
>   If you don't, I won't.
> Will your fancy friends really be there?
>   Probably not.
> Just remember ... I sincerely care.
> Sorry but I don't need your kind of love.
> You've given me the last and final shove.
> Now I must say goodbye.
>   I feel your love for me was just a lie.
> So finally I bid my farewell.
>   You can go straight to hell.
> Till someday, I pray,
>   you'll want me again, friend.

"He signed it 'From, Nobody'—meaning I treated

him like a nobody, I guess. It expresses a curious mixture of emotions. In one line he's telling me he sincerely still cares, in another that I can go to hell. There's some hope for revenge in that part about 'crashing down from oh so high,' but he sums it up saying he prays I'll want him again. Why would I ever want to go back to someone who told me, in writing, to go straight to hell?" Eve asked with a raised brow and comical grin.

"What else is in the folder, Eve? Are those all poems from Doug?" I asked.

"Oh, God, no." she replied. "There are a couple more he wrote, but this a mish-mosh collection of poems, love notes, and fan mail from that phase of my life. I don't recall getting much of this type of thing until after my break-up with Luke. I don't know why I started saving them. Some were too sweet, others too funny, to toss in the trash.

"There's an aspect of dancers that is rarely acknowledged—our role as muse. I didn't always take the notes personally. Sometimes I was just a conduit for a guy to have a romantic focus, that he wasn't necessarily involved with, to express himself creatively.

"Think about it—a guy has a closet talent for writing. He goes to the local everyday bar, where there are no dancers. What's he gonna write about? How golden and sparkly his beer looks crowned by a halo of angelic frothy foam? Not much inspiration there. Then he goes to the Squire and sees a fantasy woman: young, curvy, exotic, enticing, and the poetry flows, driven by hormones running amok. He knows there's little chance she'll respond, but he has to get it out of him or he'll explode. He grapples around his pocket for a pen, then grabs the nearest piece of paper he can find—usually a bar napkin—and begins to write." Eve reached into the blue folder, grabbed a bar napkin and read:

> I have fallen into orbit around you.
> I've fallen in love with you a hundred times.
> The last dozen times were different and once
>   it became permanent.
> In the beginning I loved what you were, now
> - I realize in my life this feeling will
>   never be replaced.

"It wasn't exactly signed—this guy used to draw a symbol for his signature. It was like an eye with a heart in the center. He came in often, usually with a buddy. They were part of the regular lunchtime landscape. I might have talked to him once or twice. That's why it was such a surprise to get these notes from him. He was a clever guy. I wish I had gotten to know him a little better. Another one he wrote was one of my favorites. It's a bit long, but I think you'll get a kick out of it."

"Sure, please go ahead." I replied.

Eve pulled the note from the folder. It was handwritten on two lined sheets, stapled in the upper left corner. Their left sides were tattered from being torn out of a small spiral-bound notebook. She said, "He started by writing our horoscopes from the daily paper. I'll skip that part and begin with his commentary. It's dated—most of these notes aren't—Thursday, August 22, 1984:

Crossed? Not exactly. Conjunctive? No. I miss you. That healing, soothing, blessed substance in your visitations. The ex-kwisit curve of your neck escaping from your shoulders—a foot away. The irreproducible sound of only your voice. The details of your beauty I can only see when you are near.

Maybe you don't understand. Maybe you understand and you think it's a burden. Remember,

The passions that we feel contract it, those that we inspire expand it.

Think of it that way.

Scenario: I die. They burn my body. The ashes are sifted through a grate. One shining silver piece remains like some charm-bracelet trinket. It spells "Lisa".

Scenario: In his basement, Mr. X begins to build a liking. For what someone is, for what they represent, for what they stand for. One day it is too big to get out the door. So he gives it a coat or two of varnish and it stays.

"At this point there's a break," Eve said, as she turned the paper so I could see what she referred to. There were a few lines a third of the way down the page with a border inked around them. To the right of this manually written 'text box' a small heart was drawn. He had written '1/100' inside the heart, and above it 'Just Fan mail.' Eve read the passage that had been set aside from the rest of the page:

> Where others cloy
>   the appetites they feed,
> She makes hungry
>   where most she satisfies

"I wish I could ask him what he meant by this. Or maybe it's best that I can't," she said, then smiled.

"Eve, do you have any idea what the heart symbol with 1/100 inside it means?" I asked.

"Yes, I do Stella," she replied. "He and his buddy gave me a silver charm-bracelet heart one day. They said it was because I was the 'Winner of a Hundred Hearts.' I was tickled by the gift and the tagline that came with it. I wore it for years, but not on a bracelet. I put it on a safety pin and wore it on my shirts and jackets, sometimes on my sleeve for a laugh. I still have it after all these years. Anyway, this is my favorite part coming up." Eve took a sip of water and continued reading:

In the midst of a broken chaotic flurry of

dream sequence there is a peaceful bit in a well-lit cafe. Plain tables but clean. Natural lighting through clear curtained windows. All kinds of people. Pleasant busy buzzing conversation. The major topic — excitement over a new batch of Lisa-dolls that you are making. Hand made. Hand painted. Everybody wants one. No two exactly alike but those who have one already will tell you eagerly how it has just a touch of sunshine in its eyes. The batch is only a dozen. Every one is bought and paid for long before it's made. I can plainly see how they enrich the lives of those who own them. I see these things in a minute because this is a dream. I am only passing through.

The little old ladies in flower print dresses with hats and handbags and sturdy shoes adore Lisa. Those who have one of the dolls cherish it like a fairy granddaughter. One has brought the doll with her today and brought her own flesh and blood visiting granddaughter to meet Lisa in the cafe in the prairie sunlight.

The dolls appear immune to wear and tear. You can tell the difference between an old and new one but not by any sign of degradation in its appearance.

Someone starts talking to me and the dream scene changes.

"It's not what you'd expect from a strip-club regular, is it?" Eve shook her head as her lips formed a wry grin. "That dark club was far from prairie sunlight, and never the kind of place little old ladies in flower print dresses would frequent. What an imagination! I probably wouldn't have called you to help me with this book if I could write like him.

"Quite a contrast to this next little tidbit. This guy must have been trying to see how many bad pick-up lines he could cram onto one cocktail napkin. I'll let you scan this one yourself, Stella. It's too adolescent to warrant reading aloud."

Eve reached across the table and handed me a small square napkin. What appeared to be coffee stains made some of the words barely legible. Covering both sides, printed in pencil, were the following lines:

> I want to make us both feel good
> Let's Make Love
> I want to screw you
> I just want to get laid
> Let's make our body's one
> Let's Fuck
> I want your body
> I want to jump your bones
> Let's have sex
> I'm horny, please help me relieve the tension
> I'm a straight man,
>   who wants to get straightened out

Let's get it on
Let's Do It! Let's make it!
Let's get lucky
Let's have intercourse
    (social as well as physical)
Let's make whooppee!
I'm looking to share a joint venture with you
Let's shack up
Let's fool around
Let's spend the night together
If I get a room will you join me?
I want to park my car in your garage
I Want You
My place or yours?
Let's copulate
This may be a stiff approach,
    but it softens up with time

"Yes, Eve, I see what you mean," I said, as I handed back the scribbled list of sexual clichés.

"What's impressive is how he fit all that garbage onto one tiny napkin." Eve said. "My first impulse was to throw it in the trash, but I decided it belonged in the archive, part of my history whether I like it or not. It's a great illustration of what I was talking about before: One guy sees you as an angel floating in the clouds, your mere presence sending waves of beautiful healing light; another sees you as a gutter wench, something to satisfy his crudest desires with before he tosses you back into the slime pit. If I have to choose between these two unrealistic images, I'd rather be the one hanging out in the prairie sunlight.

"Most of my 'fan mail' was handed to me directly by the author, or sent backstage with the help of a cocktail waitress. This one came through the U.S. Postal Service," said Eve, as she held up an 8 x 11 sheet of white paper. It had a light green stain across the top edge, but otherwise was clean and neatly typed. She continued, "It was simply addressed to: Lisa, Squire Club, Revere, MA. I was amused before I even opened the envelope, marveling that it managed to get to me at all—no last name, no street, no zip code. I guess every postman from Bangor to Boston knows where the Squire is.

"A week or two prior to getting this letter, there had been a flurry of excitement in the club. Several club patrons and employees said the guy sitting at the bar, near the front entrance, looked like the author Stephen King. The man was gone before I came out of the dressing room, but I had noticed him from the stage. There weren't many people there that day, so it was easy to spot a newcomer amongst the regulars. This man had an interesting aura about him. I was sad he was gone. It would have been refreshing to talk to someone who wore coke-bottle glasses and looked like he could have a conversation about something other than the wasteland babble I was used to in that place. This letter was dated, Feb. 23, 83:

Dear Lisa,

I have never written a fan letter before, so you should know from this one that I think you're very special. You have a charming act, dance beautifully, project a wonderful personality, and look lovely. You are definitely the class act at the Squire Lounge and for that matter one of the best ecdysiasts I've ever seen, and I'm a connoisseur.

Even though you are not supposed to be able to improve on perfection, I hope you will not mind if I make a suggestion. I think you should dance all of the last act, or at least part of it, completely nude. Leaving the cape on just does not give the same effect that total nudity does. The part of your act where you are nude except for the cape is charming and cute, and you ought definitely to keep it. But it would be great if it were the next to the last thing in your act rather than last. So I suggest taking the cape off and hanging it up behind the curtain, just as you do with the rest of your costume, and then dancing for at least a few minutes completely nude.

To do this would not in the least spoil the high tone of your act or make it just like anyone else's. I know that lots of the other girls dance nude, but you are not lots of the other girls. They can't dance as well, are not as beautiful, and don't have your personality. If you would look at it as a challenge to continue to be distinctive in your charming way, yet dance totally nude, I think you might find it very interesting. I suppose the reason that I am hung up on this is that I am a great believer in the aesthetic principle of "resolution." You know the dissatisfied feeling that you have when someone lifts a needle off the record just before it ends. Similarly, the ending to your act at present seems to come too soon.

I probably won't be able to get back to the Squire for a few weeks, but I will identify myself to you as the writer of this letter next time I am there. If you want to talk this over, it would be my pleasure. Meanwhile, you might ask some of the other customers what they think about this.

"It was signed 'Sincerely yours, An Admirer.' He never did show up and identify himself. Maybe he came in on my day off, or sobered up and thought better of it. Since that day in 1983 I have wondered if it *was* Mr. King who wrote the letter. I wrote to him not long ago to ask him. I hope he got a good chuckle out of it, but I'm not surprised I never got an answer.

"Whoever wrote it, I want them to know I was just about rolling on the dressing room floor after I received it. It was certainly quite flattering, but the analogy of the needle being lifted off the record had me in stitches. That someone felt so strongly about my avoiding total nudity—they would take the time to write such an eloquent discourse—really tickled my funny bone.

"Wherever that guy is now, he must be in 'connoisseur heaven.' From what I've heard, the whole business has changed. No more shows and fancy costumes. The girls are one hundred percent nude by the end of the first song. Where do you go from there? It's all stripping and no teasing, bending over and showing strangers your private gateway to heaven. For me, that would have been hell.

"The tease was the main tool in my toolbox. Take that from me and it's like asking a carpenter to build without hammer and nails. I had a hard enough time getting close to naked. If I couldn't put a negligee on before ditching my G-string I never would have lasted ten years in that business. I would have felt far too vulnerable being completely nude. I wasn't confident enough about my dancing, didn't know what to do naked if I couldn't twirl and swirl diaphanous fabric around. My hats off to the ladies who are comfortable enough in their skin not to need any props.

"I never was cut out to be a stripper, but that was true of most every other job I've had before and since. Whether I was a waitress, office clerk, or salesperson, I always felt like I was putting on an act. I've always envied people who found careers that really suited them, who could earn a livelihood doing something they are truly passionate about. I'm over fifty now and still trying to decide what I want to be when I grow up."

"Eve, what do think it was that made the business change, and move away from the Burlesque-like shows?" I asked.

"Tipping," she replied. "I'm pretty sure that was it, Stella. When I worked at the Squire there was a sign clearly posted that said 'No Tipping.' The clubs up Route One were allowing it. The Squire was having a harder time keeping talent once girls got hip they could make a lot more at clubs that allowed guys to tip the dancers. They also noticed the guys didn't usually tip until they started shedding their clothes. They could make more tips if they dropped most of their costume earlier in the show.

"Some patrons must be happy with it that way, but I know others who genuinely enjoyed our creativity in the old days. I'm sure I was too tame for those who like a hard-core show. I never showed any 'pink,' which disappointed a few customers. But others liked my semi-modest style. I remember a couple of dudes one day who were begging me to never change. One of them told me that I was sexy enough to turn him on, but ladylike enough to take home to his mother, a combination he found much more appealing than if I had shown him every last part of my anatomy.

"I must have been doing something right to inspire this kind of sweet sentiment," Eve said, as she pulled out a piece of light green paper the size of a large index card and began to read:

now it's my time to flirt!
you were a phantom of delight,
when first you gleamed upon my sight,
a lovely apparition sent,
to be a moment's ornament!

"So that guy wasn't disappointed that I didn't gyrate on the floor and spread my legs." Eve shrugged, then pulled out another sheet of paper and held it so it faced me. It was typed, and broken into several four-line verses. She said, "I want to include one more before we wrap it up for the day, Stella. This one was written by one of my most special club buddies. It's hard to explain why I felt so close to him almost as soon as we met. Maybe because he was an artist. I often gravitated toward people with artistic talent. He wrote scads of poetry. He signed everything 'Brian Christian,' but that was not his real name. He told me he used to write song lyrics for some well-known rock 'n roll stars. Whatever magic it was, he was comfortable for me to be around. It wasn't a sexual thing, at least not for me.

"Brian was one of the few club buddies I saw outside of the club. We'd have lunch or dinner every so often. He was married, which made it easier for me to keep it platonic. After we had been friends for about five years, he said to me, 'I've been trying to figure out what this is, this thing between us. In the beginning I was hoping for more, but now I'm grateful you didn't feel that way, because I really didn't want to cheat on my wife. Now when I think of you, the word 'sister' comes to mind. I'm just sad that you can't meet my wife, because I think you two would like each other. But it would be too hard to explain you to her.'

"I went on seeing him occasionally for about ten years after I quit dancing. Eventually, it felt awkward having this friendship that he had to keep hidden from his wife—intimacy doesn't have to be physical to feel like infidelity. I don't think what we did was totally wrong. I believe our relationship was important for us both, for our personal growth and for the blessed gift of having someone in your life who understands you intuitively. The visits with my 'brother' Brian eventually dwindled off. After I re-married and moved out of state we lost touch.

"He brought many poems into the club to show me. Some were romantic, but those were not written for me. He knew I wouldn't approve of that. This one is a tongue-in-cheek take on the Squire, from a dancer's point of view, titled 'April Fool':

> I work short hours for lots of money.
> Feel like a bear with a tree of honey.
> I'm given free drinks all day long,
> Always entertained by the latest song.
>
> Nicest guys sit in the front row
> There to support an artistic show.

They must know I'm really quite shy
Their kind looks never meet my eye.

Never a complaint from management here.
The lady in charge is really a dear.
She's so sweet, soft spoken and kind.
If I'm sick or late she really won't mind.

That Ernie's a gentleman, hope he's not mad,
I'm sure it's my hand he meant to grab.
My breasts are my own,
   they may not be much,
So it couldn't be them he was trying to touch.

Paid vacations with a full medical plan
Working here's easy and whenever we can
We rest in the back, take in the show
Enjoy such freedom: Free to come and go.

Atmosphere, in Revere,
   this place has such class.
A superb menu includes pheasant under glass,
Complimented by choice liquors
   and fine old wines
No water in the drinks can anyone find.

Sound from the speakers
   is a quiet background.
With easy conversation and couples around
Well-appointed tables and comfortable chairs.

A refuge without worldly cares.

Yes, when all is said and told
Think I'll stay here 'till I've grown old.
Now, if you really believe all this shit
You can come over and kiss my left ___.

Eve drew a line in the air with her finger to indicate the last 'word' was a blank. As she slipped the poem back into the blue folder, she said, "In this case, it was the club itself that was his muse. I wonder if he wrote about his own workplace with the same enthusiasm. I doubt it.

"I wasn't the only one who got fan mail. My friends Sindy and Spicy each gave me a pile of their own, in case I wanted to use them. They don't fit into my memoir, but perhaps we can put together a scrapbook of stripper fan mail once we finish this. There must be stacks of similar notes, poems, and propositions written to exotic dancers all over the world, a mountain of cocktail napkins and assorted scraps of paper that pay tribute to striptease artists.

"Maybe there is a special Muse in charge of this particular branch of literature. Her name might be something like 'Ecdysiastia.' Yes, I like that." Eve raised her arms, with the palms of her hands facing upward. Her voice grew loud and deep, like a priestess of an ancient temple, as she declared, "Hail Ecdysiastia, Great Muse of Strip Literature!"

17. SIZZLE SISTERS

"I got a bit off track from my story line pulling out the fan mail yesterday. *Where was I?*" Eve said as she settled in on the sofa. I prompted her by reading my notes from the previous day.

She nodded and said, "Thanks Stella, that was helpful. As I mentioned, I didn't have a precise plan about how I would transition out of being a striptease dancer. I followed my instincts, which led me through a convoluted trail of events. Sometimes events moved me toward my goal when I least expected it, when I let go of thinking about it and focused on something else.

"One of the girls I worked with—we called her Crazy Lacey—was turning thirty, and was pretty blue about it. She asked me, and a few of the other dancers, to go out to a club on Lansdowne Street called 'Spit.' I wanted to pull Lacey out of her gloom and make it a memorable night for her. I put all my thinking about changing careers on hold and did what I could to cheer up my friend.

"I conspired with the other three girls and customized T-shirts to wear for Lacey's birthday. We had different sayings on each one, and jazzed them up by adding beads and fringe to the bottoms and sleeves. We wore spandex pants that looked like they were spray-painted on. Mine were neon pink, with a white shirt that said, 'Whose Party is it Anyway?' Raven's pants were leopard print, and her shirt said, 'What are you staring at?' Dawn's pants were silver. Her lipstick-red shirt said 'Never a Dull Moment.'

"We couldn't go out in a normal automobile looking so flamboyant. We needed a vehicle to match our pizzazz. A designated driver would probably be a good idea too. I asked Keith, a regular club patron, if we could rent one of his limos. When he found out it was for Lacey, he gave us the limo for the night, no charge, and threw in a dozen roses and a bottle of Dom Perignon. Turns out he had a 'thing' for Lacey, and was glad to help make it a special night.

"Lacey had no idea what was cooking. I had gone to Spit beforehand and decorated a little corner of the club with pink and black streamers and balloons. I had a 'Happy 30th' birthday cake made with pink and black icing. Pink and black were Lacey's trademark colors.

"When we got to Lacey's house, she was in a dilemma about what to wear. I handed her a black T-shirt, fringed and beaded with sparkly pink beads. Pink letters spelled out, 'It's MY Party ...' on the front, with pink rhinestones twinkling on 'MY.' On the back more pink letters said, '... and I'll Cry if I want to.' Lacey's eyes lit up when I gave her the shirt. She forgot all about her birthday blues — thirty schmirty — so what?! She was going out with the girls to rock the town. She paired a black mini skirt and fishnet stockings with her glittery birthday T-shirt.

"I told her to look out her window at the car we had for the night. She jumped up and down on her bed and did a few back-flips — she was quite the gymnast. We hadn't even gotten out the door of her house and she was already as bubbly as a glass of champagne.

"We caused quite a scene pulling up to Spit in a limo, spilling out of it in our custom-made party duds. Our spirits were soaring as we drank, danced, and held court in the corner of the club I had partitioned off with the black and pink streamers.

"Then I saw Patrick, the owner of the club. He had an intense, stern look on his face. He came over to me and asked, *'Who did this?'* as he waved his hand toward the streamers and balloons. From the tone of his voice, I thought he disapproved of the decor. I feared he would make us take it down, or even kick us out. I couldn't answer him. Thoughts of doom raced through my head. I worried about how Lacey would feel if he flipped the 'off' switch on her party.

"'It was *you*, wasn't it?' He asked. *Oh, great*, I thought, *he'll ban me from the club.* I nodded yes and explained that I came in earlier to set it up, and the manager said it was okay. He wasn't upset at all, as my pot-induced paranoia would have me think. He said, 'The streamers, balloons, cake, and the way you all are dressed — *you're quite a talented coordinator.'* I heaved a sigh of relief that we weren't going to be expelled. We could carry on with Crazy Lacey's party and the commotion we were causing with our flashy outfits.

"Lacey's bash, with all its little surprises, was my special gift to her. But I got a gift myself that night. When Patrick singled me out and complimented me on my talent to make it all happen, it was more of a boon than he could have imagined. He was a successful entrepreneur and well-respected businessman. I had gotten a lot of attention as a dancer for my looks, and tons of applause for baring it all. To have someone of his caliber recognize me for being talented and creative in a context that had nothing to do with being a stripper lifted my spirits a mile high. I had never thought of the word 'coordinator' to describe myself, but I liked the sound of it.

"Around that time I was putting together a modeling portfolio. I never thought I was pretty enough, tall enough, or photogenic enough to be a model. When I thought of models, I pictured ultra-tall, skin-and-bones fashion models with chiseled features. My acting classes made me aware they were using all types of people for TV commercials and print ads. I was branching out and exploring different possibilities, so I gave it a shot.

"I went to a black-tie dinner with people from the photography studio who were doing my portfolio shoots. They thought it might help me to make connections for my modeling career. I had never been to anything like that before. Tables draped in white, adorned with bright bouquets and sparkling crystal, filled a room so big you needed binoculars to see from one end to the other. The men were in dark suits and tuxes, an elegant backdrop to the ladies they escorted who looked ready to go to the Oscars.

"The evening was a fundraiser for the National Kidney Foundation. Festivities centered on an award ceremony for local citizens who had made significant contributions to the community. There was entertainment, singers, dancers and such, but I can't remember much of it. I was too busy watching a young woman with long blond hair.

"She wore an unadorned black dress and simple strand of pearls. Her outfit was a subdued contrast to all the glitz and glitter. She seemed invisible to all but me. She moved through the tables, holding a clipboard. Occasionally she leaned over to chat briefly with an audience member before dashing off to her next task. I was more intrigued by her than all the fanfare on the stage, or the 'Who's Who of Boston' that surrounded me.

"I asked my escort from the photography studio if he knew who she was. 'Oh, yes,' he said, 'that's Laura. She works for the Kidney Foundation. She's the coordinator for this whole thing. Would you like me to introduce you?' *Coordinator,* I thought, *there's that word again.* 'Sure, I'd love to meet her,' I replied. I was fascinated that this one inconspicuous person had been responsible for putting together the elaborate event, from the banquet to the entertainment. I met her briefly and got her card.

"I figured the best way to find out more about her, and what a coordinator does, was to volunteer to help her. I called and asked Laura if I could take her to lunch to discuss how I might be of service to her organization. I let her know I was interested in learning about what she does, and I was willing to help in any way I could, if she was open to helping me in my 'research.' She was pleased by my offer. She said most nonprofits are notoriously understaffed and hers was no exception.

"When we met for lunch, I felt I had to take a chance and be up-front with her about my occupation. I felt my stomach tighten as I said, 'Just one thing I want you to know about me, before we go any further—I am currently earning my living as a striptease dancer.' I held my breath, waiting for her reaction. She raised an eyebrow slightly, shrugged, and said, 'So what? That wouldn't stop me from accepting your help. What made you feel compelled to share that with me?' I told her I was not ashamed of it, but was aware of the social stigma that goes along with being a stripper. I said I just wanted her to know, so if she heard it from someone else it wouldn't be a shock, or put her in an awkward position with her superiors. She appeared to take it in stride and not make any judgment about me. She said she was very appreciative of my honesty, but saw no reason why it should be an obstacle to signing me up as a volunteer.

"Laura was a classy lady. Class is truly about how

you treat people. If she did think any less of me for being a stripper, she certainly never let it show. She was generous sharing information with me and showing me how she put events together. I was enthusiastic and gave my all to any task she asked of me, from helping with large mailings to running errands. I never felt she took advantage of my willingness to help. It was a fair trade for what I was learning from her.

"One day Laura asked if I would be interested in serving on a committee for an upcoming fundraiser. I told her I would be honored, but that I was surprised she asked me. The committee was mostly wealthy and accomplished people, and I wasn't sure I'd fit it with the local 'movers and shakers.' She said that many of them may be on the 'Who's Who' list, but some signed up for committees only so they could see their names in print. She needed people who would actually DO something, people like me. I was so thrilled, you'd think I'd just got promoted in a paying job. It didn't matter that it was volunteer work. I felt good contributing my time to a good cause, and expanding my horizons at the same time.

"The more I embraced my new activities, the harder it was to be Lisa Doolittle. There had been times in the past when going to work in the clubs was an oasis from my personal life. It had been an escape from Eddie's abuse, an exciting contrast to my wholesome housewife life with Jake, and a refuge from the crushing loneliness of marriage to Luke. As my personal life became more fulfilling and exhilarating, my days at work dragged on endlessly. I was getting too fidgety to keep stripping five or six days a week, with so many more interesting paths to pursue. I had been dancing for more than eight years, the longest I had stayed in any occupation. Still didn't know what else to do. I needed more time to myself to figure out who I was and where I was going.

"I told Norma I was going to cut back on my days, with a mind to transition out of the business in a year or so. She had a hard time fathoming that I would want to leave. *'What are talking about?'* she screeched at me, *'You've got a better body than most of the eighteen-year-olds! Why the hell would you want to leave this business?!'* 'Thanks for the compliment,' I said, 'I may still look okay on the outside, but my knees and back can't take many more years of dancing in high heels. I don't want to end up in a wheel chair by the time I'm forty 'cause I didn't know when to quit.' My reply fell on deaf ears, as most of what you said to Norma did. I didn't bother telling her my soul felt like it was shriveling up, like the feet of the Wicked Witch of the East after Dorothy dropped the house on her.

"I hooked up with one of the nighttime dancers, Spicy, to share an apartment with. Splitting the bills made it possible to cut down to four days a week. Her sister, Sindy, was one of my buddies on the day shift. They were both very creative and made most of their costumes. I admired them for their talent at putting shows together. We all shared a quirky sense of humor. They were two of my favorite co-workers. One day they approached me with a special announcement.

"It was the first time I had done my 'Unknown Stripper' show. They both came into the dressing room after the show. With mischievous grins, they said, 'Well, now that you make your own costumes too, and since everyone thinks you're our sister anyway, we've decided to adopt you.' Then they told me I just needed a new name. 'Hmm,' I said, as I considered what this new name should be. 'No, no, no,' they said, 'we've already picked one for you — since *Sindy* and *Spicy* start with an S, we'll just add an S to your name and make it *Slisa.*' To which I replied, 'If Sindy, Spicy, and Slisa are our first names, what's our last name, Sizzle?' We all burst out laughing. Our trio became 'The Sizzle Sisters' from that day on. I still have a fringed and beaded T-Shirt, bright red with pink letters and silver beads, that says 'Sizzle' on it. We had a lot of fun and complete silliness being The Sizzle Sisters.

"They even put together a *Sizzle Family Album.* They used photos from the dressing room, and from parties we had — not flattering photos, but the dorky ones you hope no one ever sees. They added captions from magazine clippings to make them even more hilarious. I brought it with me to show you, but I don't think we can use any of the photos in the book. We'd need signed releases. I'm not sure some of the people in these photos would want them published, even if I could track them down. I'd like you to see it anyway, Stella. It's a great reminder of how much fun we made to get ourselves through it all. Our comic insanity helped us to keep our sanity." Eve excused herself to retrieve the photo album from the guest room.

When she returned, she motioned for me to join her on the sofa to look through the thick black binder. The opening page featured a man dressed in a black suit with a derby hat, and shoes that looked two sizes too big. He was bent over looking through the viewer of an old-fashioned camera — the kind we associate with the Victorian era, where the photographer drapes a cloth over their head to peer through a mysterious black box with an accordion-like protrusion. Under the image of the large camera and Charlie Chaplin-like photographer was a caption pieced together from various clippings that read, 'Sizzle Family Album, The New Revised Edition.'

"Sindy used to do a show where she'd dress up like Charlie Chaplin," Eve explained. "She found this picture and knew it had to be the title page. She did an awesome Chaplin too. Some of the guys looked bewildered when she'd come out on the stage in a derby hat and mustache, twirling a cane around, but she managed to pull it off. Sometimes I wondered if we all knew each other in a past life. Perhaps we were in Vaudeville together, the way we liked to ham it up."

Eve continued to flip through the pages, sometimes

explaining the context of the photos, other times letting the images speak for themselves. There was an entertaining mix of photos from parties in their private homes to backstage antics in the strip club. The fun-filled pictures were embellished with words, cartoons, and other images clipped from magazines and newspapers. The clever way it was put together showcased the talent of the two sisters who created it. There was surprisingly little nudity, for a photo album of striptease dancers. I commented on this to Eve.

"I was careful about that, Stella, as were many of my co-workers. I didn't want nude pictures of myself turning up years later to haunt me. I didn't know where my career might end up. I wanted to make sure I had control over any photos of myself that could be incriminating someday. So yeah, there's that one of three of us baring one breast backstage, and several of us mooning the photographer at our parties where all you see is a row of anonymous naked butts.

"And this one here—of me and Dawn in Sindy's house on New Year's Eve. Most of the partygoers were strippers and their boyfriends, who had all seen us nude in the club. There were also a few of Sindy's husband's friends, so we wanted to keep it campy but clean. We just did it for a laugh, and to create a little fanfare when the clock turned midnight. We came down the staircase wearing trench coats, to spoof on the cliché of the 'flasher' who shocks people by opening his raincoat and exposing his naked body to unsuspecting strangers. When we opened our coats, we had pasties covering our nipples and wore G-strings, garter belts, and stockings—pretty tame by today's standards.

"I never was a shutterbug. Thank God Sindy and Spicy were handy with their cameras and were able to document those wild times. These photos make it look like it was all fun and games, but they don't tell the whole story. Everyone had their share of heartaches and headaches in that business, but that's not the stuff you tend to photograph." Eve closed the *Sizzle Family Album* and we decided to break for lunch.

18. PUMPKIN LADY

After lunch, Eve continued reminiscing, "My 'Sizzle Sisters,' and other dancer friends, helped me cope with the tedium of stripping. They were also instrumental in my transition out. I hadn't realized how much, until I reflected on the disjointed chain of events that led me out of the labyrinth. I was guided mostly by instinct, like an inchworm who can't see where it's headed, but keeps taking the next step hoping it will lead to the treetop.

"I had a hunch the clubs on Lansdowne Street, and the enigmatic Patrick who owned them, held the key to my escape from Stripperland. Damned if I knew how or why they would figure into my nebulous plan. Yet, it felt important to build on the attention I had gotten from Patrick over Lacey's party.

"On October thirty-first I would turn thirty-one, and wanted my Halloween birthday to be special that year. I decided to enter the costume contest at the Metro. I asked my wild 'n crazy girlfriends to join me.

"I made a stuffed pumpkin out of orange fabric that fit over the trunk of my body, and used the black lace leggings and arm pieces from my saloon-girl striptease costume. My hair was teased out like

Phyllis Diller's and sprayed neon orange. I painted black stars around my eyes and smeared my lips with black lipstick, which made me look like a female member of the band 'KISS.' The look was completed with a mask my 'Sizzle Sisters' made. It was hand-held, so I could cover my face or remove it as I wished. They had dressed it up with sequins, beads, and bright fluffy feathers. My arms, legs, hair and makeup looked exotic. The rotund pumpkin covering my curves was a comical contrast to the rest of my racy outfit.

"When my friends showed up at my apartment I was blown away. They knew I was wearing an orange and black costume and going as the 'Pumpkin Lady.' I hadn't asked them to wear anything specific. They all showed up in mostly black, with a few animal prints thrown into the mix. Each of them looked bewitching in sleek outfits, adorned with flirty fringes of beads, bangles, and spangles.

"Ashley looked wicked in her pointy hat, black spandex pants, and beaded 'Witches are Bitches' T-shirt. Spicy fit her name well, decked out in a skimpy leopard-print tunic. Sindy looked ready to fly in her hooded bat-cape and sparkly top that said, 'Bat's Where it's At.' Maxine wore thigh-high boots and a rhinestoned jacket, without much else. Lacey let her punk-girl go wild in black leather and fishnet stockings, with handcuffs dangling from her waist. Raven was sassy in a shiny leopard cat suit with the words 'Snaggle Puss' across her chest.

"'The whole is greater than the sum of its parts,' rang in my head when I saw the seven of us together.

"We had been earning a living dressing up our bodies to tease and entice. This night we were vamping it up for sheer fun and frivolity. Each one of them had enough pizzazz to take center stage. Instead, they all wore what they thought would be a good backdrop to my Pumpkin Lady outfit, rather than compete with it. They said it was my night, that I was the star and they were like the back-up band. It was generous of them to push me to the forefront like that. I told them we were the 'All-Star Team.' We smoked weed and drank champagne, but I was more buzzed on our friendship, and the energy we created in our bedazzling outfits, than on drink or drug.

"Halloween is a night filled with spectacle, not easy to stand out in a crowd, but jaws dropped when we spilled out of the limo and into the Metro. Any one of us might have turned heads, but the group of us together made them spin around like people possessed. As we paraded into the club, I saw Patrick.

"I approached him covering my face with the mask, then let it fall away to see if he recognized me. 'Oh, it's *you*,' he said. I couldn't tell if he was glad to see me or not. 'Where's your costume?' I asked. 'I'm not a costume kind of guy,' he answered. 'That's what I thought,' I said, 'but since you're hosting this Halloween bash, I thought you should have one, so I made this for you.' I reached into the bosom of my stuffed pumpkin, pulled something out and handed it to Patrick. As he unrolled the large black T-shirt, his face changed from curiosity, to shock, then to an amused grin. The T-shirt had 'Pumpkin Eater' splashed across the chest in orange letters. I had sewn a few scraps of orange fabric below the letters, as if bits of pumpkin had been dribbled on it.

Patrick grabbed my hand and pulled me into a nearby janitor's closet. He leaned over to kiss me, but stopped short, saying, 'It's hard to kiss someone who's wearing black lipstick.' His hand reached for my thigh and landed on a patch of skin right above my lace leggings. 'What's this — *bare flesh?*' he asked. 'Never mind about that,' I said, pushing his hand away. 'I just have a favor to ask — can you make sure I get into the costume contest?' 'Why should I do that?' he replied. 'Because it's my birthday,' I said. 'Well, okay,' he said, 'but all I can promise is that you'll get in. No guarantees on winning.' 'I don't care about winning,' I said, 'I just want to be in it.'

"There were over a thousand people in the nightclub. Only thirty would be chosen to be in the costume contest. I had to use whatever edge I could to get in, but I couldn't have flirted with Patrick like that unless I was truly attracted to him. Nonetheless, I wasn't about to make-out with him on the spot and become a broom-closet bimbo. I rejoined my friends and we danced, drank, and partied until the costume contest was announced.

"One by one the contestants stepped forward on the stage as the emcee announced them. When he summoned me, I turned my back to the crowd, and asked the emcee to pull the string above my shoulder. When he did, the big stuffed pumpkin fell to my feet. Under the puffy outer costume, I had a skimpy orange tunic-length T-shirt. A strand of beaded fringe crossed my upper back, and more beads sparkled around the edges of a large cut-out that exposed my back. Then I turned around and stretched my arms out, showing off the front of the T-shirt. 'Pumpkin Lady' was spelled out in black letters across my chest.

"After ditching the bulbous pumpkin shell, I was as sleek and sexy as the rest of my entourage. The crowd was taken by surprise. A thousand people gasped at once, then followed with thunderous applause.

"I had done a striptease without actually taking anything off. I didn't win the contest, but the crowd's enthusiasm was reward enough for me. I went there to make a scene, cause a little commotion, get noticed. It worked.

"Patrick didn't know what to make of me, but he knew I wasn't someone to overlook. He was not an easy person to impress. A lot of people were vying for his attention. His practiced arrogance was the armor he wore to distance himself from the riff-raff.

"I wasn't sure what I would do once I got his attention, but it felt important not to be invisible to him. I wonder what he ever did with that 'Pumpkin Eater' T-shirt?" Eve said, smiling and shaking her head. "God, I was a silly woman, but *damn*, it sure was fun!" Her smile broadened for a moment. She paused to drink some water, gazing out the window to collect her thoughts.

"That was quite a year. My friend Brian wrote a poem about that post-divorce phase of my life. He asked Sindy to jazz it up. She was an excellent calligrapher, a multi-talented artist."

Eve handed me a parchment-colored page titled *Thirty-First Year*. On the right side was a delicately penned illustration of a tree with a pumpkin at the base of it, and a small owl sitting on one of the bare branches. A few autumn leaves clung to the tree, some were scattered on the ground. Near the tree-top a crescent moon and a star glittered with a dusting of iridescent sparkles. I read the verses aloud, as Eve had requested:

Now I'm thirty-one
My life has just begun
Old strength flows back,
I'm on the right track.

The help of friends and a little time
Brought a peace, a life that's mine.
Went to Maui, with sea so blue,
Saw London town and Paris too.

Brothers, sisters, Dad and me
Quiet lake, warm days, cool tall trees
Time with family, this month of June
Camping and quiet came none too soon.

New horizons for she who dances.
Modeling, acting, both are chances.
They now seem real where once before
Cold despair nearly closed the door.

Nothing's perfect some problems remain
I'm better now, can stand the strain.
Future looks bright with feet on the ground,
My thirty-second year will soon come around.

"It's lovely, Eve. What a special memento," I said. "You talked about your trip to Maui, but what are these other references? Did you go to Europe that year too? And camping with your family?"

"Yes to both, Stella. Dad and several of my siblings had been going to the Adirondacks for years. I needed time with my family and the healing peace of natural wilderness to soothe my bruised and battered spirit. In spite of my fondness for glitz and glamour, I was most comfortable and happy in jeans and a flannel shirt, poking a campfire. Dad instilled us with a love of the outdoors. He had been taking us camping, and on day trips to state parks, since we were big enough to walk. We spent a week on the peninsula of a lake, far from anyone but our little clan. The fresh air, stunning beauty of the forest, and easy company were a galaxy away from the dark smoky barrooms I made my living in. I put my Lisa Doolittle costumes away and reverted back to being

Eve-Marie for a week. I don't know if my siblings knew at the time how I made my living. I told my parents years before this, but we never talked about it after that.

"As for Europe—that was a real hoot.

"When I broke up with Charles, the Brit I dated on the rebound from Luke, I asked one favor of him. I told him I would like to remain friends, but said it would really irk me if he went after any of my closest friends. He seemed to take delight in irking me, and straightaway made a play for Ashley. She came to me and asked how I was with that. I told her to go ahead and date him. I wasn't in love with the guy, after all, and sure wasn't going to let it ruin my friendship with her.

"A few months later he invited Ashley to go to England for a week. She had a boyfriend she lived with, and told Charles it would be easier if she could bring a friend along. It would be a cover for her so her boyfriend wouldn't get jealous. 'Anyone you want,' he said. 'Anytime you're ready. I'm a man of my word. You can bring anyone you want, and I'll pay her way too.' Ashley said Charles nearly fell off his barstool when she told him the friend she wanted to take was *me*. He was 'a man of his word,' and wouldn't back out of it. I knew he was hurt when I dumped him, or at least had a bruised ego. But he was a good sport and let bygones be bygones. So off we went. Charles was already in England when it was time for our trip.

"Ashley and I flew together. We were asked to fill out information cards to go through security. 'Hmm ... what are you putting down for occupation, Ash?' I asked. 'Entertainer,' she replied. I decided to be more specific. I wrote 'Ecdysiast.' I wished I had a movie camera to record the scene when we landed at Heathrow. I handed my 'landing card' to the security officer. The conversation went like this:

(Eve recited the security officer's lines in a fairly good Cockney accent.)

He: 'ow long ya gonna be in London, then?
Me: About four days, then we're going to Paris.
He: Can I see your tickets to Paris?
Me: We don't have them yet.
He: Well, where ya staying then?
Me: We're not sure.
He: 'ow much money 'ave ya got?
Me: About a hundred bucks each.

"At this point, his eyes bugged out of his head. I thought he was about to arrest us for vagrancy. It did sound preposterous to be planning a week in Europe with almost no cash, no tickets to Paris, and no idea where we were staying. He shot questions at me before I could clarify that our friend Charles was picking us up, taking us to his home somewhere north of London, and paying all expenses, including Paris.

"I never did get a chance to explain.

"His widened eyes quickly scanned down my information card. Then his head jerked up as he blurted out, 'What the 'ells *ecdysiast* mean?' I looked him straight in the eye and said, 'It means *striptease artist.'* His eyebrows went up, he took a step backward, and looked us both up and down. Then he stepped aside, waved us through with an elegant gesture and said, 'Go ahead ladies, you'll do alright, then!'

"I suppose he figured if times got tough, we could do a sultry dance on the sidewalk and pass the hat around. Good thing for us Charles was 'a man of his word,' or we might have found out what that security officer meant by 'You'll do alright then.'

"Charles met us at the airport and took us to his lovely country estate. He had a new girlfriend, Julie, he had been seeing for a month. It was a little awkward when he had to tell her he'd invited two young American women to visit for a week. He'd already invited us before he met Julie. She relaxed when it became clear neither one of us was carrying on with Charles.

"I don't want to turn this into a travelogue of my week in Europe, Stella. Suffice it to say we were riding high. Julie's sister joined us for the weekend escapades in Paris. Charles was the center of attention escorting four lovely young women, who were dressed to the nines, to all the Paris hot spots. Ashley and I were gaga over the shows we saw at the Moulin Rouge and the Lido. They made us feel like we were still in striptease kindergarten. Yet, the costumes and choreography would have been over-the-top for the Boston suburbs. It was an exhilarating trip—a healing and renewing adventure after the bumpy ride of the previous few years. I had been so low about my marriage breaking up, but that year life was showing me a world of new possibilities.

"I appreciated the experience of living the high life that week—the best restaurants, chauffeur service, primo champagne for breakfast, if I wanted. Yet, it also confirmed what I already suspected about myself.

"I needed something in my life deeper and more meaningful than anything money could buy. I was looking for a way out of dancing, but beyond that I was looking for something that would make me feel more fulfilled, no matter how I might earn my living." Eve stood up, yawned, and stretched. "If you don't mind, Stella, I'm pretty beat right now," she said. "How about if we save my explorations into the occult for tomorrow?" Eve smiled, winked, shut the recorder off, and headed upstairs to rest before dinner.

19. Celestial Bodies

"Good Morning, Stella!" Eve greeted me with a cheery grin as she poured a cup of coffee, then asked, "Did you sleep well?"

"Actually Eve, that line you left me with yesterday—about the occult—had me tossing and turning a bit," I replied. She picked up from my sideways glance and slight smile that I was joking.

"You should know me well enough by now to know I'm a *good* Witch!" Eve said, as she mimicked my playful expression. I nodded 'yes' in reply. We settled in to our respective places in the parlor.

"I have been called a Witch as far back as I can remember, because of my Halloween birthday," said Eve. "My siblings tried to taunt me by calling me a Witch, but it had the opposite effect. It made me feel special. Witches are mysterious and powerful. Why wouldn't a shy, insecure young girl want to be one? I never fantasized about being wicked, like the famous Witch of 'Oz.' Samantha from 'Bewitched' was more my ideal. She was sweet, and pretty, and could control anything life tossed her way with a mere twitch of her cute little nose.

"Yet, my gullible young mind couldn't shake a slight fear that the story my babysitter, Betty Lou, told me when I was eight would someday prove true.

Betty Lou was alone with me in the kitchen of the house I grew up in. As she told the story, her voice deepened, and she spoke slowly, staring into my eyes like a vampire hypnotizing her victim. She told me that when I turned forty, the Witches would come for me. They would fly me to the top of their secret mountain, force me to drink a foaming green potion, and turn me into one of them.

"I had seen hip teenagers in movies, but Betty Lou was my real-life role model. She was the Queen of Cool in her bubble hairdo and tight clamdiggers, blasting '50s bee-bop tunes on her portable radio. She knew so much more about life than I did. So I thought, *maybe she wasn't just putting me on.* Part of me wished it was true, the other part terrified that it might be. She probably forgot about her fairy tale the next day, but it fascinated and haunted me for years afterward.

"In my thirty-first year I was opening to all kinds of new experiences. I became curious about what it truly means to be a Witch. I knew there were people who called themselves Witches in our modern world. What the media projects and what the mass populace thinks Witches believe or practice was not the real story. I wanted to know the truth, but had no idea where to go to find the answers. When I got serious about it, the answers started coming, as if by magic. I would meet someone who would tell me about a book to read, or where I could take a class, that kind of thing. I followed the clues like a bird following a trail of breadcrumbs.

"I read a book called The Spiral Dance, subtitled '*A Rebirth of the Ancient Religion of the Great Goddess*' by Starhawk. That book wrapped loving arms around me and welcomed me home. The philosophy of seeing nature as sacred resonated deep within my soul. Envisioning deity as female was empowering and healing after living with a lifetime of patriarchy. I loved the idea that I could be a priestess, and create my own prayers and rituals to communicate with the Divine.

"In the church I grew up in, priests were men, and only boys could assist them in the Holy Mass. The women and girls had to sit quietly on the sidelines and live with the implication that we were unworthy to serve the Lord in the sacred ceremonies.

"I was fed up with anything that would reinforce my low self-esteem, whether it was an individual, a powerful organization like the Catholic Church, or a societal double standard. After years of feeling estranged from anything resembling religion, I found a spiritual path that felt right for me. And I wanted to connect with other people who felt it was right for them.

"At the adult-ed center where I took my first acting lesson, I found a course that was an introduction to Witchcraft and Paganism. There was a mix of people from different age groups, and various levels of interest. Some were there to satisfy a passing curiosity.

"I was part of a small group—all women—who followed the teacher, Andras Corban-Arthen, to his car after every class, badgering him with questions. Andras patiently answered us, but didn't slow his pace. When he'd reach his car he'd bid us good evening, speed off, and leave us, with our voracious minds, on the sidewalk. One night, too hungry to wait until the next class, we decided to go out to a local pub to keep the conversation about 'Magick' going.

"That was the beginning of my connection to a larger community of Witches and Neo-Pagans. I went to my first gathering with that core group. There were hundreds of us, all there to re-plant the roots of our souls deep into the rich soil of the earth. All there to reach out to the stars with our hearts and let our spirits soar to the heavens. Well, maybe not all of us—some were there strictly for the party."

"Eve, this all sounds intriguing, but what does it have to do with your life as a striptease dancer?" I asked.

"Great question, Stella," Eve replied. "I can't tell my story without including it. It was an important piece of the puzzle, and will make sense to you soon enough." Eve scrunched her face and rolled her hands over each other. She imitated the shrill and sinister voice of the Wicked Witch of the West and said, *"All in good time, my little pretty—all in good time,"* and finished with a chilling cackle.

Resuming her normal voice, Eve continued, "It was a melting pot—a magical cauldron of people and events swirling around — that directed the course of my life after the divorce. An idea began to stir that took me on a whirlwind of new activity, and connected many diverse aspects of my life.

"I was blessed to have lots of friends who wanted to celebrate my birthday with me. Halloween, as it happens, is a favorite holiday of many people and an easy birthday for them to remember. Friends showed up at my house with bottles of champagne as early as a month before October thirty-first. Many of them said, 'I know how busy you get around your birthday, so I thought we could celebrate early.' I wanted to stay focused on my new activities, but I could not turn down their thoughtful offers to whoop it up.

"It was fun, but exhausting. Before my next birthday rolled around, I needed to do something, or it would end up becoming a two-month stretch of endless partying. I decided to get everyone together and have one big Halloween / birthday party. Then I thought about all the clubs in Boston that made a ton of money at Halloween. I wondered if I could create an event that would take some of that money and steer it toward a good cause.

"I talked to Spicy about my ideas, which included getting some of the other dancers to dress up as phases of the moon and do a brief show to kick off the festivities. She said, 'Why limit it to phases of the moon? Why not include other heavenly bodies?' We joined forces with our other Sizzle Sister, Sindy, and designed several costumes, based on the concept of my Pumpkin Lady ensemble. They would all have two basic parts—a large outer costume that hid our feminine curves, which would be shed at some point to reveal sleek and skimpy outfits.

"The result was more campy and brilliant than anything I had imagined. When Spicy mentioned other heavenly bodies, we were both thinking 'planets.' We were open to hearing ideas from the other dancers we recruited. We ended up with seven wild costumes: the Earth, the Moon, a Shooting Star, Mars, the Milky Way, the Weather, and Heaven's Little Angel.

"Liana was the Earth. Under her stuffed blue planet, she wore a fiery red leotard. A white strip of fabric with the words, 'Center of the Earth's Red-Hot Core' snaked around her body and ended up pointing to her G-spot.

"I was the Moon. Under my silver-sequined moon, I wore a tunic-length T-shirt and navy blue tights. Bands of white sequins streamed across the white T-shirt, like moonbeams. The back was cut out, beaded and fringed around my derriere, with the words 'Lunar Eclipse' spelled out in blue rhinestones across my back. My crazy take on a lunar eclipse—you kinda see the 'moon,' but you kinda don't.

"Spicy was a Shooting Star. A puffy silver star graced the trunk of her body. Underneath, she wore a slinky fringed and beaded tee over shimmery tights. She glowed bright enough to light up the night sky.

"Ashley's outer costume looked like a Milky Way candy wrapper. When it came off, her body was in skin-tight black. A cascade of rhinestones, like a thousand stars, twinkled across her torso and scattered down her shapely legs.

"Cheryl's Mars costume was a stuffed red disc, with crisscross lines and green circles. Someone said it looked more like a pizza with anchovies than the red planet. When she ditched the 'pizza,' she was in a black leotard. Like a beauty pageant queen, a gold sash draped across her body, made to resemble a Mars candy bar label.

"Sindy was the Weather. Half of her head was dripping with silver beads—rain. The other half, draped with multi-colored beads—a rainbow. Her outer costume was a puffy silver cloud. Under it, she wore a pale blue tank top and tights. A rainbow of bright sequins coming out of a cloud was splashed across her chest. I would have loved to see the local weatherman track the storm she was brewing up in that outfit.

"Roxie wouldn't wear a big outer costume. Puffy sleeves were as far as she would go. She looked innocent in her silver and white fairy-princess frock and white angel wings. Under it, she wore silver tights and a skimpy camisole with 'Heaven's Little Angel' glimmering from her midriff. If you knew Roxie like we all did, you'd understand how funny that was. This was a woman who always matched her underwear to her dress, as she was likely to do an impromptu handstand at any given moment, regardless of where she was or who was watching. Her impish personality made her more like Heaven's *Devilish* Angel.

"We were the 'Celestial Bodies in Orbit,' and we were out to dazzle the universe, if only for a night!

"The event would be called 'Video Magic Night.' I recruited artists through the Boston Film/Video Foundation, a nonprofit that fostered talent in film and video arts. I hired them to shoot film, video, and still photos, which would later be edited into a short video. The plan was to do another party in a year and show the video. I hoped it would build a following for the event—all the people who attended the first one would bring their friends the next year to see the video. It was the early '80s. MTV was just becoming a household word. Cell phones that could record images were not even on the radar. The idea of making a video out of our party was cutting-edge, and did the trick to create a buzz.

"All the pieces of the puzzle were falling into place. There was just one problem—I hadn't booked the club yet. I had been trying to reach Patrick, the owner of Spit and Metro. He was playing hard to get, like some high school prom queen prima donna.

"I didn't blame him for not returning my calls. I had been using some unconventional tactics to get his attention—showing up in wild outfits with my high-spirited friends at the clubs, and sending campy pictures of myself to his office to keep my face fresh in his mind. So, I got him to notice me, but he thought I was this crazy chick. He seemed amused by my antics when I confined them to the nighttime club scene, but during the day, in his office, he was all about business. He must have thought I was only about monkey business.

"The night of the party was only three weeks away. If I didn't secure the location soon, there would be no lead-time to promote it. I had all these people helping me put this thing together. If I couldn't book the club, I wouldn't be able to show my face to them again. My career as an event coordinator would be over before it started. My fingernails became my favorite snack.

"I gave up trying to call Patrick. I parked my fanny in the waiting room of his office for three days straight until he found time to see me. I think he was in shock when I told him what I was there for — shock, and disappointment. He was probably hoping I wanted to crawl under his desk and do something cheap and superficial with him, not book his nightclub for a Halloween charity event." Eve paused a moment to change her position on the sofa.

"What made you think he expected, as you put it, 'monkey business'?" I asked.

"I wasn't just imagining it, Stella, if that's what you're thinking," Eve replied. "We were alone in his office. He put his arms around me and said, 'You look like the type that likes to be cuddled.' He leaned over and was about to kiss me. My heart stood just about still, my body was on fire. I wanted to melt into his broad shoulders. It took all my inner strength to push his arms away. I said, 'Yes, I am, but I'm particular about who I'm cuddling with, and where.' He backed off right away. I explained that, much as I was attracted to him, I had no intention of becoming a backroom bimbo. He nodded, as if to say I was right—I would have been tossed aside like a candy wrapper after he'd had his sugar fix.

"He listened to my ideas for 'Video Magic Night' and hooked me up with the club manager to work out the details. He could only offer a Monday night, at Spit, the smaller of the two clubs. It was perfect. With only two weeks to promote it, I didn't think I could get a big enough crowd for the Metro anyway.

"There wasn't enough lead-time to make it a charity event for a bona fide nonprofit, but I wanted to set a precedent for future events. We billed it, 'On Behalf of Independent Film/Video Artists' and said the $5.00 donation was for the production of the video.

"The next two weeks were a flurry of activity—finishing costumes, rehearsing, mailing invites—and working my day job, stripping. Days I had to work in the club I felt like a caged tiger. I couldn't wait until I was free again to keep working on my little event.

"I was doing whatever I could to promote 'Video Magic Night.' I went to the Metro a few nights before the event with a stack of postcards. I passed them out to anyone who looked cool to invite them to the party. I was in a panic, afraid there wouldn't be enough people to make it a success.

"Maybe it was lack of sleep, or my obsessive state of mind, or a slight buzz from smoking and drinking. Pushing my way through the nightclub, looking for the next person to hand an invite to, I failed to see the step down in front of me. I landed sprawled out face down across a wide set of carpeted stairs. My legs were splayed out behind me, my left foot twisted at a very disturbing angle.

"Three days before my big night, I mangled my ankle. It wasn't broken, but badly sprained. *Damn the luck!* The doctor said to keep it elevated for a few days and stay off of it—as if that was going to happen. I'd been through it before: being hurt and still muddling my way through a performance. I taped it up, and threw a band of sequins around it to make it look like part of my costume. Then I downed a couple shots of tequila to numb the pain. I had pulled too many people into it, and staked too much of my hope on that night to let a gimpy ankle hold me back.

"Thanks once again to Keith, we arrived in high style. He contributed a couple of limos to transport me and the other 'Celestial Bodies' to the club. The planning, sewing and rehearsing took countless hours, but our ten-minute show was worth the effort. It jump-started the party and gave the film crew a sparkly spectacle to shoot.

"The show was simple. We came out on the stage one by one, dancing around in our comically puffy costumes. The last to parade onto the stage was Spicy, in her 'Shooting Star.' She appeared when the song

'Lucky Star' by Madonna started playing. Then we lined up, side by side across the stage. We danced in our 'chorus line' until there was a break in the song where Madonna is singing, '... shine your heavenly body tonight ...' That was our cue to drop our outer costumes and reveal the campy, body-hugging attire underneath. The crowd went berserk, applauding, hooting, and hollering as we finished up the act dancing around in our sexy little outfits.

"All of us ladies had been cheered for years for baring it all on stage. It was exhilarating to get the applause and still be dressed. We had managed to pull off a striptease, of sorts, without getting naked.

"The event felt like a success, except for one thing: I had hoped we'd pull in a bigger crowd. With a short time frame to promote it, and a very teeny budget, we got about a hundred and fifty people. Later that night I found out the club manager was very impressed that we got so many people on a Monday night. He told me we were sharing the club with another event, which was sponsored by a clothing store. They didn't pull anyone in, even with an advertising budget that bought them radio ads. Monday night was a dead zone for parties, so I guess we did okay after all.

"The crowd may have been small, but their enthusiasm wasn't. The energy throughout the night was electric. We called it 'Video Magic Night' and it truly was magical. Our stage performance was part of that, but it was the spirit of the people who came that really carried the night. I made enough money to cover the costs, and staged my first public event. It was successful enough to encourage me to plan another one.

"I still didn't know how it would lead me out of stripping, but it gave me something to latch on to. I grabbed hold of the Halloween party idea like it was a life-preserver that would save me from drowning in the dark sea of strip club life."

20. NEW IDENTITY

After lunch, Eve continued describing her serpentine journey out of the strip club world. "I wouldn't have known about the Boston Film/Video Foundation if it wasn't for my acting coach," she said. "Eleanor encouraged her students to take a course at BF/VF, called 'From Script To Screen—The Production Process.' She said it might help our acting to have an overview of the fundamentals of creating a film.

"Besides meeting the video artists who helped me document 'Video Magic Night,' I made other connections through BF/VF, and volunteered to work on a film and video conference. I met a man named Gene at the conference, who I ended up having a brief affair with. He wasn't the usual kind of guy I was into dating. Sticking to 'my type' hadn't worked out too well. I was trying to broaden my horizons. He was tall, a bit handsome, and worked on Wall Street. He was married, but separated from his wife and three daughters. As our affair progressed, he confessed he had a girlfriend he lived with in New York. I wasn't interested in being a third wheel, so I cut the relationship off.

"Before we broke up, he mentioned a man in the investment business whom he had great admiration for. He was often prattling on about business bigwigs, but I wasn't particularly interested in them merely because they were wealthy. Gene had read an article about Dean in *Fortune Magazine* that said he was interested in the I Ching. I wanted to meet anyone who explored the wisdom of the great sage, even if he was a millionaire. I wrote to him and sent him a copy of Carol Anthony's book on the I Ching. Dean sent me a lovely thank-you note and asked to meet me.

"Gene was all wrong for me—a neurotic three-timing liar and cheat, who was also delusional. He thought I would want to give him more children. He must have been wearing earplugs when told him I never wanted kids. Yet, I will always be grateful to him. I never would have heard of Dean if it had not been for Gene. Dean became a very special friend who played a significant role in my transition out of stripping.

"The first time we met was in his office. I felt quite out of place riding the elevator to the twelfth floor of the Federal Reserve Bank Building. I wore the most business-like dress I owned—a beige silk shift with a Native American-style print, belted at the waist. I still looked bohemian, with wavy hair flowing wild and free, and strappy high heels. I wasn't the three-piece suit type, but this was a social call, not a job interview.

"My acting skills stepped up to the plate. I put on my 'serene and regal' mask as I approached the receptionist. No one but me knew my palms were drenched and my stomach was tight as a drum. I was led to a room that overlooked Boston Harbor and all of Southie. Left to wait at a large conference table, I was so out of my element I was ready to bolt. When Dean walked in, my apprehension dissolved. There was such warmth coming from those aquamarine blues, I felt I'd known him all my life.

"We were an unlikely pair—a strip tease dancer with no more than a high-school education, and a genius, Harvard MBA lion of the investment world. He never made me feel small or insignificant—quite the opposite. I felt exalted around him. It wasn't his money. That provided us with a pleasant backdrop for our get-togethers, but it wasn't the essential thing that drew me to him. It was the sparkle in his eyes, his keen intelligence. He looked at the world with both childlike curiosity and the deep comprehension of a mystical wise man.

"I loved him, not only for who he was, but also for the way he made me see myself. I was blonde, and a stripper—two things strongly, and wrongly, associated with the word d-u-m-b. Having the attention of a man as intelligent as Dean was validation that I was no dummy. He believed in me, and that helped me to believe in myself.

"As far as what he saw in me, well, he was a man, and I *was* pretty dishy back then. He probably had his pick of gorgeous women who were more appropriate for him—educated, rich, and socially connected. I think he had a rebellious streak in him that took delight in dating someone his peers might have raised an eyebrow over. It wasn't just my occupation that was unconventional. He seemed to get a kick out of hearing about my spiritual explorations too. I don't suppose he met many women in the investment world who were into Wicca—at least any who could risk being open about it.

"My friends couldn't figure out what I saw in this 'straight-laced' businessman who was nearly twenty years older than me. They thought I should find someone who had more time for me. He was divorced from the mother of his two children, and re-married to his business. We only saw each other a few times a month. That was perfect for me. I was focused on making my way out of the strip-tease life. Seeing him occasionally gave me someone special to channel my romantic energies and fantasies toward, without monopolizing my time. The time we did spend together always felt like an oasis. We escaped from our diverse worlds and their cares, and lost ourselves in the easy and uplifting company of each other.

"He took me to some upscale places, including the Harvard Club, elite hangout of the Boston aristocracy. I followed his lead on which of the ten pieces of silverware I should use first. Dean was a class act—not because of his money, but because he chose to treat people who didn't have it with the same courtesy and respect as those who did. He encouraged me not to be apologetic about my profession. If society in general were as open-minded as he was, I may not have felt the need to be so guarded about my stripping.

"That was close to thirty years ago. I don't think striptease dancers have gained much ground in social status since then. The world has a love/hate relationship with them. Societal attitudes contributed to my own mixed feelings about stripping. I never lived my life based on what society thinks. But I longed to find out if I was capable of being/doing/becoming more than what that life offered me." Eve paused a minute to stretch and sip some lemonade.

"Sounds like this guy Dean was in a position to set you up in a new life, Eve. Is that what you were hoping for?" I asked.

"I had hopes and dreams, Stella, but they didn't center around Dean, or any other man. Occasionally I played with the idea of marrying him, trying it on the way one would try on a dress to see if it fit. I could never get a clear vision in my daydreams of what that would look like. All the material comforts would be there, but beyond that it felt empty. He'd be busy with his business and I'd spend my time—*doing what? Finding new ways to spend his money?* Toying with the idea helped reaffirm that what I was looking for had to do with self-fulfillment, with discovering what, besides undressing creatively, my talents were.

"When I wasn't dancing or seeing Dean, I kept myself busy with acting classes, and my explorations into Wicca and goddess religion. I also spent much of my time taking the Halloween party to the next level.

"In the months following 'Video Magic Night' I met with my friend Dan to edit the material my film crew had shot into a short video. There were hours of video and super-eight film. We had to condense it and try to make it interesting. Dan was my hero. He donated a good deal of his time. He had also earned hours of studio time, through volunteering at BF/VF, which he generously used to help me.

"Many nights we worked 'til three a.m., in a closet-sized room, editing until our eyes went blurry. When we got the visuals to a place we were happy with, Dan said, 'Now we have to think about a soundtrack.' I said, 'Oh, I've already been kicking some ideas around.' I showed him my selection of songs. I knew exactly where I wanted to use them, and fade out and segue to the next. I even had a tape of someone playing a saw for a weird sci-fi 'wah-wah' effect. Dan said I had a real knack for putting sets of music together. He told me I could probably get a job in broadcasting if I wanted to.

"He had no idea I was a stripper, and had been putting sets of music together for my shows for years. I paused for a moment, deciding whether or not to tell him how I developed my special talent for programming music. I trusted Dan. I knew he wouldn't think less of me. But I decided if I was going to leave 'Stripper-World' behind, it didn't serve me to keep telling new people I met about my profession.

"His comment stayed with me. It made me aware that I had been building skills and talents through my striptease job that could be applied to other things. It helped me to appreciate how every job I've ever had added to my repertoire. Even jobs that felt like a depressing waste of time contributed knowledge that would turn out to be useful in the long run. Sometimes it was knowledge that helped me in another job—other times, knowledge that led to a deeper understanding of life.

"Staging that first party, and planning the next, was a roll-your-shirtsleeves-up endeavor. I had such a passion for it that it didn't seem like hard work. Once I became committed to taking the Halloween party further, the universe magically provided me with all I needed to make it happen.

"My 'Celestial Bodies' buddies had already done so much to help. I wanted them to just attend the next party and enjoy themselves. I had to look elsewhere for talent. It was Dan's idea to recruit some of the BF/VF artists to showcase their videos, along with the one we created. We would kick-off the festivities with a ninety-minute screening of several videos. That was a good start, but I needed some hot music to rock the party.

"I met a guy named Jonathan one night in Spit. We were the only two on the dance floor without partners, dancing wild and free in our own energy fields until we nearly collided. After taking a few more spins around, we went out to my car and hung in the parking lot shooting the breeze. Jonathan might be the zingiest guy I ever met. I was instantly attracted to him. Not as a lover, I was content with Dean for that. In the middle of our conversation he reached toward my face. I thought he was going to grab me and start making out. I was about to put on the brakes, give him the 'I just wanna be friends' speech, when he grabbed something I hadn't expected. He pulled two chopsticks from my hair, unraveling my blond curls from the bun they held in place. Then he started drumming all over the dashboard of my car with them.

"He was a drummer. He could resist the urge to kiss me, but couldn't pass up a shot to ratta-tat-tat with my makeshift drumsticks. I loved the silly sweet surprise of that moment. We became buddies and hung out from time to time. That chance meeting added another piece of the puzzle to my party plans. His band, 'Judy's Tiny Head,' would play at the next Halloween party.

"More key players came from the connections I was making in the Wiccan and Neo-Pagan community. One new friend was a professional dancer—jazz and modern, not stripping. She recruited several other dancers to perform a couple of numbers that would bewitch the partygoers. A woman in the dance show, Paula, knew a bit about publicity and offered to help with that as well.

"The line-up for the night was rounded out with a street performer, 'Alexander, King of Jesters.' When I spotted him in Faneuil Hall riding a unicycle, juggling swords, and playing the flute all at the same time, I had to recruit him. I enlisted Bradley J, a DJ from the local rock station, to emcee the evening and host the costume contest.

"It was all falling into place, but it wasn't going to be the event I dreamed of unless it was a charity fundraiser. I went to my friend Stan, the Secretary of the Boston Film/Video Foundation. BF/VF artists had been instrumental in the success my first Halloween party. I thought their organization should benefit from the next, which I decided to call the 'Pumpkin Lady's Ball.' Stan thought the idea was great. He told me to come back with a written proposal and the means to fund the production costs.

"This was virgin territory. The first party was planned using the 'fly-by-the-seat-of-your-pants' method. I had never written a proposal before. No one ever asked me for one to apply for a striptease job. I did my best to organize my chaotic thoughts onto a few sheets of paper, typed out on an old IBM Selectric. Petrified of looking like the amateur I was, I asked my acting coach, Eleanor, to look it over before I brought it to BF/VF.

"She read it in silence. I waited across the room, fidgeting with a handkerchief. When Eleanor finished scanning it, she glared at me and said, *'Who taught you to do this?'* Her demeanor was so intense, I thought there was something drastically wrong with my proposal. I figured she wanted to know who to blame for misguiding me. I took so long to answer that she finally said, *'Nobody – am I right? You did it all yourself?'* I squeaked out a sheepish, 'Yes.' To my great relief she went on to praise my effort, saying that I had great instincts and a heap of common sense. She told me those qualities would also aid my work in acting, if I chose to pursue it.

"In the months that followed, I became more interested in the behind-the-scenes production end of things. I tapered off on my acting classes, but the knowledge and self-confidence I gained from my time with Eleanor were an integral part of the new person I was becoming.

"My proposal was approved by the BF/VF Board, contingent on my ability to raise the funds. Once again, I was playing 'beat the clock.' I needed about two thousand dollars to produce the Ball. Two grand went a lot further in 1985 than it does now, but it was still beyond my reach.

"I had no experience soliciting sponsors. My lead-time to promote the event would evaporate while I was pounding the pavement to drum up the money. Dean came to my rescue. He made a donation to BF/VF to cover the costs, but made it clear it was a one-time favor. He had enough charities on his gift list already, but wanted to help jump-start my new career.

"Many fortuitous circumstances contributed to the creation of the Pumpkin Lady's Ball. The Fairy Godmother of Serendipity was watching over me. She put people in my path, and ideas in my head, that were the magic ingredients leading to my success. It's hard to call it *my* success, as I have so many people to thank for making it possible.

"The event connected people from many facets of my life. Fellow striptease dancers, acting and film connections, movers and shakers I met through networking, and scores of Witches and Pagans came together. We joined forces to build the event into one of the hottest Halloween happenings Boston had ever seen.

"I was moving farther away from my 'Lisa Doolittle' persona and embracing 'The Pumpkin Lady' as my new identity."

21. THE GOODBYE GIRL

"Eve, you mentioned that your explorations into Wicca were an integral part of your transition out of stripping. Were you referring to the connections you made that helped you with the Pumpkin Lady's Ball?" I asked.

"They were indeed a major factor, Stella," she replied. "One connection in particular, Paula, was pivotal in raising the bar on the event. I met her in a class I took on Witchcraft. She saw the potential of the Ball after helping with the second one. She partnered with me to produce the next two.

"We learned a lot from each other. I learned a great deal from her about the administrative aspects of running a big event. She learned what a pain-in-the-wazoo it was to co-produce with an alcoholic pothead.

"It's a miracle that we accomplished as much as we did, given that I still had some serious growing up to do. The event flourished, and our friendship survived, in spite of my chronic substance abuse. I can't imagine what we could have accomplished had I gotten clean and sober then, instead of waiting several years. Goddess bless her for hanging in there with me!

"Many people I met through the Wiccan/Pagan

community volunteered to help. Countless others attended the Ball. Those connections were vital to the success of the event. There were also other facets to my spiritual explorations into Wicca, which helped me in my transition. I had experiences that opened up my consciousness and expanded my perceptions in ways that are difficult to articulate. If I *could* describe them to you, it would fill another book.

"Most relevant to my life as an ecdysiast, was the change in my attitudes toward sexuality. I came of age during the 'Free Love' movement of the '60s. I stripped and enticed men for a living for ten years. Yet through it all, my Catholic guilt and the Puritan attitudes of our culture told me I should be ashamed. I wasn't totally ashamed, but I was never completely comfortable with sex, or stripping, either.

"The Wiccan philosophy of seeing nature as sacred struck a chord deep within my psyche. If everything in nature that comes in pairs is having sexual intercourse, how could it be dirty and disgusting? Sex isn't vulgar—it's our minds that are. I don't mean sex when used as a weapon, such as cases of rape. Sexual assault is beyond vulgar.

"Consensual adults sharing pleasure through sexual union can be sordid or sacred, depending on one's perspective. My earliest views had been formed by the Catholic Church, which considered sex outside of marriage a sin. It implied even marital sex was unclean by demanding that clergy remain unmarried and celibate.

"I embraced the life-affirming beliefs of The Craft and Neo-Paganism that validated my sexuality as something to be divinely celebrated. I found myself onstage contemplating the link between modern strip-tease dancers and the temple priestesses of ancient cultures, who danced sacred dances to raise energy for healing and prosperity. Some guys in the audience may have been there to suck down a beer and jerk off over a naked chick, but that didn't mean I couldn't secretly channel some healing energy their way. Whether it worked or not, I'll never know, but it helped me get through those final months of stripping to have something more noble to focus on.

"When I began to explore Wicca, I discovered that several of my co-workers were curious about it as well. Some already considered themselves Witches. I wasn't surprised. Strippers have the same yearning for, or indifference to, spiritual connection as anyone else might. Why wouldn't they be drawn toward a religion that was more accepting of people living alternative lifestyles?

"I remember some of us talking about it in the dressing room one day, wondering if we had been in a coven together in a past life. The ideal in a coven is to join together 'In Perfect Love and Perfect Trust.' That is the kind of bond I felt with my closest stripper friends. Perhaps our kinship *had* started centuries before we ended up in the Squire together.

"Through my new spiritual path I found tools for healing my past wounds. I came to understand that hanging on to anger, such as I still carried for Eddie, was detrimental to my well-being. Through ritual and prayer I was able to forgive him. As I did, the aches and pains in my body from his brutality began to subside.

"No matter how badly I wanted to quit stripping, it's what I was used to. I was tethered to that life like an infant feeding on mother's milk. Having a newfound spirituality, and community of like-minded people, eased my transition. It provided a path as soft and solid as the earth herself to journey forth on. It helped me to replace fear with faith and move toward a life of positive self-transformation.

"A basic tenet of Wicca is the 'Threefold Law of Return'—whatever you do comes back to you three times as great. It's about taking responsibility for your actions. No sinning all week, then going to confession to have your sins erased like chalk on a blackboard. It's much like the Hindu and Buddhist concept of karma.

"'No one will know the difference twenty years from now,' used to be my excuse to take dangerous risks—like trying LSD, or leaving my hometown with an ex-convict. Now I believe everything we do sends out ripples that may last through eternity. My Pagan path helped me to choose health, wholeness, light, and love as the ripples I wish to send out to the universe.

"Not that I, or my life, became perfect at the wave of a magic wand. The changes were gradual, and often subtle. It wasn't until I was ready to quit the

'Biz' that I reflected on how far I had come since I first stepped onto the striptease stage. I remembered my paralyzing stage fright, which was surpassed by my desperation to escape from Eddie. Quite the contrast to the confident woman I had become, who looked forward to the next chapter of her life with exuberant optimism." Eve stood up to stretch, smiling as she reached toward the ceiling. She spread her fingers out in a gesture that seemed to invite sunbeams and rainbows to shower her. "Much better to have hope and joy motivate you than fear and anxiety," she added.

"The time had finally come to move on. It was between the second and third Pumpkin Lady Balls—in 1986. I don't remember the exact month. I wasn't earning more than a stipend from producing the event. No money saved to make the transition. One of my 'club buddies,' 'Little Lou,' offered to help me until I could make it on my own. He swore I would owe him nothing for the favor. I looked for other work right away, but having him to fall back on gave me the incentive to take the leap.

"I went to Norma to give my notice. She actually said, 'What do you mean, *quit? You can't quit!* If you need a break that's okay, but you'll come back after that, *right?'* I told her I wasn't just leaving the Squire, I was leaving *the business*. She looked through me like I was already a ghost. I was flattered she thought me so valuable that she was in denial about my resignation, but it was bizarre at the same time. The beginning and middle of my dancing career felt surreal, why shouldn't the end? I assumed from her response she wouldn't be throwing me a 'bon-voyage' party.

"During the next couple of weeks, many of my fellow dancers wished me farewell. As we shared good-bye hugs backstage, I was struck by how many times I heard, 'You've helped me so much ...' I never thought I had done much for anyone, except maybe Toni.

"She was a dancer I had met years before, at the Checkmate. Toni was a salt-of-the-earth type whose life had taken some nasty turns. She got strung out on dope after surgery left her hooked on morphine. She was one of the most giving people I ever met. Then she ran head-on into some of the biggest takers. They took everything she had, leaving her a shell of her former self. She landed in a mental hospital after trying to jump off a roof.

"When I found out, I went to the looney bin to visit her. She was so wasted on Thorazine she hardly recognized me. She made it out of there and into a halfway house. When I went to see her there, she was getting her spark back. I told her she was welcome to stay with me until she got back on her feet. She would be eligible to get financial help from Social Services, but not without an address. I didn't want her to end up back on the street, so I took her in for about three months.

"Toni and I lost touch for a few years after that.

Then I bumped into her when I went to a clinic for a routine physical. She was working there as a counselor, helping other addicts recover. She hugged me so tight she nearly squeezed the stuffings out of me, and told me I saved her life. She had been ready to pack it in, felt no reason to live. I was the only person to visit her in the mental hospital after her suicide attempt. She said she had always looked up to me. So, if I thought she was special enough to go to that hell-hole to see her, then maybe her life was worth living after all. I had thrown a life preserver to her, and there she was, years later, throwing one out to others.

"What my other friends were referring to wasn't as dramatic as Toni's story. As I asked each one what help I had given them, the answers varied. Sometimes it was a shoulder to cry on. Others said they saw how I was turning my life around and it inspired them to make changes in their own.

"One told me I always had a safety pin handy when she needed one. We laughed as we hugged good-bye, trying not to let misty eyes streak our mascara.

"I was taken back to that day ten years before, sitting at the bar in the Surf, wondering what I was doing in that decrepit place, and hearing that voice that said, 'If you help one person, that is why you are here.' The person I helped most was me, but somehow the ripple effect of healing myself blessed others along the way.

"My co-workers couldn't let my last day end with a

fizzle. They took me out for Mexican to celebrate. There were about twelve of us wild and crazy ladies, guzzling champagne and Margaritas. In the midst of the festivities I couldn't help but think back to my early days in the business—how insecure and alone I had been. I'm sure I had a toke or two, and a few drinks in me, but I was higher on the love I was feeling that night than anything else. As they showered me with humorous cards and good-luck gifts, I felt a cascade of appreciation for the treasures I would take with me. I was leaving the business rich in friendship and memories.

"Ten years after I first danced in spiked heels, I was wiser and healthier than I'd ever been. I had learned many lessons, gained confidence in my talents and abilities. I had developed an inner strength that comes from surviving hardship and despair. That should be the natural progression of maturing. Maybe it would have happened anyway, if I hadn't become a striptease dancer." Eve shrugged and then added, "Not that I was entirely grown-up at that point. That's a life-long process for some of us 'kids.'"

"Eve, you described your first time on stage so vividly, do you remember your last show?" I asked.

"I don't recall my last dance with the same clarity as that first one," Eve replied. "The emotional intensity wasn't the same. I certainly wasn't terrified like I was that first day. In many ways it was just another routine show. I kept a low profile about it being my last day, because of the way Norma was acting. She wasn't pleased that I was leaving, so I didn't tell a lot of the regulars. I remember looking out at them from the stage, thinking how strange it was that they didn't know it was the last song of my last striptease.

"I thought The Goodbye Girl by David Gates was my last song—it came to mind when I was trying to recall my final show. That song got my friend Ashley all choked up. I went backstage after it played to find her teary-eyed, holding my pair of silver spikes. She asked me if she could take them to have them bronzed—then she would return them. I never saw those shoes again, but she and I had a good laugh over it years later. What would I have done with a pair of bronzed stripper shoes? They'd make nice bookends, I suppose. They would also have raised a lot of questions I might not want to answer.

"I recently went through my box of tapes and found the cassette with that song on it. It was one of my softer, more romantic sets. I wore my 'Valentine' costume. The bra, jock, and G-string were white lace, edged with ruffles, and topped with red sequined hearts. Over it I wore a negligee of sheer red, trimmed with ruffled white lace. I looked like something you'd unwrap for Valentine's Day expecting to find a box of chocolates.

"The first song of my last set was *Going Out of My Head* by Little Anthony and the Imperials. I danced the entire song with my complete outfit on. I used the negligee for part of the second song, *Show Me Some*

Affection by Dave Mason. I was down to my under-pieces for *Can't Take Love for Granted* by Graham Parker. I ditched my bra on that song, covering and uncovering my breasts with my arms in my usual teasing way. Never got used to being bare-chested and bare-assed after all those years.

"Then I danced to *The Goodbye Girl* and stripped down to my G-string. One last time I disregarded the fan letter that urged me to dance the last part of my act completely naked.

"I put on my negligee before I shed my G-string, swirling layers of diaphanous red fabric around my naked body. I floated like a love goddess in red spiked heels for the final time to the song *Since I Don't Have You* by Art Garfunkel. That was the final tune I swayed around to as 'Lisa Doolittle.'"

After a long silence, Eve reached across the coffee table and shut the tape recorder off.

22. SHADY PAST

When I woke the next morning, Eve was sitting on the patio enjoying her coffee. Dawn lit the garden with a golden mist. She looked so serene, I didn't want to disturb her. As if she could feel my eyes on her, she turned my way. She smiled and waved for me to join her.

"You looked so deep in thought, Eve, I figured I should leave you alone," I said.

"Oh no, Stella, it's too early to be deep into anything but my magic wake-up brew. *Cheers!*" She said, clinking her mug against mine. "I reckon we're nearly finished with our recording sessions. I'm going to miss your garden and our little talks. My husband must be wondering if I'm ever coming home. You're probably wondering if I'm ever going to leave!"

We talked about the next steps to turn the tapes into a book. I asked Eve if she could stay one more week, to read the first draft before she left. Then we could continue the work long-distance.

After breakfast and showers we settled into our familiar places in my parlor. I turned the tape recorder on for our final session.

"So, Eve, what did you do after your exit from

dancing?" I asked.

"I was still intent on producing the Pumpkin Lady's Ball," she began. "I was used to the rush of being on stage. The manic energy it took to coordinate a big event filled an adrenaline void after I hung up my dancing shoes. My obsessing paid off. I didn't earn a living at it, but eventually I was able to build a resume with my event planning and charity work as the keystone. That Halloween event was the bridge that led to a 'real-world' livelihood.

"I needed most of my daytime hours free, to attend business meetings and do other organizational work on the Ball. I went back to something I thought I'd never do—waiting tables. I began cocktail waitressing at an upscale steak house. Shortly after I started, they offered me an assistant bookkeeper job as well. I made more money waiting tables, but the office job was a better resume-builder. It was also a nice balance to being out on the floor.

"It was a hopping place, especially on weekends. The lounge was a holding pen for people waiting to be seated for dinner. They often had a two-hour wait, even with reservations. Folks get ornery when they're hungry, and biding their time swilling liquor. All those years practicing the fake 'Lisa' smile came in handy, dealing with obnoxious drunks asking for the tenth time, *'Miss, why isn't our table ready yet?'*

"It was a blessing to go down to the basement, far away from the din of the restaurant, to count cash and balance the daily sales reports. I worked alone most of the time in my bookkeeper role. That suited me just fine.

"I had a slight fear that someone would recognize me from the clubs, and my new boss and co-workers would find out about my 'shady past.' I wasn't overly concerned. Most likely if a guy came in who knew me from a strip club he would be with his wife or girlfriend. He'd be squirming more than me over a potential encounter.

"It never happened at the restaurant, but I did see someone I knew from the Squire at a mall one day. The guy was with his wife and kids. He had a look on his face like the world was about to end when he spotted me. I smiled and winked at him and saw the color coming back to his face as I walked on by.

"The incident amused me, but also made me wonder how many times I might have been recognized by a customer who ducked out of sight before I could notice him. All this shame and secrecy—I wonder if it will ever change? There must be a few wives who know and accept that their men frequent strip clubs, but they would be an exception. For most of the married or otherwise committed guys, it is a secret pleasure—a part of their lives they share with their buddies, but not with their women.

"I left the business, but it's hard to shake the stigma that comes with having been a striptease dancer. It's not something you go around blurting out to people if you're trying to make it in 'polite society.' Yet, after ten years it was hard to stop feeling like a stripper. It was part of my nature. It had forged me, like a steel sword, into the person I was. I didn't feel personal shame about it. I kept it hidden because I knew the way the world works. Some people are open-minded and don't judge you on it, others think it's scandalous. The uncertainty about people's reactions kept me tight-lipped in my subsequent jobs.

"There was something I enjoyed about having a secret past, especially when I left the restaurant to work at an insurance company. I could hardly have picked a more conservative arena than the life insurance business as my next career move. It's an atmosphere that encourages conformity and frowns upon extremes of individual expression.

"I've read about women who wear sexy lingerie under their business attire so they can smile to themselves throughout the day thinking, *'If only my straight-laced co-workers knew about the other side of me ...'* There are men who look quite conventional, but under their Brooks Brothers suits they are tattooed from their neck to their wrists.

"These people, like me, chafe at the constraints of the office cubicle and yearn to keep a connection to something primal and untamed in themselves. I wore my 'shady past' beneath my office-appropriate costume like a secret lace garter belt that helped me remember I was still wild and free.

"Perhaps that is part of the fascination people have for strippers—we are able to shed inhibitions and break taboos that are programmed into us. Our freedom of expression can be alluring to some, and threatening to others. That might explain the love/hate attitudes of society toward strippers.

"A similar need to connect with the essence of who I am drew me to a spiritual path that some call the 'Old Religion.' There was no going back to my Catholic roots—wearing a flowered hat, clutching a hymnal with my little white gloves, as I watched the priest and altar boys on stage.

"I felt a deeper connection to the Divine dancing half-naked around a bonfire in an oak grove than I ever did kneeling in church pews, cut off from the beauty of nature by thick stone walls. I don't mean to put down organized religion, I'm just saying it no longer worked for *me*. I've kept the tenets of my original faith that resonate with me—the teachings of Christ in their purest form—but left the man-made rules and regulations of Catholicism behind. I do believe that 'Jesus Saves,' but so does the Goddess, Buddha, Allah, Vishnu, and the Great Spirit. Even atheists can find salvation through connecting to the goodness in their hearts." Eve excused herself to get another cup of coffee.

When she returned, I commented on how she often brought up the subject of religion, and her spiritual path.

"I'm sure it's not what one expects in a stripper's memoir, Stella. Yet, my story would lack the dimension and truth of who I was, and am, without it. I was on a self-destructive path even before I became a dancer. After having my body broken by Eddie, and my heart broken by Luke, I could easily have escalated my drinking and drugging to the point of no return.

"If I believed *all* we humans *are* is flesh alone—without a soul or divine aspect to us—I may have packed it in. Throughout the roller-coaster life I was living, I never moved so far away from the core being that I am—that I think we all are—that I was in real danger of falling into the abyss. Remembering my connection to spirit kept me striving to heal, improve myself, and move toward becoming whole and happy. That evolution continues for me. Looking back on my striptease days has given me an appreciation for the progress I have made. Life does get better when we choose what's best for us. Ah, but that's the trick, isn't it? Sometimes we don't know what's best for us until it's too late." Eve grinned and shook her head, then paused to drink her coffee.

"You ended up working at an insurance company, Eve. Is that what you have been doing since?" I asked.

"I worked there for about six years," she replied. "I've had a patchwork career in the years since I left dancing. Nothing I could get juiced about, no jobs that were as spicy as stripping. The two jobs I've enjoyed the most were striptease dancing and event coordination. What they had in common were the way they tapped into my creativity. They were also roles where I felt I had the most control. Not that I didn't have to overcome a lot of fear to do either one.

"That's another skill I acquired during that phase of my life—how to push through fear. After the first time I drew back that velvet curtain, fear never gripped me quite the same way. That moment became a point of reference that helped me take other risks. The first time I had to perform in front of my acting class my knees were buckling. I thought, *How bad is this compared to dancing naked?* and had a good laugh at myself. Time and again I was terrified of rejection when I was seeking support for my Halloween event. Then I'd think, *What's the worst that can happen? Can't be as bad as what I've been through already.*

"About a year after I left dancing, love asked me to open my heart. I was nearly in a panic that I might be hurt again. I didn't let it stop me. I knew I would survive, no matter what the outcome. Nothing is more worthy of tossing fear aside for than love.

"I was in that relationship for four years—doubled my previous record! I was indeed hurt when it was over, but it also became a turning point. I was so heartsick over that break-up that I reverted back to drinking too much, once again. I hit a bottom I knew I couldn't climb out of alone, and finally went to AA.

"Turning the doorknob to enter that first 12-Step meeting is on my list of 'The Top Ten Scariest Things I've Ever Done.' It also tops the list of 'The Best Things I've Ever Done.' It helped me to go deeper into myself to heal and grow. I re-discovered my core being, which I had distanced myself from by alcohol abuse. The serenity I found through recovery gave me a solid foundation to re-build my life.

"Five years after my first AA meeting I met my husband. We've been happily married for eighteen years. One of the keys to our happiness is that we had each worked on ourselves and had found our own inner peace before we met.

"Overcoming self-doubt and fear was a reward in itself. It led me to a life that was richer and fuller than I had imagined. The bonus was that it also led me to being in a deeply loving relationship, for which I feel truly blessed.

"Putting heavy boots on and stomping your way through fear is a metamorphic experience. My life is considerably more serene these days. Just so I don't become too complacent, I try to do something that shakes me up and wakes me up every few years, like the time I ended up camping all alone in the woods for a week.

"I was at a Pagan retreat. By accident, I pitched my tent a mile from the nearest person. I could have moved it, but used the mistake to overcome my fear of the dark. All day I was with hundreds of others at the main camp. Each night I walked a mile through the woods, the bright stream of my flashlight my only company. Every owl hoot and leaf rustle was amplified tenfold in the pitch dark. The tension in my body eased a little more each night I made the solitary trek to my campsite. By the end of the week, I felt as much at home in those shadowy woods as in my own living room.

"I tromped through fear again when I worked at a furniture store, and talked four guys into dressing in drag to do a show for an employee fun night. We did a comic spoof where I lip-synched *Diamonds Are a Girl's Best Friend*, dressed like Marilyn Monroe. I dreaded it would be a flop, or that I'd lose my balance in those '50s-style heels and land on my butt. It had been twenty years since I dealt with stage fright. I felt triumphant when it was done, not just because the crowd loved it, but because I pushed through my fears and doubts to make it happen.

"None of these things are earth-shaking accomplishments. Maybe those are yet to come for me. In the meantime, I've learned to celebrate my small achievements. It took years to break the chains of self-doubt that kept me imprisoned by fear. Each minor triumph has helped build my confidence. I've learned that when you have a burning desire to do something, not to let fear hold you back. The only real failure is not trying."

"Have you done anything lately that scared you, that pushed your boundaries?" I asked.

"Yes, indeed, Stella, something that scared me more than doing my first striptease."

"What was it, Eve?"

"I told you my story and asked you to write a book about it," Eve replied. Then she winked and shot me an impish grin as she reached for the tape recorder to click the 'off' button one last time.

EPILOGUE

One more from my friend Brian -

"Twenty Minutes"

Clock says one, it's time to go
My turn now to put on the show
Flash on stage and feel the flow
Head held high, watch faces glow
I must be smooth, can't let them know
It's lonely here with strangers all below

Old and young, bold in the night
Men try to catch me in mid-flight
Never stand still, dance lightly away
My breasts are bare but still I play
To the guy in the back, his tie askew
He watches me, his drink, the barmaid too.

Smiling bright, must look pretty in this light
To their dismay and my delight
The beads and strings all stay on tight
As I bend and stretch and watch them fight
To see what's hidden from their sight
Those parts I share with lovers at night

The fun's all gone, the last song's due
Can't hide now, what's there is true.
A thin gauze gown can hardly hide
What men desire to hold with pride.
It's mine alone, not theirs to take.
Wonder if they know this smile is fake

Thru the curtain at twenty past one
Applause dies out, another show's done.
Put on some clothes and smoke a joint
At times I wonder what's all the point.
Must soon go out, go thru the door
Say, Smile, my friend, next show's at four.

— Brian Christian

ABOUT THE AUTHOR

Eve Littlepage danced in strip clubs in the suburbs of Boston during the 70s and 80s, when there were still traces of Old Burlesque in the business. She also created The Pumpkin Lady Ball, a Halloween charity event that benefitted Boston-area organizations in the late 1980s, raising funds and public awareness for Arts Organizations, Victims of Domestic Abuse, Homeless People, and Endangered Wildlife, among other causes.

Eve is happily married to an artist whom she met at a dance in 1993. She still likes to dance, though these days she prefers being clothed and barefoot to dancing naked and in high-heels. She hopes that when she's reincarnated she can have a Halloween birthday again, because it's been so much fun this time around.

Learn more about Eve on her blog, Eve's Little Page: EveLittlePage.com or contact: eve@evelittlepage.com

Made in the USA
Columbia, SC
16 April 2022

59078482R00183